Financial Aid
for the
Utterly Confused

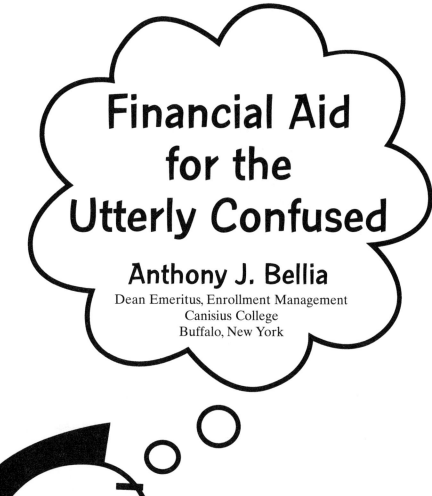

Financial Aid
for the
Utterly Confused

Anthony J. Bellia

Dean Emeritus, Enrollment Management
Canisius College
Buffalo, New York

McGraw-Hill

New York   Chicago   San Francisco   Lisbon   London   Madrid
Mexico City   Milan   New Delhi   San Juan   Seoul
Singapore   Sydney   Toronto

Over the years, my wife Maureen has been the guiding light in our family. I dedicate this book to her; and to my children, Anna, A.J., Claire, and Sarah; to my daughter-in-law, Tricia; and to my granddaughters, Katherine Anna and Mary Elizabeth. I also dedicate this book to my parents, who taught me what is important in life.

Disclaimer

The material in this book has been carefully researched so that it is accurate and as up to date as possible as of the date of publication. Some of the material was compiled from the U.S. Department of Education, National Association of Student Financial Aid Administrators, the College Board, Sallie Mae, finaid.org, fastweb.com, ncaa.org, naia.org, rotary.org, and other national student aid publications and websites. Material not listed in this disclaimer or footnotes was obtained from rendily accessible reference works and databases. Due to the nature of federal, state, and institutional guidelines affecting student aid programs, the information is subject to change without notice. Use this guide to make general plans; then follow the specific direction of each institution, federal, and state agency and private scholarship organizations.

Contents

Acknowledgments   xv
Introduction   xvii

Chapter 1   Early Financial Planning Strategies   1

             Early Financial Planning Strategies   2
             Estimating Future College Cost   2
             Developing a Savings Plan   4
             College Savings Plan Worksheet   6

             Savings Tips   7

             College Savings and Investment Plans   9
             529 State College Savings Plans   9
             529 State Prepaid Plans   10
             Independent 529 Plan   10
             Coverdell Education Savings Account   11
             Custodial Accounts   12
             Savings Bonds   12
             Roth IRA   12
             Taxable Accounts   13

             Education Tax Credit   13
             The Hope Scholarship (Tax Credit)   13
             The Lifetime Learning Tax Credit   13

	State Prepaid Tuition and/or State College Savings Plan	17
	Some Tips for Maximizing Your Aid Eligibility	28
	Tips	28
	Collection of Additional Information by Colleges	30
Chapter 2	The Real Cost of a College Education	33
	The Real Cost of College	34
	Affordability Facts	34
	The Wide Range of College Options	35
	Two-Year College Option	43
	Tuition Charges at Public Colleges and Universities for Non-State Residents	43
	Estimating the Sticker Price of a College	45
	Sticker Price versus Net Price	46
	Colleges' Concerns about Sticker Price	49
	Financial Need Varies According to College Cost	49
	Student Financial Aid: Myth and Reality	50
	Myth One: College Is Just Too Expensive for Our Family	51
	Myth Two: There Is Less Aid Available Than There Used to Be	51
	Myth Three: You Have to Be a Minority to Get Aid	52
	Myth Four: My Parents' Income Is Too High to Qualify for Aid	52
	Myth Five: The Financial Aid Form Is Too Hard to Fill Out	53
	Myth Six: My Parents Saved for College, so We Won't Qualify	53
	Myth Seven: Only Students with Good Grades Get Financial Aid	54
	Myth Eight: If I Apply for a Loan, Then I Have to Take It	54
	Myth Nine: Working Will Hurt My Academic Success	54
	Myth Ten: I Should Live at Home to Cut Costs	55
	Myth Eleven: Private Schools Are Out of Reach for My Family	55
	Myth Twelve: Millions of Dollars in Scholarships Go Unused Every Year	55
	Myth Thirteen: My Folks Will Have to Sell Their Home	56
Chapter 3	Student Aid Programs	59
	Submitting Your Application: the FAFSA	60
	Annual Submission	60

Contents

The FAFSA   60

Processing the FAFSA   61
What Happens After You Submit the Financial Aid Forms?   62

Federal Verification for Federal Student Aid Programs   63

Supplemental Aid   70
CSS/Profile Form   70
Institutional Aid Application   70

General State Residency Guidelines   71

Student Financial Aid Programs   73
Federal Student Aid   73
State Aid Programs   77

Other Ways to Save Tuition Dollars at Public Colleges   82
New England Regional Student Program (RSP)   82
Academic Common Market   83
Midwest Student Exchange Program   84
Western Interstate Commission for Higher Education   85

College-Sponsored Aid Programs   86

Athletic Money   87
National Collegiate Athletic Association (NCAA)   87
National Association of Intercollegiate Athletics (NAIA)   90

Military Financial Assistance Opportunities   91
Montgomery GI Bill (MGIB)   92
Montgomery GI Bill for Selected Reserve Training (MGIR-SR)   92
Tuition Assistance Top-Up Benefit   92
Reserve Officer Training Corps (ROTC)   93
Health-Related Programs   93
United States Military Academies   93
College Loan Repayment Programs   95
College Fund Program   95
State Educational Assistance   95

Rotary International Scholarships   96
Ambassadorial Scholarships   96
Application Procedure   97

Aid for Students With Disabilities   97
Where to Look   97

Other Sources of Funds 101

College Planning Calendar, Middle School
to High School Senior Year 101
Middle School 102
Grade 9: Freshman Year 102
Grade 10: Sophomore Year 102
Grade 11: Junior Year—Fall/Winter 103
Grade 11: Junior Year—Spring 104
Summer before Grade 12: Senior Year 104
Grade 12: Senior Year—Fall (September to December) 104
Grade 12: Senior Year—Winter (January to March) 105
Grade 12: Senior Year—Spring (April to May) 106
Summer Before College 106

Summary: Financial Aid Applications 107
November/December 107
January/February 107

Chapter 4 Your Share of the Cost of a College Education 111

Federal Methodology 112

Institutional Methodology 112

Calculating the Expected Family Contribution
Under federal Methodology 113
Principles of Need Analysis 113
Calculating the Expected Family Contribution 114
Financial Need Calculation 128

Simplified Need Analysis Formula 128
Dependent Students 128
Independent Students 129
Who Automatically Qualifies for a Zero EFC? 129
Independent Students 130

Who is Considered a Parent? 130
Definitions 130
Non-Custodial Parent 131
Home Schoolers and Federal Student Aid 131
Independent versus Dependent Status 132

Special Circumstances 133

Chapter 5	Student Financial Aid Office and Award Notification Process	135
	The Role of the College Student Financial Aid Office	136
	Award Letter Notification	137
	Determining Student Financial Need	137
	Reviewing the Award Letter	139
	Case Studies: How Aid Packages Will Differ	142
	Fictional Case Study 1	143
	Fictional Case Study 2	145
	Fictional Case Study 3	147
	"Let's Make a Deal": Appealing the Aid Package	148
	How Outside Private Scholarships Affect the Aid Package	149
	How Will the Receipt of an Outside Scholarship Affect My Financial Aid Package?	150
	Post-Enrollment Activity With The Financial Aid Office	151
Chapter 6	Student Debt: An Investment in Your Future	155
	Investment with a Return	156
	What Is Reasonable Debt?	157
	Tips for Borrowing	158
	Incentives from Lenders	158
	Loan Repayment Plans	159
	Standard Repayment Loan Plan	159
	Graduated Repayment Plan	159
	Loan Consolidation Plans	159
	Income Sensitive Plan	160
	The Extended Repayment Plan	160
	Other Financial Terms	160
	Calculating Estimated Loan Repayments	161
	Alternative Loan Programs	161
	Websites and Telephone Numbers for the Private Student Loan Lenders	164
Chapter 7	Controlling the Cost of a College Education	169
	Cell Phones	170
	Credit Cards	171

	Leave the Car at Home	172
	Purchasing School Supplies	172
	Selecting the Right Meal Plan	173
	Travel to and from College	173
	Checking Accounts	173
	Preventing Identity Theft	174
	Three-Year BA/BS Programs	175
	What Are the Benefits of Graduating in Three Years?	175
	Advanced Placement/College Credit Courses	175
	Some Other Tips	176
Chapter 8	Options for Paying College Expenses	179
	Loan Programs to Finance Parental Contribution and Unmet Need	180
	Your Credit Score	181
	Financing Options	181
	College-Sponsored Payment And Loan Programs	182
	Home Equity Lines of Credit/Home Equity Loans	183
	Home Equity Line of Credit	184
	Home Equity Loan	185
	Federal Loan	185
	Federal Plus Loan	186
	Alternative Loans	187
	Other Financing Options	188
	Retirement/IRA Plans	188
	Life Insurance Loans	189
	Will Loans Impact the Student Aid Formula?	189
Chapter 9	Consultants, Scholarship Search Companies and Other Resources	193
	Financial Aid Consultants	194
	Selling Points for Financial Aid Consulting Companies	195
	Consultant Services	195

Guidelines to Consider Before Hiring a Consultant   198
Negative Experiences   199

Financial Aid Source Books   199

Scholarship Search Companies: Private Scholarships   200
Scholarship Assistance   201
Materials to Submit   201
Scholarship Letter Tips   202
How to Identify a Scholarship Scam Company   202

Internet Resources   203

Financial Aid Resources in Spanish   207
Websites   207
Sample of Publications and Aid Applications   208

Chapter 10 Tips: College search and Financial Aid Process   211

High School First Steps   212

Understanding Tuition Costs   212

Applying for Student Financial Aid   213

Merit, Athletic, and Private Scholarship Opportunities   214

College Selection/Award Letter Process   214

Renewing Financial Aid/Individual College Policy   215

Student Loans   215

Cutting College Costs   216

Parents   216

Appendix   219
Glossary   231
Index   261

Acknowledgments

The student aid profession has been a part of my life and my family's life since 1967. For over 38 years, I have been directly or indirectly involved in this field. This profession is fortunate to have dedicated professionals who are available to assist students, their parents, school counselors, and others.

I am grateful to friends and colleagues who were willing to assist me in this publication. Michele Rizzo, Assistant Director, Financial Aid, Canisius College, assisted me throughout the process in organizing the book as well as providing technical expertise. Joseph Russo, a long-time friend and colleague, Director, Student Financial Strategies, University of Notre Dame, provided me with editorial advice. Curt Gaume, Director, Student Financial Aid, Canisius College, provided me with technical assistance. Tony Goodwin, Director, Educational Lending, M&T Bank, Buffalo, New York, and Lea Nicholson, Assistant Director, Student Financial Aid, Canisius College, reviewed the two chapters on loans. Joan Kader, Financial Aid Technician, and Patricia Deganis, Financial Aid Technician, Student Financial Aid Office, Canisius College, provided financial aid tips. I also want to thank Renee Lefrancois for her continued patience while assisting me in the editing of this book. I thank Patrick Prosser, Director, Student Financial Aid, John Carroll University, and William R. Burke, Director, Student Financial Aid, University of Scranton, for allowing me to use printed material. Finally, I would like to thank the capable staff at McGraw-Hill, especially Adrinda Kelly, who guided me through the publication process. Special thanks to Barbara Gilson, Editorial Director, for allowing me to publish this book, and to Grace Freedson, my agent, for guiding me and answering all of my questions.

I am grateful to my wife, Maureen, for her support and encouragement during the research and writing of this book. Most of all, I am grateful to her for four decades of love and support, and the nurturing of our children Anna, A.J., Claire, and Sarah during the time that financial aid meetings and seminars and evening financial aid presentations took me away from the family.

Anthony J. Bellia

Introduction

This book provides a comprehensive guide on how to finance a college education. *You can afford a college education.* While you can afford to go to college, there are several things you must understand. First, you must understand the real cost of a college education. In many instances, this price is *less* than what a college education might appear at first glance to cost. Second, you must understand the financial aid programs that are available to help you to pay for college. Third, you must understand how to apply for student financial aid. No one will come to you and offer you money to help you pay for college—you must ask for it. Finally, you must understand the things that you can do to save money for college or, if it is too late for that, to help you afford the costs of college that will soon fall upon you.

This book is divided into several chapters. Each addresses a specific question regarding the financing of a college education. You would do well to read the book from start to finish. You will gain from it a thorough understanding of what you can do to afford a college education. That said, each chapter stands alone as an independent reference guide to the matter it addresses. Thus, if you have only specific questions about how to finance a college education, this book will be useful to you as well.

It is well worth repeating that you can afford a college education. Student aid programs exist to make a college education affordable to those who cannot pay for it on their own. Financial aid programs are designed to take your individual circumstances into account. No family should consider itself too poor or too rich to apply for student financial aid.

This book addresses each of the following questions:

- How do I save money for a college education?
- What is the real cost of a college education?
- How do I get cash to attend college?
- How much will I have to pay?
- What happens after I submit the financial aid forms?
- Why is a college education worth the cost?
- Can I control the out-of-pocket costs of a college education?
- What are the options to pay for college if student aid is not enough?
- Do I need to hire a financial aid consultant?

This book answers these questions with the most up-to-date information available, and includes review questions at the end of each chapter. It will guide you on this exciting and interesting journey you are about to begin.

Early Financial Planning Strategies

Do I Need to Read This Chapter?

You need to read this chapter if you are a parent of a preschooler or have a child in school and need to learn about

➡ Early financial planning strategies with worksheets

➡ Different savings vehicles

➡ College savings plan with worksheet

➡ How these savings vehicles can affect eligibility for student financial aid

➡ How to estimate future college cost with worksheets

➡ Tips to maximize your aid eligibility

The McGraw·Hill Companies

Library of Congress Cataloging-in-Publication Data

Bellia, Anthony J.
    Financial aid for the utterly confused / Anthony J. Bellia.
        p.   cm.
    ISBN-13: 978-0-07-146731-5
    ISBN-10: 0-07-146731-9
    1. Student aid—United States.   2. College student orientation—United States.
    I. Title.

    LB2337.4.B455   2007
    378.3—dc22   2006021423

1 2 3 4 5 6 7 8 9 0   DOC/DOC   0 1 2 1 0 9 8 7 6

ISBN-13: 978-0-07-146731-5
ISBN-10: 0-07-146731-9

The sponsoring editor for this book was Barbara Gilson and the production supervisor was Pamela A. Pelton. It was set in Times Ten by International Typesetting and Composition. The art director for the cover was Handel Low.

Printed and bound by RR Donnelley.

McGraw-Hill books are available at special quantity discounts to use as premiums and sales promotions, or for use in corporate training programs. For more information, please write to the Director of Special Sales, McGraw-Hill Professional, Two Penn Plaza, New York, NY 10121-2298. Or contact your local bookstore.

This book is printed on acid-free paper.

Early Financial Planning Strategies

Investment strategies to save for college will vary from family to family. Any savings strategy you develop should reduce your anxiety about paying college bills and potentially reduce your family's loan indebtedness. It will also result in less expense and more choices. Since there are many savings vehicles for a family to choose from, in developing your investment plan it is important to consider the projected cost of college. That projection will depend on the number of years until your child will attend college and the rate of inflation.

Estimating Future College Cost

Table 1-1 offers some guidance on projected tuition at both public and private four-year colleges. It provides estimates of future costs for four years of college, including tuition and fees, room and board, transportation, books and supplies,

TABLE 1-1   Estimating Future College Cost

Number of Years Before Starting College	Year You Will Begin College	Total Projected Cost for Four Years at an In-State Public University	Total Projected Cost for Four Years at a Private College
Current	2005–2006	$61,530	$127,239
1	2006–2007	$64,606	$133,600
2	2007–2008	$67,836	$140,280
3	2008–2009	$71,228	$147,295
4	2009–2010	$74,790	$154,659
5	2010–2011	$78,529	$162,392
6	2011–2012	$82,846	$170,512
7	2012–2013	$86,578	$179,038
8	2013–2014	$90,907	$187,989
9	2014–2015	$95,543	$197,388
10	2015–2016	$100,225	$207,257
11	2016–2017	$105,237	$217,620
12	2017–2018	$110,499	$228,500
13	2018–2019	$116,023	$239,926
14	2019–2020	$121,825	$251,923
15	2020–2021	$127,916	$264,519
16	2021–2022	$134,312	$277,745
17	2022–2023	$141,027	$291,632

Source: Prepared by Anthony J. Bellia, July 2005.

and other personal expenses. These estimates are based on the College Board's annual survey and assume an average annual 5% increase in college costs. (For academic year 2004–2005, increases in tuition and fees and room and board at four-year public and private colleges averaged between approximately 6.6% and 5.7%, respectively.) Note that actual increases may turn out to be lower or higher, and the college your child attends may be more or less expensive than the average.

Table 1-2 is an inflation factor chart that allows you to select from a range of annual rate increases, yielding an *inflation rate factor* that you can use to project future college cost. For example, if the cost to attend a particular institution is $15,000 and your child has ten years before enrolling in college, and you are

TABLE 1-2   Inflation Factors

Years Before Starting College	Inflation Rate				
	5%	6%	7%	8%	9%
1	1.10	1.12	1.07	1.08	1.09
2	1.16	1.19	1.15	1.17	1.19
3	1.22	1.26	1.23	1.59	1.30
4	1.28	1.34	1.31	1.71	1.41
5	1.34	1.42	1.40	1.85	1.54
6	1.41	1.50	1.50	2.00	1.68
7	1.48	1.59	1.61	2.16	1.83
8	1.55	1.69	1.72	2.33	1.99
9	1.63	1.70	1.84	2.52	2.17
10	1.71	1.90	1.97	2.72	2.40
11	1.80	2.01	2.11	2.94	2.58
12	1.89	2.13	2.25	3.17	2.81
13	1.98	2.26	2.41	3.42	3.07
14	2.08	2.40	2.58	3.70	3.34
15	2.19	2.54	2.76	3.99	3.64
16	2.29	2.69	2.95	4.31	3.97
17	2.41	2.84	3.16	4.66	4.33
18	2.53	3.03	3.62	5.03	4.72

Source: Reprinted with permission by the authors, Joseph A. Russo, Director of Student Financial Strategies, University of Notre Dame, and James A. Belvin, University Director of Financial Aid, Duke University, from *How to Save for College From Day One*, The Princeton Review/Random House, New York, 2004.

assuming a 6% inflation rate, you would calculate an estimated future college cost as follows:

$15,000	Current Tuition
× 1.90	Inflation Rate (Table 1-2)
$28,500	Projected Cost for One Year
× 4	Years
$114,000	Projected Tuition Cost*

Developing a Savings Plan

As you consider projected tuition costs, you need to consider a savings plan. No matter where you invest your money, it needs to work for you.

The Power of Compounding

When you're investing in a savings plan, the power of compounding is most important. The earlier you begin saving, the more the power of compounding will work for you. Table 1-3 illustrates the power of compounding by measuring the return on an investment of $1,000 at different rates of return.

TABLE 1-3   Rate of Return

Year	5%	6%	7%	8%	9%
1	$1,050	$1,060	$1,070	$1,080	$1,090
2	1,103	1,123	1,143	1,163	1,183
3	1,158	1,191	1,225	1,260	1,295
4	1,256	1,263	1,310	1,360	1,411
5	1,276	1,338	1,403	1,469	1,539
6	1,340	1,418	1,501	1,587	1,677
7	1,407	1,504	1,606	1,714	1,828
8	1,477	1,594	1,719	1,851	1,993
9	1,551	1,689	1,838	1,999	2,172
10	1,629	1,791	1,956	2,159	2,367
11	1,710	1,898	2,105	2,332	2,580
12	1,796	2,012	2,252	2,518	2,813
13	1,886	2,133	2,410	2,720	3,065
14	1,980	2,261	2,579	2,937	3,342
15	2,079	2,397	2,759	3,172	3,642
16	2,183	2,540	2,952	3,426	3,970
17	2,293	2,693	3,159	3,700	4,328
18	2,407	2,854	3,380	3,996	4,717

Source: Prepared by Anthony J. Bellia, October 2005.

*This projection does not include fees, room and board, or books and supplies.

Tools for Estimating College Savings

The earlier you develop a regular savings plan for college, the more money you will have set aside for college expenses. The longer the investment time frame, the better your savings plan should tolerate the frequent ups and downs in the marketplace. The following are two tools to assist you in estimating how much money you will have available at given interest rates.

Rule of 72: First, the "rule of 72" provides a rule of thumb for calculating how long it will take you to double your money at a given interest rate:

$$\frac{72}{\text{Interest rate}} = \text{Years to double investment}$$

For example, if you want to estimate how long it will take to double your money at 5%, divide the interest rate 5% into 72 to obtain the number of years:

$$\frac{72}{5\%} = 14.4 \text{ years}$$

The rule of 72 also allows you to estimate what rate of return you must earn to double your money in a given time period. You simply use the formula backwards. For example, "My child has eleven years before she attends college. What is the rate of return I will need to double my money?"

$$\frac{72}{11 \text{ Years}} = 6.54\% \text{ Rate of Return}$$

The rule of 72 merely provides an approximation of how long it will take to double your money, but the approximation is a fairly accurate one. Table 1-4 lists the number of years it will take, in actuality and as approximated by the rule of 72, to double your money.

TABLE 1-4   Rule of 72

Interest Rate*	Actual Years	Rule of 72 Years
4%	17.67	18
5%	14.21	14.4
6%	11.90	12.00
7%	10.24	10.29
8%	9.01	9
9%	8.04	8.00
10%	7.27	7.2

*Assumption is that interest is compounded annually.

TABLE 1-5   Interest Compounded Annually

Years Before Starting College	Return Rate				
	6%	7%	8%	9%	10%
1	.60	.70	.80	.90	1.00
2	1.24	1.45	1.66	1.88	2.10
3	1.91	2.25	2.60	2.95	3.31
4	2.63	3.11	3.61	4.12	4.64
5	3.38	4.03	4.69	5.39	6.10
6	4.19	5.01	5.87	6.77	7.71
7	5.04	6.06	7.14	8.28	9.49
8	5.94	7.18	8.51	9.93	11.43
9	6.90	8.39	9.99	11.72	13.58
10	7.91	9.67	11.59	13.67	15.94
11	8.98	11.05	13.32	15.80	18.53
12	10.12	12.52	15.18	18.13	21.38
13	11.33	14.10	17.20	20.66	24.52
14	12.61	15.79	19.37	23.42	27.98
15	13.97	17.59	21.72	26.43	31.77
16	15.40	19.52	24.26	29.70	35.95
17	16.93	21.59	27.00	33.28	40.55
18	18.54	23.80	29.96	37.17	45.60

Source: Reprinted with permission by the authors, Joseph A. Russo, Director of Student Financial Strategies, University of Notre Dame, and James A. Belvin, University Director of Financial Aid, Duke University, from *How to Save for College From Day One*, The Princeton Review/Random House, New York, 2004.

Rate of Return: Table 1-5 illustrates how much interest your money will earn over a given number of years at annual rates of return from 6% to 10%.

College Savings Plan Worksheet

The following is a sample of a college savings plan and an opportunity to calculate your own plan:

Example		Your Child
1. Child's current age	5	$_____
2. Years before starting college (age 18)	13	_____
3. Current annual cost (tuition, fees, room and board)	$12,000	_____

4. College cost inflation rate; e.g., 5%, choose one from inflation factors chart (Table 1-2)	1.98%	_____
5. Future annual cost (multiply line 3 by line 4)	$23,760	_____
6. Total cost for 4 years of college (multiply line 5 by 4 years)	$95,040	_____
7. Select a rate of return from the return rate chart (Table 1-5)	14.10%	_____
8. Your savings/investment per year (divide step 6 by step 7)	$6,740	_____
9. Amount you must save per month (divide line 8 by line 12 months)	$561	_____

This example assumes no savings. If there are savings, subtract the amount of savings from the total four-year cost (line 6) and then continue with the calculation, as follows:

	line 6	$95,040	_____
		−10,000	
		$85,040	
Select rate of return from the return rate chart	line 7	14.10	_____
Divide step 6 by step 7	line 8	6,031	_____
Amount you must save (divide step 8 by 12 months)	line 9	502	_____

Savings Tips

Now that you have a projection of future costs and how much you may need to save, here are some tips to consider in choosing a plan.

1. You want an investment plan that has flexibility. Consider how much you can contribute to the account; what percentage of expenses the plan will cover; what restrictions, if any, there are on in-state versus out-of-state colleges; and what time limits, if any, there are on when the money must be used. What separates good plans from poorer ones is the flexibility of the plan.

2. Make sure to read the enrollment agreement to determine the fee structure, including both sign-up fees and annual fees. Obviously, the smaller the fee structure, the more money you will have for college expenses.

3. Your tolerance for risk is a major consideration. Some plans may be too conservative or some too aggressive for you. Also, the fund's historical performance should be reviewed very carefully to determine both volatility and investment return.

4. Weighing the tax benefits of each plan will help you narrow down the options.

5. Some financial planners question whether you should invest in your child's education or invest in your own retirement plan. College saving plans, state-sponsored 529 plans, independent 529 plans, and mutual funds are considered by the federal government in determining eligibility for federal student aid. Later in this chapter, we will discuss how these plans affect the student financial aid formula. Currently, however, the federal government excludes retirement funds, such as IRAs and 401(k)s, in the methodology it uses to determine your eligibility for financial aid.

Dean's Tip

Effective July 1, 2007, the assessment of student assets in Federal Methodology will decrease from 35% to 20% for dependent students, independent students without dependents other than a spouse, and independent students with dependents other than spouse.

6. Your choice may be influenced by understanding how the financial aid regulations for treatment of parent and student assets can affect federal financial aid eligibility. On the Free Application for Federal Student Aid (FAFSA), the form that institutions use to calculate students' eligibility for certain federal aid, for example, parents' assets are assessed up to 5.6%, (not including equity in primary residence) and students' assets are currently assessed at 35%. However, effective July 1, 2007, students assets will be reduced from 35% to 20% for both dependent students and independent students with and without dependents other than a spouse. So, if the student has $10,000 in assets as of the date of completing the FAFSA, Federal Methodology will use $3,500 as a resource when determining the expected family contribution ($10,000 × 35 = $3,500), effectively reducing the student's eligibility for need-based federal aid by $3,500. After July 1, 2007, the calculation is $10,000 × 20% = $2,000. This means the student asset contribution will be $2,000 instead of $3,500.

7. Some financial planners suggest that parents should investigate whether they are eligible for aid when their child is an infant. The assumption is if you are ineligible now, you most likely will be ineligible in the future. I strongly

disagree with this advice. Who can predict the future? Who knows what the state and federal student aid regulations will be in ten to fifteen years? Also, students may be eligible for merit aid. The number of children in college concurrently may impact aid eligibility. In my view, you should ignore financial aid eligibility of an infant in forming your savings strategy.

8. Generally, families are at their peak income when their children begin college. For many, their cash flow will enable them to pay some of the educational bills. Some college financial planners recommend that college funding should come from three sources: one-third from savings, one-third from current disposable income, and one-third from borrowing (future income).

It is critical to discuss your financial situation with a qualified investment specialist and in some cases with an attorney and an accountant. For each of the savings vehicles described here, you should understand what tax consequences it has, how flexible it is, and what qualified educational expenses the plan will pay.

College Savings and Investment Plans

There are numerous college savings plans and tax credit programs for you to consider. Deciding on how to invest will depend on the child's age, your income, and the impact of a plan on your future eligibility for student aid. The following are some general questions that you need to ask before you select a plan:

- What are the fees associated with the plan?
- What are the state tax benefits?
- Who are the fund managers?
- What are the investment opportunities?
- What commission will the broker earn (if you use a broker)?

Now let's review some of these savings and investment plans.

529 State College Savings Plans

- These programs allow you to save money for college through state-sponsored investment accounts.
- You can use the funds at most accredited public or private colleges or universities in the United States. Also, some plans allow you to use the money at accredited vocational and international colleges.
- The beneficiary of the program can be changed without penalty to certain other family members.

- Funds can be used for *qualified educational expenses* such as tuition, fees, room and board, books, and supplies.
- Earnings and withdrawals, if used for qualified educational expenses, are exempt from federal taxes. Also, some states waive taxes for residents or let parents deduct a portion of the annual contribution.
- The purchaser of a 529 program retains full ownership regardless of beneficiary age.
- **Financial Aid Impact:** Funds are treated as parental assets—current financial aid formulas count up to only 5.6% percent of parental assets when calculating the student's financial need. Consequently, this investment has a limited effect on how much financial aid you will get.

529 State Prepaid Plans

- These programs allow you to buy future tuition at public state colleges at today's price. Earnings are guaranteed by the state to match or exceed annual in-state public college tuition inflation. The cost of a plan can vary, depending on the age of the child.
- Most programs allow accumulated funds to be transferred to private or out-of-state schools, but then require you to pay the difference between the prepaid tuition price and the current price of tuition at the out-of-state school. Also, some plans will allow funds to be used only for tuition and fees. You need to check out the specific provisions of each state plan.
- **Financial Aid Impact:** Federal legislation passed in February 2006 allows prepaid tuition program distributions to be treated as an asset of the parents. Federal financial aid formulas count up to only 5.6% of parental assets when calculating the student's financial need. Consequently, this investment will now have a limited effect on how much financial aid you will get.
- **Note:** Refer to the chart in Table 1-7 (later in this chapter) of state prepaid tuition plans and state college savings plans.

Independent 529 Plan

This plan enable you to prepay tuition or a part of it at over 250 participating private colleges. Some of the colleges participating in this plan include Stanford University, Vanderbilt University, University of Notre Dame, Canisius College, Amherst College, Carnegie Mellon University, Massachusetts Institute of Technology, and Princeton University. Through this plan, you purchase certificates that can be used to pay the percent of tuition you pre-purchased. Check the website (www.independent529plan.com) or call 1-888-718-7878 for more information and a complete list of participating private colleges. This program is administered by TIAA-CREF Tuition Financing Inc.

According to its website, this plan offers the following:

- The same federal tax consideration as any 529 prepaid plan
- The flexibility of a national program at any member college at which the beneficiary is admitted and becomes enrolled
- Freedom from entry, annual, exit, and maintenance fees
- Freedom from market risk and federal income taxes
- The security of a guarantee against tuition inflation
- A special discount provided by each participating school

Financial Aid Impact

Federal regulations enacted in February 2006 changed the treatment of this 529 Prepaid Tuition Plan. It will now be treated as a parental asset. Federal financial aid formulas count up to only 5.6% of parental assets when calculating the student's financial need. This investment will now have a limited effect on how much financial aid you will get.

You should also check the following websites for additional information on 529 plans:

- www.independent529plan.com
- www.savingforcollege.com
- www.moneycentral.msn.com
- www.collegeboard.com
- www.nasd.com/investor

Coverdell Education Savings Account

Formerly known as the Education IRA, this account is similar to an IRA but it is used for education costs. It is not a retirement account.

- These accounts let families put away $2,000 per beneficiary per year and use the money—tax free—to pay for qualified college expenses for the designated beneficiary.
- You can now use Coverdell funds to pay for elementary or secondary education costs as well.
- There are income restrictions to make full contributions to a Coverdell account—check the latest IRS regulations.
- Grandparents, aunts and uncles, and friends can contribute to a Coverdell account.

- **Financial Aid Impact:** Coverdell "parent-owned" accounts are counted as a parent's asset, assessed up to 5.6% in calculating the student's need. (Treatment as a parental asset is a U.S. Department of Education ruling in January 2004.) These funds, similar to 529 College Savings Programs, will have a limited effect on how much federal need-based aid the student will be eligible to receive.

Custodial Accounts

Also known as the Uniform Gifts or Transfers to Minors Act Accounts, custodial accounts deserve a close look due to the latest tax cuts. There is now greater flexibility in custodial accounts regarding spending the money for the child's expenses other than college-related costs. However, children get control of the money when they become adults.

Financial Aid Impact: Treated as student assets, these accounts will be assessed currently at 35% and can significantly reduce the amount of aid a student will get. Check the Dean's Tip in this chapter for the latest regulation.

Savings Bonds

These bonds provide a safe investment, with low returns, but interest earned is tax free for qualified higher education expenses. Certain income guidelines apply.

Financial Aid Impact: Funds in the parents' name are treated as a parental asset, are assessed up to 5.6% when calculating the student's need, and will have a limited effect on how much aid the student will get. However, savings bonds in the student's name will be currently assessed at 35% and may significantly affect aid eligibility. Check the Dean's Tip in this chapter for the latest regulation.

Roth IRA

The Roth IRA is different from other retirement savings plans. All earnings are tax free when the investor or beneficiary meets certain criteria.

- You may withdraw contributions to a Roth IRA to pay for college expenses without having to pay other income tax or the 10% early withdrawal penalty that generally applies to IRAs.

- Any investment earnings in your Roth IRA are also available for withdrawal without the 10% penalty but are subject to regular income tax. You may withdraw investment earnings tax free if you're over 59 1/2 and you have had your Roth IRA for at least five years.

- **Financial Aid Impact:** Funds are treated as a parental asset, are assessed at up to 5.6 percent when calculating the student's need, and will have a limited effect on how much aid the student will get.

Taxable Accounts

This is money invested in a regular brokerage account, allowing unlimited contributions and with the flexibility to use the money for any purpose.

Financial Aid Impact: Funds are treated as a parental assets, are assessed at up to 5.6% when calculating the student's need, and will have a limited effect on how much aid the student will get. However, funds placed in the student's name will be assessed at currently 35% and may have a significant impact on financial aid eligibility. Check the Dean's Tip in this chapter for the latest regulation.

Education Tax Credit

As you get closer to the time you will actually be paying for college expenses, you need to investigate the federal government's education tax credits. These tax credits can help offset college expenses. The Hope Scholarship and Lifetime Learning Tax Credit programs, if you are eligible, will assist you in paying for college costs. You must meet certain income conditions in order to qualify for these tax credits. A tax credit allows you to subtract the amount of the tax credit from your total federal income tax, not just from your taxable income. As a result, tax credits allow for greater total savings than tax deductions.

The Hope Scholarship (Tax Credit)

This $1,500 tax credit per student applies to tuition and fees for the first two years of post-secondary education. To claim a Hope Scholarship Tax Credit, the student must be enrolled at least half time for at least one academic period, and must not have completed the first two years of undergraduate study. The amount of the credit is 100% of the first $1,000 of qualified tuition and fees (not room and board costs) per student plus 50% of the next $1,000 of qualified tuition and fees. The expenses must be paid by the taxpayer and the taxpayer must list the student as a dependent on his/her income tax return. Scholarships and grants (not student loans) reduce the amount of qualified tuition and fees that the taxpayer can claim in applying for this tax credit. Gifts, inheritances, and bequests do count as income by the taxpayer. "as paid" or "as income". Check IRS Publication 970, "Tax Benefits for Higher Education," for the definition of modified adjusted gross income, and for the most up-to-date guidelines and income qualifications.

For a student's parents to claim a Hope Scholarship Tax Credit for tuition and fees, parents must also claim the student as a dependent. If parents do not claim the student as an exemption, the student can claim the Hope Scholarship Tax Credit. Finally, if the student has been convicted of a felony, the credit will be denied. You need to complete IRS Form 8863 with Form 1040 or 1040A to claim the tax credit.

The Lifetime Learning Tax Credit

This credit is available to college juniors and seniors, students pursuing graduate and professional degrees, and for courses (even a single course) to acquire or improve job skills. It is mainly intended to help defray college costs after the first two years, when the Hope Scholarship Tax Credit is no longer allowed.

Like the Hope Scholarship Tax Credit, the Lifetime Learning Tax Credit can be used only for tuition and fees. You cannot claim both the Hope and Lifetime Credits for the same student in the same year. The Lifetime Learning Tax Credit equals 20% of the amount of qualified tuition and fees up to $10,000 for a maximum credit of $2,000 per tax return for all eligible students. Note: This is a $2,000 limit per return, not per student. You don't get another tax credit for each additional child.

The family income limits to qualify for the Lifetime Learning Credit are the same as for the Hope Scholarship program. The amount of the credit is gradually reduced based on your Adjusted Gross Income. Check IRS Publication 970 for the definition of Modified Adjusted Gross Income and for the most up to date guidelines or income qualifications. Colleges will issue an IRS Form 1098-T before January 31 of the next calendar year. You need to complete IRS Form 8863 with Form 1040 or 1040A to claim the tax credit.

Don't Forget...

Consult IRS Publication 970, "Tax Benefits for Higher Education," for specific rules on eligibility and claiming these tax credits. Visit the website (www.IRS.gov) or call toll free at 1-800-TAX-FORM (1-800-829-3676) to obtain more information.

IRS Publications

- Publication 970 (PDF), Tax Benefits for Higher Education: www.irs.gov/pub/irs-pdf/p970.pdf[1]

- Form 8863 and Instructions (PDF), Education Credits (Hope Scholarship and Lifetime Learning Tax Credits): www.irs.gov/ pub/irs-pdf/f8863.pdf

- Tax Topic 605, Education Credits: www.irs.gov/taxtopics/ tc605.html

- Frequently Asked Questions and Answers from the IRS, Education Tax Credits: www.irs.gov/faqs/faq-kw52.html

The College Savings chart in Table 1-6 compares different savings plans for calendar year 2005.

[1]Internal Revenue Service IRS.gov, Section 6. Publication 970 (2004) Tuition and Fees Deduction

TABLE 1-6 College Savings Plans Comparison Chart for Calendar Year 2005

	Contribution Limit	Income Restrictions	Tax Breaks	Flexibility of Funds Used	Federal Financial Aid Impact	Potential Sunset Changes	Offered By
529 College Savings Plans	Up to total of about $300,000 for some plans; may pay gift taxes if more than $11,000 a year. Can donate up to $55,000 at one time.	None	Qualified distributions tax-free. (Some states may also offer tax breaks.)	Tuition, fees, room, board, and graduate school.	Considered parents' assets, assessed up to 5.6%.	Earnings withdrawals will be taxed at child's rate after 2010.	States–supported with help from financial services companies.
529 State Prepaid Plan	Maximum varies by state, but plans cover, in general, up to five years of college costs.	None	Qualified distributions tax-free. (Some states may also offer tax breaks.)	For most plans, tuition, fees, room, and board.	Considered parents' assets. Assessed up to 5.6%.	Earnings withdrawals will be taxed at child's rate after 2010.	States
Indepen-dent 529 Plan	Up to five years' tuition at the groups' most expensive college (currently $137,000).	None	Qualified distributions tax-free.	Tuition and mandatory fees.	Considered parents' assets. Assessed up to 5.6%.	Earnings withdrawals will be taxed at child's rate after 2010.	250+ private colleges and universities.

(Continued)

TABLE 1-6 College Savings Plans Comparison Chart for Calendar Year 2005 (*Continued*)

	Contribution Limit	Income Restrictions	Tax Breaks	Flexibility of Funds Used	Federal Financial Aid Impact	Potential Sunset Changes	Offered By
Coverdell Education Savings Account	Up to $2000 a year.	Check latest IRS regulations.	Qualified distributions tax-free as long as used for eligible school cost.	Post-secondary costs; K-12 costs.	Considered student's assets, assessed at 35%. Effective July 1, 2007, assessed at 20%.	Contribution limits would revert to $500 after 2010.	Banks, mutual funds, and company brokerages.
Custodial Accounts	No total maximum, but may pay gift taxes if more than $11,000 a year.	None	For minors over 14, earnings taxed at child's rate; under 14, earnings less than $800 are tax-free, over $1,600 taxed at parents' rate.	Unlimited	Considered student's assets, assessed at 35%. Effective July 1, 2007, assessed at 20%.	Favorable 5% tax rate set to expire in 2009.	Banks, mutual funds, and company brokerages.
Savings Bonds, such as Series EE bonds	Annual limit of $60,000 per owner, $30,000 in paper bonds and $30,000 in treasury direct bonds.	Check latest IRS publications.	Interest earned is tax-free if used for qualified higher-education purposes.	Tuition and mandatory fees.	Considered asset of bond owner.	None	Banks and credit unions.
Mutual Funds	Unlimited	None	Earnings and gains taxed in year realized.	Unlimited	Considered asset of owner.	Favorable 15% rate also set to expire in 2009.	Brokerage firms and banks.

Source: This table was updated in February 2006. The original chart was published in the *Wall Street Journal*, September 24, 2003, page D3.

Each savings plan needs careful evaluation by each individual family. As tax laws are constantly changing, parents should start saving whatever they can as possible. There is no silver bullet for just the right investment plan. For some families, it may be a combination of more than one savings vehicle.

State Prepaid Tuition and/or State College Savings Plan

The National Association of Student Financial Aid Administrators (NASFAA)[2] has created a portion of the chart in Table 1-7, which provides basic information

TABLE 1-7   State Prepaid Tuition and/or State College Savings Plans

State	Program Name and Contact Information	Plan Type	Applic. Fee	Portable	Tuition/ Fees Only?	State Tax Incentive
AL	**Prepaid Affordable College Tuition (PACT) Program** State Treasurer (800) 252-7228	Prepaid	Yes	Yes	Yes	Yes
	Alabama Higher Education 529 Fund State Treasurer (866) 529-2228 www.treasury.state.al.us	Savings	No	Yes	No	Yes
AK	**University of Alaska College Savings Plan** University of Alaska (866) 277-1005 www.uacollegesavings.com	Savings	No	Yes	No	No
AZ	**Arizona Family College Savings Program** Arizona Commission for Postsecondary Ed. (602) 258-2435 www.azhighered.org/college	Savings	Yes	Yes	No	Yes

(*Continued*)

[2]National Association of Student Financial Aid Administrators, (NASFAA), Copyright 2004. Printed with permission.

TABLE 1-7 State Prepaid Tuition and/or State College Savings Plans (*Continued*)

State	Program Name and Contact Information	Plan Type	Applic. Fee	Portable	Tuition/ Fees Only?	State Tax Incentive
AR	**GIFT College Investing Plan** Financial Data Services, Inc. (877) 615-4116 www.thegiftplan.com	Savings	No	Yes	No	Yes
CA	**Golden State ScholarShare College Savings Trust** Golden State ScholarShare (877) 728-4338 scholarshare.com	Savings	No	Yes	No	Yes
CO	**College Invest** Citigroup Inc. (888) SAVE-NOW collegeinvest.org	Savings	Yes	Yes	No	Yes
CT	**Connecticut Higher Education Trust (CHET)** TIAA-CREF (888) 799-2438 www.aboutchet.com	Savings	No	Yes	No	Yes
DC	**DC College Savings Plan** Calvert Group (800) 987-4859 www.dc529.com	Savings	Yes	Yes	No	Yes
DE	**Delaware College Investment Plan** Fidelity (800) 292-7935 www.fidelity.com/delaware	Savings	No	Yes	No	Yes
FL	**Florida Prepaid College Program** Florida Prepaid College Board (800) 552-4723 www.florida529plans.com	Prepaid	Yes	Yes	No	Yes
	Florida College Investment Plan Florida Prepaid College Board (800) 552-4723 www.florida529plans.com	Savings	Yes	Yes	No	Yes

TABLE 1-7 State Prepaid Tuition and/or State College Savings Plans (*Continued*)

State	Program Name and Contact Information	Plan Type	Applic. Fee	Portable	Tuition/ Fees Only?	State Tax Incentive
GA	**Georgia Higher Education Savings Plan** Georgia Higher Education Savings Plan (877) 424-4377 www.gacollegesavings.com	Savings	No	Yes	No	Yes
HI	**TuitionEDGE – Hawaii College Savings Plan** Delaware Investments TuitionEDGE Plan (866) 529-3343 (EDGE) www.tuitionedge.com	Savings	No	Yes	No	Yes
ID	**Ideal Idaho College Savings Program** Ideal Idaho College Savings Program (866) 433-2533 (Ideal Ed) www.idsaves.org	Savings	No	Yes	No	Yes
IL	**College Illinois!** 529 Prepaid Tuition Program (877) 877-3724 www.collegeillinois.com	Prepaid	Yes	Yes	Yes	Yes
	Bright Start College Savings Program Illinois State Treasurer's Office (877) 432-7444 www.brightstartsavings.com	Savings	No	Yes	No	Yes
IN	College Choice 529 Investment Plan One Group Dealer Services (866) 400-7526(PLAN) www.collegechoiceplan.com	Savings	No	Yes	No	Yes
IA	**College Savings Iowa— Savings Plan** Vanguard Investments— Iowa State Treasurer's Office (888) 672-9116 collegesavingsiowa.com	Savings	No	Yes	No	Yes

(*Continued*)

TABLE 1-7 State Prepaid Tuition and/or State College Savings Plans (*Continued*)

State	Program Name and Contact Information	Plan Type	Applic. Fee	Portable	Tuition/ Fees Only?	State Tax Incentive
KS	**Learning Quest Education Savings Plan Trust** American Century Investments Management, Inc. (800) 579-2203 www.learningquestsavings.com	Savings	No	Yes	No	Yes
KY	**Kentucky Education Savings Plan Trust** Kentucky Higher Ed Assistance Authority (877) 598-7878 www.kentuckytrust.org	Savings	No	Yes	No	Yes
	Kentucky's Affordable Prepaid Tuition Plan (KAPT) Kentucky Higher Ed Assistance Authority (888) 919-5278 (KAPT) www.getkapt.com	Prepaid	Yes	Yes	Yes	Yes
LA	**Student Tuition Assistance and Revenue Trust (START)** Louisiana Office of Student Financial Assistance (800) 259-5626 www.osfa.state.la.us/start.htm	Savings	No	Yes	No	Yes
ME	**NextGen College Investing Plan** Finance Authority of Maine (800) 228-3734 (877) 463-9843 www.nextgenplan.com	Savings	No	Yes	No	Yes
MD	**College Savings Plans of Maryland—Prepaid College Trust** College Savings Plans of Maryland (888) 463-4723 www.collegesavingsmd.org	Prepaid	Yes	Yes	Yes	Yes

TABLE 1-7   State Prepaid Tuition and/or State College Savings Plans (*Continued*)

State	Program Name and Contact Information	Plan Type	Applic. Fee	Portable	Tuition/ Fees Only?	State Tax Incentive
	College Savings Plans of Maryland—College Investment Plan College Savings Plans of Maryland (888) 463-4723 www.collegesavingsmd.org	Savings	Yes	Yes	No	Yes
MA	**The U. Plan** Massachusetts Education Finance Authority (800) 449-6332 www.mefa.org/savings	Prepaid	Yes	No	Yes	Yes
MI	**Michigan Education Trust (MET)** **Michigan Department of Treasury** (800) 638-4543 www.michigan.gov/treasury/ 0,1607,7-121- 1752_2235_2236—,00.html	Prepaid	Yes	Yes	Yes	Yes
	Michigan Education Savings Program (MESP) Michigan Education Savings Program (877) 861-6377 www.misaves.com	Savings	No	Yes	No	Yes
MN	**Minnesota College Savings Plan** (877) 338-4646 www.mnsaves.org	Savings	No	Yes	No	Yes
MS	**Mississippi Prepaid Affordable College Tuition (IMPACT)** Mississippi Treasury Department (800) 987-4450 www.treasury.state.ms.us/ impact.htm	Prepaid	Yes	Yes	Yes	Yes

(*Continued*)

TABLE 1-7 State Prepaid Tuition and/or State College Savings Plans (*Continued*)

State	Program Name and Contact Information	Plan Type	Applic. Fee	Portable	Tuition/ Fees Only?	State Tax Incentive
	Mississippi Affordable College Savings (MACS) Mississippi Affordable College Savings Program (800) 486-3670 (800) 987-4450 www.treasury.state.ms.us/ macs.htm	Savings	No	Yes	No	Yes
MO	**Missouri Savings For Tuition (MO$T)** Missouri State Treasurer's Office (888) 414-6678 www.missourimost.org	Savings	No	Yes	No	Yes
MT	**Montana Family Education Savings Program** Montana Commission for Higher Education (800) 888-2723 www.montana. collegesavings.com	Savings	No	Yes	No	Yes
NE	**College Savings Plan of Nebraska** Nebraska State Treasurer (888) 993-3746 www.planforcollegenow.com	Savings	No	Yes	No	Yes
NV	**The Strong 529 Plan** College Savings Plan of Nevada (877) 529-5295 www.americas529plan.com	Savings	Yes	Yes	No	Yes
	Nevada Prepaid Tuition Plan (888) 477-2677	Prepaid	Yes	Yes	No	Yes
NH	**UNIQUE College Investing Plan** Fidelity Investments (800) 544-1914 (800) 544-1722 www.nh.gov/treasury/ divisions/unique.htm	Savings	No	Yes	No	Yes

TABLE 1-7 State Prepaid Tuition and/or State College Savings Plans (*Continued*)

State	Program Name and Contact Information	Plan Type	Applic. Fee	Portable	Tuition/ Fees Only?	State Tax Incentive
NJ	**New Jersey Better Education Savings Trust (NJBEST)** Higher Education Student Assistance Authority (877) 632-2301 (877) 4NJBEST www.njbest.com/index.htm	Savings	No	Yes	No	Yes
NY	**New York's College Savings Program** State of NY, Upromise Investments, & Vanguard Mktg (877) 697-2837 www.nysaves.org	Savings	No	Yes	No	Yes
NM	**The Education Plan's Prepaid Tuition Program** The Education Plan of New Mexico (800) 499-7581 www.tepum.com/lern/ NM_5_1_2.jsp	Prepaid	No	Yes	No	Yes
	The Education Plan's College Savings Program The Education Plan of New Mexico (800) 499-7581 www.tepum.com/lern/ NM_5_1_2.jsp	Savings	No	Yes	No	Yes
NC	**North Carolina's National College Savings Plan** College Foundation of North Carolina (800) 600-3453 www.cfnc.org/savings/ cv0021.jsp	Savings	No	Yes	No	Yes

(*Continued*)

TABLE 1-7   State Prepaid Tuition and/or State College Savings Plans (*Continued*)

State	Program Name and Contact Information	Plan Type	Applic. Fee	Portable	Tuition/ Fees Only?	State Tax Incentive
ND	**College SAVE** The Bank of North Dakota (866) 728-3529 www.collegesave4u.com	Savings	No	Yes	No	Yes
OH	**CollegeAdvantage** Ohio Tuition Trust Authority (800) 233-6734 www.collegeadvantage.com	Savings	No	Yes	No	Yes
OK	**Oklahoma College Savings Plan** TIAA-CREF Tuition Financing, Inc. (877) 654-7284 www.ok4savings.org	Savings	No	Yes	No	Yes
OR	**Oregon College Savings Plan** Oregon Qualified Tuition Savings Board (866) 772-8464 (503) 373-1903 www.oregoncollegesavings.com	Savings	No	Yes	No	Yes
PA	**TAP 529—Guaranteed Savings Plan** Pennsylvania State Treasurer's Office (800) 440-4000 www.patap.org	Savings	Yes	Yes	No	Yes
	TAP 529—Investment Plan Pennsylvania State Treasurer's Office (800) 440-4000 www.patap.org	Savings	No	Yes	No	Yes
RI	College Boundfund Rhode Island Higher Education Assistance Authority (800) 251-0539 (888) 324-5057 www.collegeboundfund.com	Savings	No	Yes	No	Yes

TABLE 1-7 State Prepaid Tuition and/or State College Savings Plans (*Continued*)

State	Program Name and Contact Information	Plan Type	Applic. Fee	Portable	Tuition/ Fees Only?	State Tax Incentive
SC	**South Carolina Tuition Prepayment Program** Office of State Treasurer (888) 772-4723 www.scgrad.org	Prepaid	Yes	Yes	Yes	Yes
	Future Scholar 529 Plan Bank of America (888) 244-5674 www.futurescholar.com	Savings	No	Yes	No	Yes
SD	**College Access 529 Plan** PIMCO Funds Distributors (866) 529-7462 www.collegeaccess529.com	Savings	No	Yes	No	Yes
TN	**BEST (Baccalaureate Education System Trust) Prepaid Tuition Plan** Tennessee Treasury Department (888) 486-2378 www.tnbest.org	Prepaid	No	Yes	No	Yes
	BEST (Baccalaureate Education System Trust) Savings Plan Tennessee Treasury Department (888) 486-2378 www.tnbest.org	Savings	No	Yes	No	Yes
TX	**Texas Guaranteed Tuition Plan** Texas Prepaid Higher Education Tuition Board (800) 445-4723 www.texastomorrowfunds.org	Prepaid	Yes	Yes	Yes	Yes
	Tomorrow's College Investment Plan State Comptroller's Office (800) 445-4723 www.texastomorrowfunds.org	Savings	No	Yes	No	Yes

(Continued)

TABLE 1-7   State Prepaid Tuition and/or State College Savings Plans (*Continued*)

State	Program Name and Contact Information	Plan Type	Applic. Fee	Portable	Tuition/ Fees Only?	State Tax Incentive
UT	**Utah Educational Savings Plan Trust (UESP)** Utah State Treasurer's Office (800) 418-2551 www.uesp.org	Savings	No	Yes	No	Yes
VT	**Vermont Higher Education Investment Plan** Vermont Student Assistance Corporation (800) 418-2551 www.vsac.org/ investment_plan/main.htm	Savings	No	Yes	No	Yes
VA	**Virginia Prepaid Education Program (VPEP)** Virginia College Savings Plan Board (888) 567-0540 www.virginia529.com	Prepaid	Yes	Yes	Yes	Yes
	Virginia Education Savings Trust (VEST) Virginia College Savings Plan Board (888) 567-0540 www.virginia529.com	Savings	Yes	Yes	No	Yes
WA	**GET (Guaranteed Education Tuition Program)** Committee on Advanced Tuition Payment (877) 438-8848 www.get.wa.gov	Prepaid	Yes	Yes	No	Yes
WV	**SMART 529 Prepaid Tuition Plan** West Virginia State Treasurer's Office (866) 574-3542 www.smart529.com	Prepaid	No	Yes	No	Yes

TABLE 1-7   State Prepaid Tuition and/or State College Savings Plans (*Continued*)

State	Program Name and Contact Information	Plan Type	Applic. Fee	Portable	Tuition/ Fees Only?	State Tax Incentive
	SMART 529 College Savings Plan West Virginia State Treasurer's Office (866) 574-3542 www.smart529.com	Savings	No	Yes	No	Yes
WI	**EdVest** Wisconsin Office of the State Treasurer (888) 388-3789 www.edvest.com	Savings	No	Yes	No	Yes
	Tomorrow's Scholar (College Savings Plan) (866) 677-6933	Savings	No	Yes	No	Yes
WY	**The 529 College Achievement Plan** Mercury Funds and MFS Investment Management (877) 529-2655 www.collegeachievementplan.com	Savings	No	Yes	No	Yes

Programs change frequently; information current as of 7/6/05.
Prepaid tuition plans are not reported on the FAFSA.
Savings plans are generally reported as an asset of the holder (either student or parent) on the FAFSA.
Source: National Association of Student Financial Aid Administrators, (NASFAA), Copyright © 2004. Printed with permission.

on the various state-sponsored savings and prepaid tuition programs. Table 1-7 answers the following questions:

- Is it a prepaid program or savings program?
- Are there any application or enrollment fees?
- Is the program portable?
- Does the program cover more than tuition and fees?
- Does the program offer tax incentives?

Contact information and websites are provided for more details about each program. Please note that information about these programs changes frequently. For more information see www.collegesavings.org. This website is updated frequently.

Some Tips for Maximizing Your Aid Eligibility

As you develop a strategy to increase your financial aid eligibility, you should ask yourself whether using a specific investment strategy is consistent with your ethical values as well as your long-term financial goals.

As you think about financial strategies to increase aid eligibility, please remember that federal, state, and institutional aid is not unlimited and there is only so much money to assist all potential aid applicants. Also, as you consider these tips, honesty is always the best policy.

In the following tips section, the FAFSA is mentioned. This federal financial aid application is used by colleges and universities to award federal grants, loans, and work-study. In many cases, colleges and universities use this form to award their own institutional funds. Chapter 3 will thoroughly explain the FAFSA.

Tips

Your goal is to lower the Expected Family Contribution (EFC), which is calculated from the FAFSA. The lower the EFC, the greater the possibility of student aid, which may include grants, federal student loans, and employment.

1. **Timetable:** In order to maximize your planning strategies, you should implement them at least two years before the student enrolls in college. This timetable may influence the results of the federal need analysis formula for the initial FAFSA data (freshman year of college).

2. **Base-Year Income:** You should attempt to reduce your adjusted gross income and net worth for the "base year," which is the calendar year prior to requesting aid, e.g., calendar year 2005 for aid in academic year 2006–2007.

3. **Treatment of Assets:** Generally, parental assets (not including equity in primary residence for Federal Methodology) are assessed up to 5.6% and student assets at 35% as of the date the FAFSA is completed. On July 1, 2007, the 35% assessment rate is reduced to 20% for dependent students and

independent students with and without dependents other than a spouse. The key with assets is ownership. Check with your tax advisor to determine ownership of a particular asset.

4. **Noncountable Assets:** As you continue to plan for asset re-allocation, certain assets are not used in the federal need analysis formula. These assets are retirement plan assets, your personal residence, life insurance, annuities, and personal property (e.g., cars, boats, and snowmobiles). Also, consumer debt is not considered in the formula. For example, if the family has $50,000 in cash and $50,000 in consumer debt, the family net worth for aid purposes is still $50,000. Consequently, asset planning favors maximizing non-countable assets and increasing investment or business debt instead of consumer debt.

5. **Capital Gains Earnings:** You should attempt to minimize capital gains during the base-year because capital gains are treated as income.

6. **Student Assets:** If there are assets and money in the student's name, use those funds first because it will reduce the amount of future student assets reported on the FAFSA, which is assessed at 35% up to June 30, 2007. The 35% assessment rate decreases to 20% on July 1, 2007.

7. **529 Plans:** Invest in a 529 college savings plan owned by the parent because it has a smaller impact on the federal need analysis formula; one owned by a grandparent is even better because it is not used in the federal need analysis formula.

8. **Retirement Plans:** Don't use retirement funds to pay for college expenses. They are not counted in the federal need analysis formula. If possible, use liquid assets such as cash in savings accounts first. This will reduce the amount of assets reported on the FAFSA. If you need money from your retirement fund, it is wiser to borrow from the retirement fund, if possible, and avoid any penalty from withdrawing money from the fund.

9. **FAFSA Submission:** The date of submission of the FAFSA should be considered very carefully because the total amount of assets and marital status are reported as of the application date.

10. **Big Purchases:** If you have been saving money for a big-dollar purchase, such as home repairs or a new car, you should buy them before you submit the FAFSA. This purchase will reduce the assets reported on the FAFSA.

11. **Children in College:** The number of children simultaneously enrolled in college at least half time will significantly reduce the parental contribution (PC) and increase the student's need. It is better to have two in college than one. For example, if the PC is $10,000, it will be $5,000 per child if both are enrolled in college. Consequently, each child has a greater financial need. If children are one year apart in school, the older child might consider waiting

a year before starting college if expenses are a sufficiently important factor in the older child's ability to obtain the education he or she desires. Also, remember that your parental contribution is not adjusted when there is only one in college instead of two. Consequently, your financial need will decrease when one child graduates or leaves college. You need to keep this in mind when you are developing a multiyear college financing plan.

12. **Plus Loan:** After graduation, parents and graduate/professional students who borrowed through the Federal PLUS Loan or alternative loan programs may want to convert these loans to a home equity loan or line of credit in order to deduct the interest payments on their 1040 federal income tax return.

13. **Assets of Other Children:** Assets of other siblings are not reported on the applicant's FAFSA. However, when the other sibling enters college those assets will be considered in the need analysis formula for that student.

Collection of Additional Information by Colleges

Some colleges and universities use the College Scholarship Service (CSS)/Profile form, a product of the College Board that collects more comprehensive financial information than the FAFSA. For example, the CSS/Profile requests a reasonable selling price if the home is sold today (don't use assessed, insured, or tax value); how much is owed on the house, including the present mortgage; and the year purchased and the purchase price. A few colleges may ask the family additional information when allocating institutional funds. These examples are an exception to the general rule. The point is that some colleges will look at individual assets more carefully than other colleges when awarding their own institutional money.

Tax Tips to Finance Your Education

Hope Scholarship Tax Credit
This is a $1,500 tax credit per student that applies to tuition and fees for the first two years of postsecondary education.

Lifetime Learning Tax Credit
This is a tax credit up to $2,000 (for tuition and fees) for all years of post-secondary education, but cannot be used concurrently with a Hope Scholarship Tax Credit.

Student Loan Interest Deduction
A direct tax deduction up to $2,500. You do not have to itemize your deduction.

Custodial Accounts
New lower capital gains tax rate means that children will pay a 5% tax on any gains in their portfolio. Drawback: Children get control of the money when they become adults.

Coverdell Education Savings Account (Formerly Education IRA)
Allows families with adjusted gross incomes of up to $220,000 to save $2,000 per year, tax free. (For single filers, the adjusted gross income cap is $110,000.)

State 529 College Savings Plans
Allows families to save large amounts of money tax-free under Section 529 of the Internal Revenue Code. Plans vary from state to state. Check with your state agency for additional information.

Independent 529 Plan
This new prepaid plan works like the State 529 Plan. Parents and grandparents are able to lock in tuition at over 250 private colleges and universities at slightly discounted rates. Check the website: www.independent 529plan.org.

Make sure that you read the eligibility criteria for these seven programs.

It's a Wrap

Now that you understand that there are numerous savings plans and realize that college cost will increase annually, you are in position to begin or increase your monthly savings allocation. The tips outlined in this chapter will assist you in maximizing your eligibility for student aid.

Test Yourself

True or False

1. Tuition increases at both public and private universities averaged less than 4% for academic year 2003–2004.
2. Parental and student assets in the federal need analysis formula are assessed at the same percentage.
3. When considering an investment plan, the investor tolerance for risk should be a major consideration.
4. Over 250 private colleges and universities participate in the Independent 529 Plan.
5. A withdrawal from a savings plan is treated like a scholarship: it will reduce financial need on a dollar for dollar basis.
6. Savings bonds in the student's name will be assessed at 5.6%.

7. The Hope Scholarship Tax Credit applies to all four years of a postsecondary education.
8. Withdrawals from 529 College Savings Plans, 529 Prepaid Plans, and 529 Independent Plans are taxed at the child's rate of 35%.
9. Coverdell Education Savings account allow qualified distribution tax free as long as the funds are used for eligible school cost.
10. Base year income is the income in the calendar year preceding the award year.

Test Yourself

Fill in the Blanks

1. Parents will pay for college expenses from three sources: They are _____, _____, and _____.

2. 529 State Savings Plans are treated as a _____ _____ and current federal financial aid formulas will count up to _____% of the assets.

3. IRS Publication _____, Tax Benefits for Higher Education explains the rules on eligibility and how to claim tax credits.

4. Parental assets are assessed at up to _____% and student's assets are assessed at _____% up to June 30, 2007.

5. Name four noncountable assets in the Federal Need Analysis Formula: _____, _____, _____, and _____.

6. _____ _____ is not considered in the Federal Need Analysis Formula.

7. Total amount of assets and marital status are reported as of the _____ date.

8. Parental contribution is divided by the number of _____ enrolled simultaneously in college, at least _____ _____.

9. Some colleges will use _____ _____ _____ to collect personal financial information.

10. Two federal tax credit programs are _____ _____ and _____ _____.

The Real Cost of a College Education

Do I Need to Read This Chapter?

You need to read this chapter if you want to learn about

➡ The real cost of a college education

➡ The difference between a college's sticker price and its net price

➡ Public colleges' tuition for nonstate residents

➡ Financial aid myths: you can't afford college, and realities: yes, you can

➡ A broad range of college options

➡ How your financial need will vary according to college cost

➡ A two-year college option

The Real Cost of College

Over the years, many high school seniors and their parents have asked me, "How can I afford to go to the college of my choice?" Very few families, even those that plan ahead, have the financial resources available to pay for the complete cost of a college education. Most families rely on some form of student financial aid to assist them. These aid programs include need-based grants, merit scholarships (both academic and special talent), low-interest federal loans, and work opportunities to supplement the amount that students and parents can afford to pay themselves for college expenses. Indeed, "In 2002, only 19% of college students paid full tuition at private institutions. This was down from 37% in 1990."[1] As the cost of college has increased, so have available forms of financial aid.

Affordability Facts

- Four-year public and private colleges—46% of undergraduate students enrolled in institutions with published tuition and fees less than $6,000.

- Four-year public colleges and universities—about 60% of full-time students enrolled in these institutions attend institutions that charge published tuition and fees between $3,000 and $6,000.

- High-priced institutions—about 12% of full-time undergraduates attend a four-year institution with published tuition and fees of $24,000 or higher per year.

- Two-year public college—on average, full-time students pay a net price of about $400 (2005–2006 price of $2,191–$1,800 in grants and tax benefits).

There is more financial aid available today than ever before. During academic year 2004–2005, over $129 billion was distributed to undergraduate and graduate students. This was almost $10 billion more than during academic year 2003–2004. Recently, one financial aid expert stated that even Bill Gates would qualify for a federal unsubsidized loan. The bottom line is that all families should apply for student financial aid. To lower and middle income families, aid most certainly is available. Even to higher income families, aid may be available in the form of merit scholarships, low interest loans, and private scholarships.

You owe it to yourself to apply for financial aid if you believe that you need help. Although there is no guarantee that you will be eligible, you will know

[1] *New York Times*, November 9, 2003.

with certainty only if you apply. Even if you do not receive aid during your first year of school, you should reapply in subsequent years. Aid eligibility may increase when family circumstances change.

Simply put, financial aid makes college affordable. Williams College, located in Williamstown, Massachusetts, had a price tag for academic year 2004–2005 of $40,600 (which included tuition, fees, room and board, books and supplies, transportation, and personal expenses). Nonetheless, it is considered a "Best Value" according to the *U.S. News & World Report*, 2006 Edition, "America's Best Colleges."[2] The reason is that Williams has generous student financial aid policies. Since 2001–2002 Princeton University has met 100% of financial need through university grants, scholarships, and campus jobs. No Princeton student, domestic or international, is required to take out a loan to pay Princeton's costs. At Canisius College, in Buffalo, New York, the average net cost for tuition and fees ($23,297) for a freshman student in academic year 2005–2006 was $4,529. The average need-based financial aid package consisted of $14,550 in scholarship/grant money, $3,258 in loans, and $960 in campus work. These examples are intended simply to demonstrate why a student should never say that "college is too expensive."

The Wide Range of College Options

There are over 4,000 colleges and universities in the United States. They range from traditional four-year colleges and universities to two-year junior colleges to specialized proprietary schools (for example, schools of cosmetology or computer training). Admission policies across this range of schools vary from open admission to very selective admission. The point is that there is a college to suit most any motivated student who wants a postsecondary education. Table 2-1 provides the numbers of different kinds of collegiate opportunities in the United States.

Table 2-2 illustrates how college costs vary among different schools in each state.

TABLE 2-1   Kinds of Colleges in the United States

Two-Year Colleges		Four-Year Colleges/Universities	
Public	Private	Public	Private
1081	127	631	1538
Two-year proprietary colleges (for profit)		**Four-year proprietary colleges (for profit)**	
494		297	

[2]*U.S. News & World Report*, 2006 Edition, "America's Best Colleges," page 64.

TABLE 2-2 Sample College Costs (Academic Year 2005–2006)

State & School	Tuition and Fees (in State/ out of State)	Room & Board[1]	Transpor-tation	Books & Supplies	Personal	Total Costs (in State/ out of State)
Alabama						
Tuskegee U.	$12,045	$6,150	$381	$873	$1,596	$21,045
U. of Alabama	$4684/13,516	$5,204	$736	$800	$1,690	$12,934/21,766
Alaska						
U. of Alaska (Fairbanks)	$3976/11,566	$5,580	NA	$700	$300	$10,556/18,146[2]
Alaska Pacific U.	$18,342	$6,900	$1,300	$840	$1,111	$28,493
Arizona						
Arizona State U.	$4407/15,095	$7,150	$1,000	$700	$2,992	$16,249/26,937
U. of Arizona	$4487/13,671	$7,460	$520	$714	$2,212	$15,394/24,578
Arkansas						
U. of Arkansas (Fayetteville)	$5495/13,222	$5,696	$1,090	$892	$1,812	$14,985/22,712
Harding University	$11,200	$5,312	NA	$1,200	$300	$18,012[2]
California						
Santa Clara	$29,159	$10,032	$612	$1,260	$1,828	$42,819
U. of California (Los Angeles)	$6505/24,324	$11,928	$729	$1,483	$2,075	$23,020/40,839
Colorado						
U. of Colorado (Boulder)	$5,372/22,826	$7,980	$567	$1,163	$2,673	$17,755/35,209
U. of Denver	$28,410	$8,748	$576	$1,187	$1,044	$39,965
Connecticut						
U. of Connecticut	$7,912/20,416	$7,848	$900	$725	$1,500	$18,885/31,389
Fairfield University	$30,235	$9,600	$1,000	$500	$900	$42,235
Delaware						
Wesley College	$15,739	$6,980	$500	$1,000	$750	$24,453
U. of Delaware	$7,318/17,474	$6,824	NA	$800	$1,500	$16,442/26,598[2]

District of Columbia					
Georgetown U.	$32,024	$10,739	$410	$980	$1,522	$45,675
U. of the District of Columbia	$2520/4710	NA	$1,260	$800	$1,600	$6180/8370[1]
Florida					
Florida State	$3,208	$6,856	$1,000	$725	$1,000	$12,789/25,921
Jacksonville U.	$19,970	$6,600	$800	$600	$600	$28,570
Georgia					
Mercer University	$23,460	$7,413	$500	$800	$715	$32,888
U. of Georgia	$4,628/16,848	$6,376	NA	$750	$1,740	$13,494/25,714[2]
Hawaii					
Hawaii Pacific U.	$11,630	$9,450	$1,000	$1,300	$800	$24,180
U. of Hawaii—Manoa	$3,697/10,177	$6,717	$243	$1,017	$1,166	$15,840/22,320
Idaho					
Boise State U.	$3,872/11,280	$4,908	$1,000	$1,000	$2,258	$13,038/20,446
Idaho State	$4,000/11,700	$4,870	$810	$800	$1,730	$12,210/19,910
Illinois					
Loyola of Chicago	$24,612	$9,060	$450	$800	$1,600	$36,522
U. of Illinois (Urbana Champaign)	$8,688/22,774	$7,176	$470	$820	$2,020	$19,174/33,260
Indiana					
Indiana U. (Bloomington)	$7,112/19,508	$6,240	$750	$740	$2,600	$17,442/29,838
U. of Notre Dame	$31,542	$8,180	$500	$850	$900	$41,972
Iowa					
Drake U.	$21,462	$6,170	$325	$700	$1,500	$30,157
U. of Iowa	$5,612/16,998	$6,073	$800	$840	$2,330	$15,655/27,041
Kansas					
Bethany College	$15,460	$5,200	$600	$900	$1,900	$24,060
U. of Kansas (Lawrence)	$5,413/13,866	$5,852	$1,304	$750	$2,032	$15,351/23,804

(*Continued*)

TABLE 2-2 Sample College Costs (Academic Year 2005–2006) (*Continued*)

State & School	Tuition and Fees (in State/ out of State)	Room & Board[1]	Transpor- tation	Books & Supplies	Personal	Total Costs (in State/ out of State)
Kentucky						
Transylvania	$19,650	$6,590	$500	$750	$1,250	$28,740
U. of Kentucky	$5,812/12,798	$5,229	$560	$600	$1,148	$13,349/20,335
Louisiana						
Louisiana State	$4,515/12,815	$6,330	$822	$1,000	$1,427	$14,094/22,394
U. and A&M						
Loyola of New Orleans	$25,246	$8,312	NA	$1,000	$1,424	$35,982[2]
Maine						
Bowdoin College	$32,970	$8,670	NA	$880	$1,190	$43,710[2]
U. of Maine (Orono)	$6,910/17,050	$6,722	$500	$700	$1,100	$15,932/26,072
Maryland						
Johns Hopkins U.	$32,120	$9,924	$700	$850	$800	$44,394
U. of Maryland (College Park)	$7,821/20,145	$8,075	$674	$909	$2,022	$19,501/31,825
Massachusetts						
Boston College	$31,438	$10,170	NA	$650	$1,000	$43,258[2]
U. of Massachusetts (Amherst)	$9,278/18,397	$6,517	$400	$1,000	$1,000	$18,195/27,314
Michigan						
U. of Detroit— Mercy	$22,470	$7,328	$790	$1,342	$2,732	$34,662[2]
U. of Michigan (Ann Arbor)	$9,213/27,601	$7,374	NA	$956	$2,060	$19,603/37,991
Minnesota						
Macalester College	$28,642	$7,858	NA	$850	$700	$38,050
U. of Minnesota (Twin Cities)	$8,622/20,252	$6,722	NA	$730	$2,392	$18,466/30,096[2]

Mississippi						
Mississippi State	$4,312/9,769	$5,770	$1,000	$800	$1,790	$13,672/19,104
U. of Mississippi	$4,320/9,744	$4,698	$600	$750	$2,000	$12,368/17,792
Missouri						
St. Louis	$24,760	$8,200	NA	$1,040	$1,050	$36,600
U. of Missouri (Columbia)	$7,745/17,522	$6,245	NA	$835	$2,436	$17,261/27,038
Montana						
Carroll College	$17,078	$6,246	$1,200	$700	$1,600	$26,824
U. of Montana (Missoula)	$4,703/13,419	$5,646	NA	$800	$3,248	$14,397/23,113[2]
Nebraska						
Creighton U.	$22,382	$7,540	$600	$1,000	$1,400	$32,922
U. of Nebraska (Lincoln)	$6,364/14,680	$5,861	NA	$850	$2,056	$15,131/23,447[2]
Nevada						
Sierra Nevada College	$19,650	$7,450	$500	$750	$2,035	$30,385
U. of Nevada (Las Vegas)	$3,060/12,527	$8,373	$610	$850	$1,800	$14,663/24,160
New Hampshire						
Franklin-Pierce	$23,710	$7,990	$520	$850	$1,094	$34,164
U. of New Hampshire (Durham)	$9,778/21,498	$7,034	$300	$1,400	$1,924	$20,436/32,156
New Jersey						
Princeton U.	$31,450	$8,763	$530	$990	$2,039	$43,771
Rutgers at New Brunswick	$9,108/16,706	$8,578	$544	$733	$1,453	$20,416/28,014
New Mexico						
St. John's College	$32,574	$7,876	$600	$275	$900	$42,225
U. of New Mexico	$5,136/16,800	$6,276	$1,396	$792	$1,562	$15,162/26,826

(Continued)

TABLE 2-2 Sample College Costs (Academic Year 2005–2006) *(Continued)*

State & School	Tuition and Fees (in State/ out of State)	Room & Board[1]	Transpor- tation	Books & Supplies	Personal	Total Costs (in State/ out of State)
New York						
Canisius College	$23,297	$8,960	$700	$700	$430	$34,087
State U. of New York (Old Westbury)	$5,071/11,331	$8,082	$750	$675	$1,210	$15,788/22,048
North Carolina						
Davidson College	$28,667	$8,158	$350	$1,000	$1,176	$39,351
U. of North Carolina (Chapel Hill)	$4,515/18,313	$6,590	$500	$900	$1,200	$13,705/27,503
North Dakota						
North Dakota State (Fargo)	$5,264/12,545	$5,130	$270	$670	$2,230	$11,554/18,835
U. of North Dakota	$5,327/12,578	$4,787	$810	$700	$2,040	$13,664/20,915
Ohio						
John Carroll	$23,630	$7,526	$800	$1,000	$750	$33,706
Ohio State U. (Columbus)	$8,082/19,305	$7,770	$120	$1,044	$3,165	$20,181/31,404
Oklahoma						
U. of Oklahoma	$4,408/12,301	$6,048	$953	$1,007	$3,100	$15,516/23,409
U. of Tulsa	$18,860	$6,488	$1,170	$1,200	$2,345	$30,063
Oregon						
Lewis & Clark College	$27,710	$7,648	$900	$1,800	$900	$38,958
U. of Oregon (Eugene)	$5,805/18,201	$7,496	NA	$900	$2,345	$16,546/28,942[2]
Pennsylvania						
Penn State	$11,508/21,744	$7,060	$378	$816	$2,016	$21,778/32,014
St. Joseph U.	$27,455	$9,940	NA	$1,250	$2,500	$41,145[2]

Puerto Rico					
U. of Puerto Rico (Bayamur)	$1,416/3,048	$6,620	NA	NA	$1,200	$9,236/11,228[2,3]
Turabo University	$4,873	NA	$1,350	$600	$2,620	$8,243[1]
Rhode Island					
Providence College	$26,050	$9,270	$1,500	$700	$1,250	$38,770
U. of Rhode Island	$7,284/19,926	$8,560	NA	$600	$1,576	$18,020/30,662[2]
South Carolina					
Furman U.	$26,352	$6,912	$970	$750	$712	$35,696
U. of South Carolina (Columbia)	$7,314/18,956	$5,766	$1,104	$720	$2,420	$17,324/28,966
South Dakota					
Augustana College	$18,860	$5,520	$200	$800	$800	$26,180
U of South Dakota	$4,829/9,816	$4,240	$1,100	$750	$2,000	$12,919/17,806
Tennessee					
Fisk U.	$13,180	$6,730	$1,450	$1,000	$2,050	$24,410
U. of Tennessee (Knoxville)	$5,290/16,060	$5,210	$2,494	$998	$2,002	$15,994/26,764
Texas					
Southern Methodist U.	$26,880	$9,610	$300	$600	$1,100	$38,490
U. of Texas (Austin)	$6,972/16,310	$6,360	$850	$800	$2,150	$17,132/26,470
Utah					
Westminster College	$19,730	$5,932	$900	$900	$1,225	$28,687
U. of Utah	$4,299/13,372	$5,678	NA	$1,086	NA	$11,063/20,136[2,4]
Vermont					
Bennington College	$33,570	$8,320	$400	$800	$1,684	$44,774
U. of Vermont	$10,748/24,934	$7,321	NA	$832	$975	$19,876/34,062[2]
Virginia					
Randolph Macon College	$23,945	$7,305	$780	$1,000	$720	$33,750
U. of Virginia	$7,133/23,877	$6,389	NA	$1,000	$1,610	$16,132/32,876[2]

(Continued)

TABLE 2-2 Sample College Costs (Academic Year 2005–2006) (*Continued*)

State & School	Tuition and Fees (in State/ out of State)	Room & Board[1]	Transpor- tation	Books & Supplies	Personal	Total Costs (in State/ out of State)
Washington						
Seattle U.	$22,905	$8,403	$1,245	$945	$1,890	$35,388
U. of Washington	$5,620/19,917	$7,164	$396	$798	$2,187	$16,166/30,463
West Virginia						
Wheeling Jesuit	$21,540	$6,610	$500	$800	$600	$30,050
West Virginia U. (Morgantown)	$4,164/12,874	$6,342	$1,294	$800	$988	$13,589/22,299
Wisconsin						
Lawrence U.	$27,924	$5,900	NA	$600	$1,005	$35,429[2]
U. of Wisconsin (Madison)	$6,220/18,972	$6,078	NA	$700	$1,388	$14,386/27,138[2]
Wyoming						
Casper College (Two year)	$1,536/4,296	$3,460	$450	$500	$900	$6,846/9,606
U. of Wyoming	$3,429/9,189	$6,240	$679	$1,000	$2,000	$13,348/19,738

[1]Room and Board not included. [2]Transportation costs not included. [3]Books & supplies not estimated. [4]Personal costs not estimated.
Source: Prepared by Anthony J. Bellia, September 2005. Information was obtained from individual college websites.

Two-Year College Option

It is not uncommon for students to move from one kind of college to another during their collegiate careers. For many students, enrolling in an accredited two-year college will be a smart and financially viable option. Tuition at two-year public colleges is significantly lower than most other kinds of colleges. The average tuition cost of a two-year college in academic year 2004–2005 was $2,076. Students planning to enroll in a two-year college should make sure that the two-year college has *articulation agreements* with four-year public and private colleges. These agreements allow students to transfer credits to a four-year college after completing the two-year degree program. Enrolling in a two-year college before attending a four-year college will likely reduce the student's overall college expenses and college loan indebtedness.

Note: For brighter students, many colleges offer entering freshmen scholarships that are significantly higher than transfer scholarships. For example, a student who was offered a $10,000 scholarship annually for four years or $40,000 in total, turns it down and enrolls elsewhere. Next year, the student wants to enroll at the school that offered the $10,000. Generally speaking, the transfer scholarship will be significantly less than the amount offered as a freshman student.

Table 2-3 compares the average total annual cost of a two-year college with the average annual costs of public and private four-year colleges.

As you begin to compare the prices of different schools, you need to know that the vast majority of students *do not pay* the published or sticker price. Students pay a *net price* after all student aid is subtracted from the published price. This topic will be discussed later in this chapter.

Tuition Charges at Public Colleges and Universities for Nonstate Residents

If you are planning to attend an out-of-state public college or university, you need to consider the tuition charged to nonstate residents. The average additional tuition charged for out-of-state or out-of-district students at public two-year colleges for academic year 2005–2006 was $4,037, and $7,291 at four-year public colleges. The examples in Table 2-4 are illustrative for academic year 2005–2006.

Keep in mind, too, that college costs have been rising on average 6% per year. If you are preparing a four-year college plan, you should take the current direct costs (tuition, fees, room and board) and multiply them by 1.06% to get a ballpark figure for the sophomore year, and do the same for the junior and senior

TABLE 2-3 Sample Average Undergraduate Budgets, 2005–2006 (Enrollment-Weighted)

	Tuition & Fees	Books & Supplies	Room & Board	Transportation	Other Expenses	Total Expenses
Two-year Public						
Resident	$2,191	$801	*	*	*	*
Commuter	$2,191	$801	$5,909	$1,175	$1,616	$11,692
Four-year public						
Resident	$5,491	$894	$6,636	$852	$1,693	$15,566
Commuter	$5,491	$894	$6,476	$1,168	$1,962	$15,991
Out-of-State	$13,164	$894	$6,636	$852	$1,693	$23,239
Four-year private						
Resident	$21,235	$904	$7,791	$691	$1,295	$31,916
Commuter	$21,235	$904	$7,249	$1,060	$1,622	$32,070

*Sample too small to provide meaningful information.

Average total expenses include room and board costs for commuter students, which are average estimated living expenses for students living off campus but not with parents. These are estimated average student expenses as reported by institutions in the College Board, *Annual Sur ey of Colleges,* 2004–2005.

Note: Four-year public resident and commuter tuition and fees levels are based on in-state charges only. Enrollment weighted tuition and fees are derived by weighting the price charged by each institution by the number of full-time students enrolled. Room and board charges are weighted by the number of students residing on campus.

Source: "Trends in College Pricing," 2005, page 6. Copyright © 2005 by The College Board. Reproduced with permission. All rights reserved. www.collegeboard.com.

TABLE 2-4 Comparison of Resident and Nonresident Tuition

State University	Resident In-State Tuition	Nonresident Tuition
California System—Los Angeles	$3,035	$13,205
Florida State	$3,208	$16,340
State University of New York—Stony Brook	$5,575	$11,835
University of Alabama—Tuscaloosa	$4,864	$13,516
University of Massachusetts—Amherst	$9,278	$18,397
University of Michigan—Ann Arbor	$9,213	$27,601
University of Oklahoma—Norman	$4,408	$12,301
University of South Carolina—Spartanburg	$6,762	$13,600
University of Utah—Salt Lake City	$4,299	$13,372
University of Vermont	$10,748	$24,934
University of Washington	$5,620	$19,917
University of Wisconsin—Madison	$6,280	$20,280

Source: Prepared by Anthony J. Bellia, August 2005, and is subject to change.

years. This is only an estimate, but it will assist you in developing a four-year plan. Here is an example of how this calculation works:

First Year	Second Year	Third Year	Fourth Year
$20,000 Tuition	$20,000	$21,200	$22,472
	× 1.06%	× 1.06%	× 1.06%
	$21,200	$22,472	$23,820

There are also college cost calculators available on the Internet. They can be found at www.collegeboard.com and www.finaid.com. Many colleges and universities have links to college-cost calculators on their websites.

Estimating the Sticker Price of a College

Over the years, numerous research studies have shown that parents and students do not really understand the actual cost of attending a particular college or university. A recent study, "Getting Ready to Pay for College," issued by The National Center for Education Statistics in August 2003, found that "both students and parents substantially overestimated tuition amounts, especially for two- and four-year public institutions."[3] The same study found, in contrast, that "parents whose students plan to attend private colleges appeared to be more aware of costs than their counterparts whose children plan to attend comparable public schools."[4]

According to a College Board publication, "Trends in College Pricing 2005," the 2005–2006 average cost of attendance at four-year public colleges and universities nationally was $15,566 ($5,419 tuition and fees) and $31,916 ($21,235 tuition and fees) at four-year private nonprofit institutions. The cost of attendance includes tuition, fees, room and board, books and supplies, transportation, and personal expenses.[5]

To understand college costs, we must differentiate between two types: direct and indirect costs.

- *Direct costs* are costs paid directly to colleges and universities. They include tuition and fees for all students and room and board for resident students.

- *Indirect costs* are costs not paid directly to the college. They include, for example, personal expenses, books, and transportation. These are costs that students and families can control to some degree.

[3,4]"Getting Ready for College" issued by the National Center for Education Statistics in August 2003, page V.
[5]"Trends in College Pricing 2005." Copyright © 2005 by The College Board. Reproduced with permission. All rights reserved. www.collegeboard.com.

Dean's Tips

- The Deficit Reduction Act of 2005 (February 2006) allows students who are enrolled less than half-time to have room and board costs added to their cost of attendance budget.

- The Act also permits a one-time inclusion of the cost of a first professional credential in the cost of attendance budget for a student in a program requiring professional licensure or certification.

- Both of these provisions are effective as of July 1, 2006 for academic year 2006–2007.

You should check college websites, college literature, and handbooks to determine college costs (refer to the Appendix for a sample college cost budget). It is important to check the academic year for which the costs are being published. Often, tuition and fee data is outdated in these resources.

The worksheet in Table 2-5 is designed to assist you in calculating the cost of attendance at institutions you may be considering. The data necessary to complete this worksheet usually can be obtained from the college's literature, its website, or the Student Financial Aid Office.

Note: If you are applying to an out-of-state public school, make sure that you use the correct out-of-state tuition for nonresidents.

Sticker Price versus Net Price

Once you estimate the cost of attending a particular school, you may experience "sticker shock." But you should never let the *sticker price* of a particular college stop you from applying for admission. You need to determine the *net cost* of attending that college. The bottom line is that going to college is a realistic option for you. Colleges will provide financial aid opportunities to students who could not otherwise afford to pay.

Student financial aid effectively serves to reduce tuition, and to meet the student's financial need. The awarding of institutional scholarship aid by colleges to bring down tuition is called *tuition discounting*. Table 2-6 provides a sampler of published tuition discounts that demonstrates the importance of looking at the net price of a college rather than the published or sticker price. In many instances, the average cost listed here will be significantly reduced by additional forms of financial aid.

TABLE 2-5   College Cost Comparison Chart

Name of the Institution	1._____	2._____	3._____
Direct Educational Costs			
Tuition* & Fees	$_____	$_____	$_____
Room	_____	_____	_____
Board	_____	_____	_____
Subtotal	$_____	$_____	$_____
Other Costs			
Books & Supplies	$_____	$_____	$_____
Transportation**	_____	_____	_____
Phone	_____	_____	_____
School Supplies	_____	_____	_____
(computers, etc.)			
Clothing	_____	_____	_____
Personal Expenses	_____	_____	_____
Health Insurance	_____	_____	_____
Study Abroad	_____	_____	_____
Handicapped Expenses	_____	_____	_____
Subtotal	$_____	$_____	$_____
Total Cost	$_____	$_____	$_____

*Make sure that the correct tuition cost is used if the student is applying to an out-of-state public college as a nonstate resident.
**Commuter students living at home should estimate the daily cost of transportation to and from the college. Resident students should estimate the cost of two to three round trips home. Remember to include the cost of going to college in the fall and returning at the end of the year.

Almost no one is paying the full sticker price of a college education. Many times, even students from high-income families do not pay the full cost. That is because there is student aid that rewards students for their high school accomplishments regardless of family income/assets. Most private colleges and universities and many public institutions offer merit scholarships based on high school average, SAT/ACT scores, rank in class, and special talents. Usually, these merit scholarships are four-year commitments. For students who are in need of additional financial assistance, the net cost will be even lower because other sources of financial aid will help meet that financial need: state grants and scholarships, institutional need-based aid, low-interest loans, and private outside scholarships.

TABLE 2-6 Sampler of Published Tuition Discounts

School	Percentage of Students Receiving Grants Based on Need	Average Cost after Receiving Grants Based on Need	Average Discount from Total Cost*
National Universities			
Boston College (MA)	36%	$22,852	45%
Carnegie Mellon (PA)	48%	$25,484	39%
Cornell U. (NY)	45%	$20,507	51%
St. Louis University (MO)	67%	$22,844	35%
U of Notre Dame (IN)	46%	$20,884	47%
Liberal Arts Colleges			
Colby College (ME)	37%	$17,597	58%
Pomona College (CA)	53%	$17,511	57%
Wabash College (IN)	67%	$17,556	47%
Wells College (NY)	74%	$12,711	45%
Williams College (MA)	42%	$16,791	59%
North			
Ithaca College (NY)	67%	$22,089	38%
LeMoyne College (NY)	81%	$16,763	44%
St. Michael's (VT)	63%	$21,144	38%
South			
Loyola of New Orleans	52%	$19,387	40%
Mississippi College	46%	$11,791	41%
Murray State U. (KY)	56%	$14,072	18%
Midwest			
John Carroll (OH)	72%	$21,120	34%
U of Evansville (IN)	67%	$15,191	48%
Valparaiso U. (IN)	67%	$16,932	43%
West			
Gonzaga U. (WA)	61%	$20,476	36%
LeTourneau University (TX)	64%	$15,278	37%
U of Portland (OR)	57%	$19,106	42%

*"Total Cost is tuition, fees, room and board, books, and other expenses for academic year 2005–06."
Source: U.S. News & World Report, 2006 Edition, America's Best Colleges, pages 64 and 65.

Colleges' Concerns about Sticker Price

Some colleges are so concerned about sticker shock that, rather than use financial aid to discount tuition, they are simply reducing tuition. The eighteen colleges in Table 2-7 have reduced their tuition. Of course, these colleges will also provide additional financial aid to students who cannot afford even the reduced tuition price.

Financial Need Varies According to College Cost

Although the student's family is expected to contribute toward payment of college costs, it is seldom true that the higher the cost of a college, the more parents and students are expected to pay. The EFC will depend not on the cost of

TABLE 2-7   Eighteen Colleges with Reduced Tuition

School	Location	Academic Year Tuition Was Reduced	Percentage Reduced
North Park University	Chicago, Illinois	2005–2006	30%
Eureka College	Eureka, Illinois	2004–2005	30%
Lourdes College	Sylvania, Ohio	2004–2005	41%
Salem International University	Salem, West Virginia	2004–2005	35%
Westminster College	Fulton, Missouri	2003–2004	20%
Alberston College of Idaho	Caldwell, Idaho	2003–2004	30%
Waldorf College	Forest City, Iowa	2003–2004	15%
Heidelberg College	Tiffin, Ohio	2002–2003	32%
Bethany College	Bethany, West Virginia	2002–2003	42%
Marlboro College	Marlboro, Vermont	1999–2000	8%
Wells College	Aurora, New York	1999–2000	30%
Bluefield College	Bluefield, Virginia	1998–1999	24%
Pine Manor College	Chestnut Hill, Massachusetts	1998–1999	34%
Queens University of Charlotte	Charlotte, North Carolina	1998–1999	28%
Sheldon Jackson College	Sitka, Alaska	1998–1999	24%
Thiel College	Greenville, Pennsylvania	1998–1999	27%
Muskingum College	New Concord, Ohio	1996–1997	29%
North Carolina Wesleyan College	Rocky Mount, North Carolina	1996–1997	23%

Source: Table completed from *The Chicago Tribune*, January 9, 2005, "Colleges out to Reduce Sticker Shock."

TABLE 2-8   Financial Need and Cost of College

	College A	College B	College C
Cost of attendance	$10,300	$23,178	$40,103
Expected family contribution	−8,000	−8,000	−8,000
Financial Need	$2,300	$15,178	$32,103

the college but on the family's financial strength. Thus, the student's financial need will vary depending on the cost of the institution. Table 2-8 illustrates how financial need will rise as the cost of a particular college increases.

Note that the expected family contribution remains the same in the three examples. Generally, the methodology that colleges use to calculate the EFC—called the Federal Need Analysis Methodology (or simply the Federal Methodology)—results in the same EFC regardless of the cost of a particular college. However, in awarding their own institutional aid some colleges may adjust the expected family contribution based on their own institutional methodology. Once a college determines the student's financial need, the financial aid office will attempt to meet all or a high percentage of the student's need.

Ultimately, what a family must pay for a college education is a net cost rather than the sticker price. In many instances, the net cost of a college is significantly lower than its sticker price.

Student Financial Aid: Myth and Reality

There are many myths about student financial aid. They relate to the types of aid available and who is eligible for aid. The United States Department of Education and the College Board have identified the following myths about student financial aid:

- College is just too expensive for our family.
- There is less aid available than there used to be.
- You have to be a minority to get financial aid.
- My parents' income is too high to qualify for aid.
- The financial aid form is too hard to fill out.
- My parents saved for college, so we won't qualify.
- Only students with good grades get financial aid.
- If I apply for a loan, I have to take it.

- Working will hurt my academic success.
- I should live at home to cut costs.
- Private schools are out of reach for my family.
- Millions of dollars in scholarships go unused every year.
- My folks will have to sell their home to pay for college.

These myths are misleading to students, parents and school counselors. All of them are generally false.[6]

Myth One: College Is Just Too Expensive for Our Family

This is almost never true. According to College Board's study, "Trends in College Pricing 2005," "46% of undergraduate students in public and private four-year colleges are enrolled in institutions with published tuition and fees less than $6,000."[7] Moreover, even with respect to "expensive" colleges, once student financial aid is taken into account, the net cost of attending a private college is substantially less than the published tuition and fees price.

Private colleges over the last decade have increased student aid by more than twice as much as tuition—197% increase in aid versus 86% increase in tuition. Consequently, the net tuition at private colleges declined by $100 over the last ten years, according to the National Association of Independent Colleges and Universities.

The lesson is plain: Both private and public colleges are awarding significant amounts of financial aid to make their colleges affordable. The key is that you have to apply for the aid. No student should rule out a college because of its sticker price. Financial aid will reduce the price according to family circumstances.

Myth Two: There Is Less Aid Available Than There Used to Be

This is not true. There was "over $129 billion in available student financial aid for academic year 2004–2005. This is almost $10 billion more than academic year 2003–2004."[8] Student aid has increased significantly at private colleges.

---

[6] "Financial Aid Myths—Don't Believe Everything You Hear." www.collegeboard.com. Copyright © 2005 by collegeboard.com reproduced with permission. All rights reserved.
[7] "Trends in College Pricing 2005," page 3. Copyright © 2005 by The College Board. Reproduced with permission. All rights reserved. www.collegeboard.com.
[8] "Trends in College Pricing." Copyright © 2005 by The College Board. Reproduced with permission. All rights reserved. www.collegeboard.com

Much of this aid is in the form of scholarships and grants, which is free money. You do not repay grants or scholarships. According to The College Board, "institutional aid constitutes about half of all grant aid received by students. After adjusting for inflation, institutional grants have doubled over the past decade. About 25 percent of full-time undergraduate students enrolled in public colleges and universities and 60 percent at private institutions receive institutional grant aid."[9] In addition to the $46 billion in grants, 10 million taxpayers benefited from federal education tax credits or tuition and fees deductions. Also, there are numerous federal, institutional, and private student loans available to students with very low interest rates.

The message resulting from the discussion of the first two myths is that, in reality, there is money available to students. All college options should be investigated when selecting a college. *Don't let the published or sticker price scare you.* Don't allow such myths to discourage you from applying to the college of your choice.

Myth Three: You Have to Be a Minority to Get Aid

This statement is simply not true. There is no criteria within federal or institutional methodology (refer to Chapter 4) that factors in minority background. Both federal and institutional need analysis systems are race neutral. The FAFSA does not even ask applicants to submit race information. Colleges will use the expected family contribution and simply subtract it from the cost of attendance to determine financial need. Also, colleges are committed to access and affordability regardless of ethnic background. During the last three to four years, some colleges have adjusted their packaging policies based on income levels, not on minority status. Of course, some specific scholarships consider racial or ethnic background, but that does not mean that other forms of aid are not available to those who do not qualify for such scholarships.

Myth Four: My Parents' Income Is Too High to Qualify for Aid

Merit scholarships are awarded based on specific criteria—for example, high school average, SAT scores, rank in class (if listed), and service. Family income is generally not a factor. The largest growth in institutional aid budgets is merit money. Colleges are competing locally, regionally, and nationally for talented, gifted students. Many colleges are offering merit money in order to improve their rankings in college guides.

---

[9] "Trends in Student Aid." Copyright © 2004 by The College Board. Reproduced with permission. All rights reserved. www.collegeboard.com

Also, both the federal and institutional need analysis formulas take into consideration family income, family size, number of students in college, federal and state taxes paid, and other factors. Finally, the key factor in determining financial need is the college's cost of attendance. As explained in this chapter, a student may demonstrate financial need at some colleges and not show financial need at other colleges.

Do not believe that you are ineligible for aid due to family income. You should apply and then allow the financial aid offices at each college to provide guidance on how to pay the college costs at their college. Any family concerned about meeting the cost of a college is encouraged to apply.

Myth Five: The Financial Aid Form Is Too Hard to Fill Out

Over the years, the Department of Education with the assistance of student financial aid administrators nationally have simplified the FAFSA. Applicants who complete the FAFSA online will discover that it is easier to do. Each section has specific directions explaining how to complete the individual questions. Once you have completed the FAFSA online and submitted it, you will have an opportunity to correct any mistakes in your original data.

You can also obtain assistance on how to complete the FAFSA and other financial aid applications from local colleges, high school counselors, and possibly community action organizations. Many colleges and high schools offer free workshops on how to complete the FAFSA. These workshops are usually held late fall or January of the student's senior year. From my experience, many sophomore and junior parents attend these workshops to get a heads up on the form and actual processing timetable. Some state student financial aid organizations, such as the New York Student Financial Aid Administrators Association (NYSFAAA), offer a toll-free hotline in January to assist parents/students in completing the FAFSA and in answering general financial aid questions. Also, in late January, NASFAA offers a call-in number. If you have questions concerning the completion of the FAFSA call 1-800-4-FED-AID (1-800-433-3243, TTY 1-800-730-8913).

Myth Six: My Parents Saved for College, so We Won't Qualify

Saving for college will provide the applicant with more opportunities, most significantly:

- Both student and parental savings will reduce student's indebtness. Remember that the largest component of student aid is low-interest loans.

- Savings will provide money to assist the family in paying both direct and indirect college costs.

- **Remember:** Parental and student assets are not counted dollar for dollar in either the federal or institutional need analysis formula.

Generally, up to 5.6% of the assets are considered available to pay for college expenses if in the parents' name and 35% if in the student's name. Consequently, planning ahead for college costs through 529 College Savings Plans and Coverdell ESA accounts is a prudent investment strategy when saving for future college expenses.

Finally, the EFC is calculated primarily on the basis of income, not family assets. Do not be afraid to save. As stated earlier, only a portion of both student and parental savings are assessed in the federal need analysis formula. Families should begin a college savings plan for their children as early as possible. In the long run, it will make it easier and less expensive to pay the college bills and reduce some anxieties associated with selecting a college.

Myth Seven: Only Students with Good Grades Get Financial Aid

Yes, many colleges award merit scholarships based on high school average, SAT score, rank in class (if reported), but they also consider service to the community, participation in the arts, athletics, and academic major as other criteria. More importantly, eligibility for student aid from the federal government and grants from individual colleges are based on the student's financial need, not academic record.

Myth Eight: If I Apply for a Loan, Then I Have to Take It

Loans are usually a significant part of aid packages, but students are not obligated to take them. In some cases, families will decide that they do not need to borrow the recommended loan amount or they will decide to borrow a smaller amount. Federal Stafford and Perkins loans are very attractive, low interest loans. Families should compare federal loans with other loan programs and select the one with the best provisions.

Myth Nine: Working Will Hurt My Academic Success

Higher education research over the years has continually reported that students who work part-time during the academic year will do well academically. The key is not to work too many hours. Students will need to develop a time management plan that includes part-time work, on-campus involvement, and obviously time for academics. Also, part-time work on and off campus will allow the student to earn money for college-related costs and possibly provide hands-on experience for a future career.

Myth Ten: I Should Live at Home to Cut Costs

It is wise to study every avenue for reducing college costs, and living at home may be a significant one. Be sure to consider commuting and parking costs when you do this calculation. Living on campus, however, may provide other benefits that are worth the cost.

Myth Eleven: Private Schools Are Out of Reach for My Family

In many cases, attending a private college or university may be more affordable than a public institution. Private colleges and universities have more institutional aid to award to students. Also, private colleges will award money to students based on academic merit and financial need in order to attract a diverse student body. This is not to imply that public colleges are not aggressive in their recruiting and student packaging practices; they are. Since private colleges and universities have higher tuition costs, applicants may demonstrate more eligibility for student financial aid than at a public college or university. Nationally, more than 70% of students attending private colleges and universities will demonstrate financial need and will receive aid packages including free money, loans, and on-campus part-time work opportunities.

Myth Twelve: Millions of Dollars in Scholarships Go Unused Every Year

This is simply not true. This myth is a banner headline used by some scholarship search companies in order to attract attention for their services. If you were to contact local scholarship foundations and civic organizations, you would discover that these organizations generally award the scholarships that they have available. Regardless, the primary sources of grant and scholarship aid opportunities are from the federal and state governments, and colleges and universities. Have these funding sources taken out ads stating that they have "millions of unused grants or scholarships" still available? To my knowledge, this has not happened. Yes, you should apply for private scholarship money. You should begin the scholarship search process as early as the freshman or sophomore year in high school.

Myth Thirteen: My Folks Will Have to Sell Their Home

The federal government does not consider the value of your primary residence in the need analysis formula. Some colleges, however, may require you to report home equity on their institutional form or the CSS/Profile if the college uses that form. These colleges are requesting the home equity information to calculate an expected family contribution for institutional grant aid, not federal student aid. **Note:** Only a few hundred colleges are requesting this additional information.

As stated previously, parental assets are assessed up to 5.6%. Neither the federal government nor colleges will expect a family to sell their home in order to pay college expenses.

The lesson in this chapter is that you should explore a broad range of options for college, regardless of published price, because families rarely pay the sticker price. Also, you should keep in mind how nonstate residents are charged a significantly higher tuition than state residents.

True or False

1. If your family makes over $80,000 a year, you cannot receive financial aid.
2. Financial aid may be used to pay for tuition, fees, and books, and also pay for food and housing.
3. If I qualify for aid, it may cost the family about the same to attend a more expensive college as it would to attend a less expensive one.
4. Students can receive financial aid only if they are going to a community college or trade school.
5. Financial aid is available only at certain colleges.
6. Financial aid is only for "poor" people.
7. The college that offers me the most money is the best one to attend.
8. Nonstate residents pay the same tuition as in-state students.
9. Direct educational costs are those paid to the college.
10. Sticker price and net price are the same amount.

Fill in the Blanks

1. Direct educational costs include _____, _____, _____, and _____.

2. Financial need varies according to _____.

3. Students attending a two-year college should make sure that there is an
   _____ agreement with four-year _____, and _____ colleges.

4. There are over _____ postsecondary institutions in the United States.

5. Over _____% of undergraduate students attend school with tuition
   fees less than $5,200.

6. _____ _____, is when institutional aid is awarded to reduce the
   tuition cost.

CHAPTER 3

Student Aid Programs

Do I Need to Read This Chapter?

You need to read this chapter if you are a student or parent and need to learn about

➡ College-sponsored aid programs (merit/need-based)

➡ Athletic scholarships

➡ Federal aid scholarships

➡ State aid scholarships

➡ Private scholarships

➡ A timetable for applying for aid

➡ Submitting the FAFSA

➡ Supplemental aid forms

➡ Verification of income on the FAFSA by aid administrators

➡ State residency guidelines

➡ Tips to save money at public colleges

➡ Preparing a college planning calendar

Financial aid, in its simplest definition, is money that is supplied by some source outside the family to help pay for the cost of the student's education. It encompasses a variety of programs funded by colleges, private organizations, and state and federal government. Financial aid is any grant, scholarship, loan, or work-study program offered to help a student meet his or her educational needs.

The purpose of this chapter is to explain the application process for federal, state, and institutional money. The chapter explores working with the financial aid office and how to evaluate and appeal a financial aid award letter. Finally, a suggested timetable for college preparation during high school is provided.

Submitting Your Application: the FAFSA

Annual Submission

Eligibility for federal student aid and institutional need-based aid is determined annually. Eligibility criteria and funding levels of federal, state, and institutional programs may change from year to year. Therefore, financial aid should be applied for every year, even if you think you don't qualify. The student financial aid office will determine your eligibility each year for low-interest federal loans, Pell Grants, Federal Supplemental Opportunity Grants, Federal Work Study, and institutional aid.

The FAFSA

The key document for applying for Federal Student Aid and institutional aid is the Free Application for Federal Student Aid (FAFSA). There is no charge for filing the FAFSA. You have to complete one FAFSA per student and you may list up to six schools. Each school will receive an electronic copy of the data analysis from the central processor. If you want to apply to more than six schools, you can add more schools after the initial FAFSA is processed. Students should consider listing their top schools on the initial FAFSA. Also, you need to check whether your state agency uses the FAFSA. If so, you should list an in-state school as one of the six possible entries in step six of the FAFSA to trigger the state application program process. (Refer to the Appendix for a sample copy of the FAFSA.)

Dean's Tips

Remembering Filing Procedures

- FAFSA (required for all colleges), and CSS/Profile (325+ colleges and scholarship organizations require it). Check if your colleges require it.
- Institutional Financial Aid Application (some colleges require this form).
- Deadlines are very important!
- Students should check with their institutions to learn which student aid forms are required.
- Submit the FAFSA and Profile forms online.

Processing the FAFSA

Your financial aid application will be processed according to the following timetable:

- As early as possible after January 1 of your senior year of high school, you submit the FAFSA electronically or mail it to the central processor in the envelope provided with the FAFSA application. Financial aid professionals strongly recommend that you submit the FAFSA electronically as it is an easier and faster way to file this form. It is also a better way to ensure that it will be done directly. To apply online, go to www.fafsa.ed.gov. Remember, the FAFSA cannot be submitted prior to January 1.

- When you begin the online process, you must obtain a personal identification number (PIN) in order to complete the FAFSA. The PIN is an electronic code number that serves as your online identifier. This PIN is good forever, so you don't need to apply for another one. It is also important that you keep it in a secure place that you will remember. You request a PIN at www.pin.ed.gov.

- Also, one of your custodial parents (refer to the Appendix for definition) must obtain a PIN. The PIN acts as the electronic signature for the parent and the applicant.

- The FAFSA is scanned and processed by the central processor.

- The central processor must verify your eligibility for federal student aid by checking selected information on the FAFSA against some national data-bases, e.g., social security benefits, homeland security, citizenship status, and (for males) selective service status.

- Once these checks are completed, the central processor will check for any inconsistencies on the FAFSA and then calculate your Expected Family Contribution (EFC). The lower the EFC, the more likely you will demonstrate need, depending on the cost of attendance of the college. (This concept was covered in Chapter 1.)

- The central processor will now send you a Student Aid Report (SAR). The SAR will indicate your family's EFC. If you mail the FAFSA, you will receive a SAR in about a month. If you submit a paper copy and include an email address, you will receive the SAR electronically. If you apply online, and provide an email address, you will receive an electronic SAR. The SAR is a multipart eligibility document. You need to review it very carefully in order to make sure that the EFC was calculated correctly. If there are any mistakes, correct the data on the SAR and return it to processor immediately. Read the directions on the SAR and follow them very carefully.

- Also, the central processor will forward your application information electronically to all the colleges listed on the FASFA as well as your state agency. In some states, this transmittal will begin the process for a state grant or scholarship. You should list an in-state school on the first FAFSA to start the process. Remember to check if the state grant or scholarship funding can be used only at an approved school located within the state or if it is portable to another state.

What Happens After You Submit the Financial Aid Forms?

- They are processed by appropriate agencies.
- Your results are shared with colleges listed on the forms.
- The college receives the results.
- College awards financial aid to you.
- Financial aid award is mailed to the student from March to April/ May.
- You and your parents evaluate the financial aid package; you either accept, decline, or seek clarification.
- Answer all correspondence requested by the Financial Aid Office in a timely fashion.

Federal Verification for Federal Student Aid Programs

In order to ensure that funds for educational assistance are awarded on an equitable basis, the U.S. Department of Education requires some applicants to complete a process known as *verification*. Through this process, the institution is asked to request documentation from the student and family of specific items reported on the student's FAFSA. Items required for verification include, but are not limited to, signed copies of federal income tax forms or statements certifying nonfiler status; documentation of child support, social security, and other forms of untaxed income; and statements to verify the number of family members in the household and the number of family members in college.

Some information requested for verification may seem redundant. Please remember, however, that federal law requires this process, and the institution must comply. You are well advised to read the institution's request for specific documentation carefully and comply as quickly as possible.

This is how the verification process works. After you submit the FAFSA, the College Processor Service will send you an SAR. If there is an asterisk following the EFC number, this means that you have been selected for verification. Consequently, the college aid office must verify selected items on the SAR. Verification is usually done by requesting signed copies of the parent and student federal income tax returns and W-2 forms if applicable from the previous year. For the academic year 2006–2007, parents/students will submit the appropriate 2005 Federal Tax form.

Colleges are required to verify 30% of the applicant pool at the college, but many colleges, particularly private schools, verify substantially more than 30%, some as high as 90–100%, of their new students.

Special Note: This verification process is a serious one. Financial Aid officers are trained to review the information carefully. They have "seen it all," so do not be creative or dishonest. Not only will you be dishonestly depriving other students of financial aid, but you will be committing a crime. The FAFSA (2005–2006) clearly states that "If you purposely give false or misleading information, you may be fined $20,000, sent to prison, or both."

The following is a form colleges or universities may use to complete the verification process.

Dependent

2006-2007 Verification Worksheet

Federal Student Aid Programs

FORM APPROVED
OMB NO. 1845-0041

U.S. Department
of Education

Your application was selected for review in a process called "Verification." In this process, your school will be comparing information from your application with signed copies of your and your parent(s)' 2005 Federal tax forms, or with W-2 forms or other financial documents. The law says we have the right to ask you for this information before awarding Federal aid. If there are differences between your application information and your financial documents, you or your school may need to make corrections electronically or by using your Student Aid Report (SAR).

Complete this verification form and submit it to your financial aid administrator as soon as possible, so that your financial aid won't be delayed. Your financial aid administrator will help you.

What you should do

1. Collect your and your parent(s)' financial documents (signed Federal income tax forms, W-2 forms, etc.).
2. Talk to your financial aid administrator if you have questions about completing this worksheet.
3. Complete and sign the worksheet—you and at least one parent.
4. Submit the completed worksheet, tax forms, and any other documents your school requests to your financial aid administrator.
5. Your financial aid administrator will compare information on this worksheet and any supporting documents with the information you submitted on your application. You may need to make corrections electronically or by using your SAR.

Your school must review the requested information, under the financial aid program rules (34 CFR, Part 668).

A. Student Information

Last name	First name	M.I.	Social Security Number

Address (include apt. no.)			Date of birth

City	State	ZIP code	Phone number (include area code)

B. Family Information

List the people in your <u>parents' household</u>, include:
- yourself and your parent(s) (including stepparent) even if you don't live with your parents, and
- your parents' other children, even if they don't live with your parent(s), if (a) your parents will provide more than half of their support from July 1, 2006 through June 30, 2007, or (b) the children would be required to provide parental information when applying for Federal Student Aid, and
- other people if they now live with your parents, and your parents provide more than half of their support and will continue to provide more than half of their support from July 1, 2006 through June 30, 2007.

Write the names of all household members in the space(s) below. Also write in the name of the college for any household member, excluding your parent(s), who will be attending college at least half time between July 1, 2006 and June 30, 2007, and will be enrolled in a degree, diploma, or certificate program. If you need more space, attach a separate page.

Full Name	Age	Relationship	College
Missy Jones (example)	18	Sister	Central University
		Self	

C. Student's Tax Forms and Income Information (all applicants)   Dependent

1. Check only one box below. Tax returns include the 2005 IRS Form 1040, 1040A, 1040EZ, a tax return from Puerto Rico or a foreign income tax return. If you did not keep a copy of your tax return, request a copy from your tax preparer or request an Internal Revenue Service form that lists tax account information.

☐   Check and attach signed tax return.

☐   Check and complete - a signed tax return will be submitted to the school by _____ (date).

☐   Check here if you will not file and are not required to file a 2005 U.S. Income Tax Return.

2. Funds received for child support and other untaxed income. (See worksheets A&B of the Free Application for Federal Student Aid-FAFSA.)

Sources of Untaxed Income	2005 Amount	Sources of Untaxed Income	2005 Amount
a. Child Support	$	d.	$
b. Social Security (non-taxed)	$	e.	$
c. Welfare (including TANF)	$	f.	$

3. If you did not file and are not required to file a 2005 Federal income tax return, list below your employer(s) and any income received in 2005 (use the W-2 form or other earnings statements if available).

Sources	2005 Amount
	$
	$
	$

D. Parent(s)' Tax Forms and Income Information

1. Check only one box below. Tax returns include the 2005 IRS Form 1040, 1040A, 1040EZ, a tax return from Puerto Rico or a foreign income tax return. If your parent(s) did not keep a copy of their tax return, request a copy from the tax preparer or request an Internal Revenue Service form that lists tax account information.

☐   Check and attach signed tax return(s).

☐   Check and complete - a signed tax return(s) will be submitted to the school by _____ (date).

☐   Check here if your parent(s) will not file and are not required to file a 2005 U.S. Income Tax Return.

2. Funds received for child support and other untaxed income. (See worksheets A & B of the Free Application for Federal Student Aid.)

Sources of Untaxed Income	2005 Amount	Sources of Untaxed Income	2005 Amount
a. Child Support	$	d.	$
b. Social Security (non-taxed)	$	e.	$
c. Welfare (including TANF)	$	f.	$

3. If your parent(s) did not file and are not required to file a 2005 Federal income tax return, list below your parent(s)' employer(s) and any income they received in 2005 (use the W-2 form or other earnings statements if available).

Sources	2005 Amount
	$
	$
	$

E. Sign this Worksheet

By signing this worksheet, we certify that all the information reported on it is complete and correct. At least one parent must sign.

> **WARNING:** If you purposely give false or misleading information on this worksheet, you may be fined, be sentenced to jail, or both.

_____   _____
Student   Date

_____   _____
Parent   Date

Do not mail this worksheet to the Department of Education. Submit this worksheet to your Financial Aid Administrator at your school. Make sure that tax forms are signed.

Independent

U.S. Department
of Education

2006-2007 Verification Worksheet

Federal Student Aid Programs

FORM APPROVED
OMB NO. 1845-0041

Your application was selected for review in a process called "Verification." In this process, your school will be comparing information from your application with signed copies of your (and your spouse's, if you are married) 2005 Federal tax forms, or with W-2 forms or other financial documents. The law says we have the right to ask you for this information before awarding Federal aid. If there are differences between your application information and your financial documents, you or your school may need to make corrections electronically or by using your Student Aid Report (SAR).

Complete this verification form and submit it to your financial aid administrator as soon as possible, so that your financial aid won't be delayed. Your financial aid administrator will help you.

What you should do

1. Collect your (and your spouse's) financial documents (signed Federal income tax forms, W-2 forms, etc.).
2. Talk to your financial aid administrator if you have questions about completing this worksheet.
3. Complete and sign the worksheet.
4. Submit the completed worksheet, tax forms, and any other documents your school requests to your financial aid administrator.
5. Your financial aid administrator will compare information on this worksheet and any supporting documents with the information you submitted on your application. You may need to make corrections electronically or by using your SAR. *Your school must review the requested information, under the financial aid program rules (34 CFR, Part 668).*

A. Student Information

Last name	First name	M.I.	Social Security Number
Address (include apt. no.)			Date of birth
City	State	ZIP code	Phone number (include area code)

B. Family Information

List the people in your household, include:

- yourself, and your spouse if you have one, and
- your children, if you will provide more than half of their support from July 1, 2006 through June 30, 2007, and
- other people if they now live with you, and you provide more than half of their support and will continue to provide more than half of their support from July 1, 2006 through June 30, 2007.

Write the names of all household members in the space(s) below. Also write in the name of the college for any household member, excluding your parent(s), who will be attending college at least half time between July 1, 2006 and June 30, 2007, and will be enrolled in a degree, diploma, or certificate program. If you need more space, attach a separate page.

Full Name	Age	Relationship	College
Martha Jones (example)	24	Wife	City University
		Self	

C. Student's Tax Forms and Income Information (all applicants)   Independent

1. Check only one of the boxes below. Tax returns include the 2005 IRS Form 1040, 1040A, 1040EZ, a tax return from Puerto Rico or a foreign income tax return. If you did not keep a copy of your tax return, request a copy from your tax preparer or request an Internal Revenue Service form that lists tax account information.

☐ Check and attach signed tax return.

☐ Check and complete - a signed tax return will be submitted to the school by _____(date).

☐ Check if you will not file and are not required to file a 2005 U.S. Income Tax Return.

2. Funds received for child support and other untaxed income. (See Worksheets A & B of the Free Application for Federal Student Aid-FAFSA.)

Sources of Untaxed Income	2005 Amount	Sources of Untaxed Income	2005 Amount
a. Child Support	$	d.	$
b. Social Security (non-taxed)	$	e.	$
c. Welfare (including TANF)	$	f.	$

3. If you did not file and are not required to file a 2005 Federal income tax return, list below your employer(s) and any income received in 2005 (use the W-2 form or other earnings statements if available).

Sources	2005 Amount
	$
	$
	$

D. Spouse's Tax Forms and Income Information (if student is married)

1. Check only one box below. Tax returns include the 2005 IRS Form 1040, 1040A, 1040EZ, a tax return from Puerto Rico or a foreign income tax return. If your spouse did not keep a copy of the tax return, request a copy from the tax preparer or request an Internal Revenue Service form that lists tax account information.

☐ Check if you and your spouse did or will file a joint return.

☐ Check and attach spouse's signed tax return if your spouse filed a separate return.

☐ Check and complete - a signed spouse's tax return will be submitted to the school by _____(date).

☐ Check if your spouse will not file and is not required to file a 2005 U.S. Income Tax Return.

2. Funds received for child support and other untaxed income. (See Worksheets A & B of the Free Application for Federal Student Aid.)

Sources of Untaxed Income	2005 Amount	Sources of Untaxed Income	2005 Amount
a. Child Support	$	d.	$
b. Social Security (non-taxed)	$	e.	$
c. Welfare (including TANF)	$	f.	$

3. If your spouse did not file and is not required to file a 2005 Federal income tax return, list below your spouse's employer(s) and any income received in 2005 (use the W-2 form or other earnings statements if available).

Sources	2005 Amount
	$
	$
	$

E. Sign this Worksheet

By signing this worksheet, I (we) certify that all the information reported on it is complete and correct. If married, spouse's signature is optional.

> **WARNING: If you purposely give false or misleading information on this worksheet, you may be fined, be sentenced to jail, or both.**

_____   _____
Student   Date

_____   _____
Spouse   Date

Do not mail this worksheet to the Department of Education. Submit this worksheet to your Financial Aid Administrator at your school. Don't forget to sign your tax forms.

Dean's Tip

The sample Federal Form 1040 is cross-referenced to questions on the FAFSA).

Referenced to Free Application for Federal Student Aid (FAFSA)

Form **1040** Department of the Treasury—Internal Revenue Service **2005** (99) IRS Use Only—Do not write or staple in this space.

U.S. Individual Income Tax Return

For the year Jan. 1–Dec. 31, 2005, or other tax year beginning _____ , 2005, ending _____ , 20 ___   OMB No. 1545-0074

Label		
(See instructions on page 16.) Use the IRS label. Otherwise, please print or type.	Your first name and initial	Last name
	If a joint return, spouse's first name and initial	Last name
	Home address (number and street). If you have a P.O. box, see page 16.	Apt. no.
	City, town or post office, state, and ZIP code. If you have a foreign address, see page 16.	

Your social security number

Spouse's social security number

▲ **You must enter your SSN(s) above.** ▲

Presidential Election Campaign ▶ Check here if you, or your spouse if filing jointly, want $3 to go to this fund (see page 16) ▶ ☐ You ☐ Spouse

Checking a box below will not change your tax or refund.

Filing Status

Check only one box.

1 ☐ Single
2 ☐ Married filing jointly (even if only one had income)
3 ☐ Married filing separately. Enter spouse's SSN above and full name here. ▶
4 ☐ Head of household (with qualifying person). (See page 17.) If the qualifying person is a child but not your dependent, enter this child's name here. ▶
5 ☐ Qualifying widow(er) with dependent child (see page 17)

Exemptions

6a ☐ Yourself. If someone can claim you as a dependent, **do not check box 6a**
b ☐ Spouse
c Dependents:

(1) First name Last name	(2) Dependent's social security number	(3) Dependent's relationship to you	(4)✓ if qualifying child for child tax credit (see page 19)
			☐
			☐
			☐
			☐

If more than four dependents, see page 19.

d Total number of exemptions claimed

Boxes checked on 6a and 6b
No. of children on 6c who:
• lived with you
• did not live with you due to divorce or separation (see page 20)
Dependents on 6c not entered above
Add numbers on lines above ▶ **75**

Income

Attach Form(s) W-2 here. Also attach Forms W-2G and 1099-R if tax was withheld.

If you did not get a W-2, see page 22.

Enclose, but do not attach, any payment. Also, please use Form 1040-V.

7 Wages, salaries, tips, etc. Attach Form(s) W-2 .... 7 **# 76/77**
8a Taxable interest. Attach Schedule B if required 8a
b Tax-exempt interest. **Do not** include on line 8a .. 8b **# 79**
9a Ordinary dividends. Attach Schedule B if required 9a
b Qualified dividends (see page 23) 9b
10 Taxable refunds, credits, or offsets of state and local income taxes (see page 23) . 10
11 Alimony received 11
12 Business income or (loss). Attach Schedule C or C-EZ .... 12 **# 76/77**
13 Capital gain or (loss). Attach Schedule D if required. If not required, check here ▶ ☐ 13
14 Other gains or (losses). Attach Form 4797 14
15a IRA distributions . . 15a **# 79** b Taxable amount (see page 25) 15b
16a Pensions and annuities 16a **# 79** b Taxable amount (see page 25) 16b
17 Rental real estate, royalties, partnerships, S corporations, trusts, etc. Attach Schedule E 17
18 Farm income or (loss). Attach Schedule F .... 18 **# 76/77**
19 Unemployment compensation 19
20a Social security benefits . 20a **# 78** b Taxable amount (see page 27) 20b
21 Other income. List type and amount (see page 29) 21
22 Add the amounts in the far right column for lines 7 through 21. This is your **total income** ▶ 22

Adjusted Gross Income

23 Educator expenses (see page 29) 23
24 Certain business expenses of reservists, performing artists, and fee-basis government officials. Attach Form 2106 or 2106-EZ 24
25 Health savings account deduction. Attach Form 8889 25
26 Moving expenses. Attach Form 3903 26
27 One-half of self-employment tax. Attach Schedule SE . 27
28 Self-employed SEP, SIMPLE, and qualified plans . . 28 **# 79**
29 Self-employed health insurance deduction (see page 30) 29
30 Penalty on early withdrawal of savings . . 30
31a Alimony paid b Recipient's SSN ▶ _____ 31a
32 IRA deduction (see page 31) ...... 32 **# 79**
33 Student loan interest deduction (see page 33) . 33
34 Tuition and fees deduction (see page 34) . . 34
35 Domestic production activities deduction. Attach Form 8903 35
36 Add lines 23 through 31a and 32 through 35 36
37 Subtract line 36 from line 22. This is your **adjusted gross income** ▶ 37 **# 73**

For Disclosure, Privacy Act, and Paperwork Reduction Act Notice, see page 78.   Cat. No. 11320B   Form **1040** (2005)

Form 1040 (2005) Page **2**

Tax and Credits	38	Amount from line 37 (adjusted gross income)	38	
	39a	Check if: ☐ You were born before January 2, 1941, ☐ Blind. ☐ Spouse was born before January 2, 1941, ☐ Blind. Total boxes checked ▶ 39a		
Standard Deduction for—	b	If your spouse itemizes on a separate return or you were a dual-status alien, see page 35 and check here ▶39b ☐		
	40	**Itemized deductions** (from Schedule A) **or your standard deduction** (see left margin) . .	40	
	41	Subtract line 40 from line 38	41	
• People who checked any box on line 39a or 39b or who can be claimed as a dependent, see page 36.	42	If line 38 is over $109,475, or you provided housing to a person displaced by Hurricane Katrina, see page 37. Otherwise, multiply $3,200 by the total number of exemptions claimed on line 6d	42	
	43	**Taxable income.** Subtract line 42 from line 41. If line 42 is more than line 41, enter -0-	43	
	44	**Tax** (see page 37). Check if any tax is from: a ☐ Form(s) 8814 b ☐ Form 4972 . .	44	
• All others:	45	**Alternative minimum tax** (see page 39). Attach Form 6251	45	
Single or Married filing separately, $5,000	46	Add lines 44 and 45 . . . . ▶	46	
	47	Foreign tax credit. Attach Form 1116 if required . .	47	
	48	Credit for child and dependent care expenses. Attach Form 2441	48	
Married filing jointly or Qualifying widow(er), $10,000	49	Credit for the elderly or the disabled. Attach Schedule R .	49	
	50	Education credits. Attach Form 8863	50	#80
	51	Retirement savings contributions credit. Attach Form 8880 .	51	
	52	Child tax credit (see page 41). Attach Form 8901 if required	52	
Head of household, $7,300	53	Adoption credit. Attach Form 8839	53	
	54	Credits from: a ☐ Form 8396 b ☐ Form 8859 . .	54	
	55	Other credits. Check applicable box(es): a ☐ Form 3800 b ☐ Form 8801 c ☐ Form _____ . .	55	
	56	Add lines 47 through 55. These are your **total credits**	56	
	57	Subtract line 56 from line 46. If line 56 is more than line 46, enter -0- . . ▶	57	# 74
Other Taxes	58	Self-employment tax. Attach Schedule SE	58	
	59	Social security and Medicare tax on tip income not reported to employer. Attach Form 4137	59	
	60	Additional tax on IRAs, other qualified retirement plans, etc. Attach Form 5329 if required .	60	
	61	Advance earned income credit payments from Form(s) W-2	61	
	62	Household employment taxes. Attach Schedule H	62	
	63	Add lines 57 through 62. This is your **total tax** . . . . ▶	63	
Payments	64	Federal income tax withheld from Forms W-2 and 1099 .	64	
	65	2005 estimated tax payments and amount applied from 2004 return	65	
If you have a qualifying child, attach Schedule EIC.	66a	Earned income credit (EIC)	66a	# 78
	b	Nontaxable combat pay election ▶ 66b		
	67	Excess social security and tier 1 RRTA tax withheld (see page 59)	67	
	68	Additional child tax credit. Attach Form 8812 . . .	68	# 78
	69	Amount paid with request for extension to file (see page 59)	69	
	70	Payments from: a ☐ Form 2439 b ☐ Form 4136 c ☐ Form 8885 .	70	
	71	Add lines 64, 65, 66a, and 67 through 70. These are your **total payments** . . . ▶	71	
Refund Direct deposit? See page 59 and fill in 73b, 73c, and 73d.	72	If line 71 is more than line 63, subtract line 63 from line 71. This is the amount you **overpaid**	72	
	73a	Amount of line 72 you want **refunded to you** . . . . ▶	73a	
	b	Routing number		
		▶ c Type: ☐ Checking ☐ Savings		
	d	Account number		
	74	Amount of line 72 you want **applied to your 2006 estimated tax** ▶	74	
Amount You Owe	75	**Amount you owe.** Subtract line 71 from line 63. For details on how to pay, see page 60 ▶	75	
	76	Estimated tax penalty (see page 60)	76	

Third Party Designee

Do you want to allow another person to discuss this return with the IRS (see page 61)? ☐ **Yes.** Complete the following. ☐ **No**

Designee's name ▶	Phone no. ▶ ( )	Personal identification number (PIN) ▶					

Sign Here

Joint return? See page 17.

Keep a copy for your records.

Under penalties of perjury, I declare that I have examined this return and accompanying schedules and statements, and to the best of my knowledge and belief, they are true, correct, and complete. Declaration of preparer (other than taxpayer) is based on all information of which preparer has any knowledge.

Your signature	Date	Your occupation	Daytime phone number ( )
Spouse's signature. If a joint return, both must sign.	Date	Spouse's occupation	

Paid Preparer's Use Only

Preparer's signature ▶	Date	Check if self-employed ☐	Preparer's SSN or PTIN
Firm's name (or yours if self-employed), address, and ZIP code ▶		EIN	
		Phone no. ( )	

Form **1040** (2005)

✶ *Printed on recycled paper*

Source: This Form 1040 with reference to the FAFSA was prepared by the Canisius College Student Financial Aid Office. Printed with permission from the Student Financial Aid Office at Canisius College, January 2006.

Supplemental Aid

CSS/Profile Form

Although the FAFSA is required for federal student aid, some colleges may require students to also submit either a CSS/Financial Aid Profile application or college financial aid application. It is important that you complete these forms according to the college's published deadlines. Unlike the FASFA you don't have to wait until January 1 to complete the Profile form. If you are asked to complete the CSS/Profile, it must be done online at www.college-board.com. There is a $5.00 nonrefundable registration fee for the CSS/Financial Aid Profile and an $18.00 processing fee for each college or program to which you want the information sent. The College Board will accept credit cards (MasterCard, Visa, American Express, and Discover), debit cards (MasterCard and Visa), and online checks. Please note that if you submit a CSS/Profile form before January 1, any estimation of federal aid by the college is unofficial until you submit a completed FAFSA on or after January 1 of your senior year.

The CSS/Profile requests substantially more financial information than reported on the FAFSA. The CSS/Profile form is used by more than 250 colleges and universities, professional schools, and scholarship programs to help them award nonfederal student aid funds.

Note: The profile is available in both English and Spanish at www.college-board.com.

Institutional Aid Application

Some colleges may require students to complete their own institutional aid application as well as a FAFSA. The purpose of this form will vary from college to college. These institutions simply want to know more about the student and family situation. They may ask for the following information and much more:

- Primary residence—year purchased, value of the home, unpaid mortgage
- More information on parents' places of employment and occupation
- Tuition at private elementary and high schools
- Unusual family financial situations
- Value of retirement accounts
- Value of insurance accounts

Remember to submit this form and all other required forms prior to each college's published deadline.

General State Residency Guidelines

You may be thinking about attending an out-of-state college and wondering how you can become a resident of that state in order to pay the lower in-state resident tuition cost. Each state has its own regulations concerning state residency. Generally, the residency of the parent is the residency of the student. Table 3-1 outlines six general residency rules for nineteen states. This chart is simply a guide to illustrate a few common requirements for state residency. Some states may have additional criteria that will be used to determine state residency.

You should check out the College Board website, www.collegeboard.com, for the state residency requirements for all states. This website also has important information for international students. Other websites to check are the individual public college websites for more information. For example, the state of Illinois allows individual colleges to set state residency requirements.

The following are some definitions to assist you in understanding the various state requirements:

- **Domicile:** The residence where you have your permanent home or principal establishment, and to where whenever you are absent, you intend to return. Every person is compelled to have one and only one domicile at a time.
- **Voter Registration:** Student is registered to vote in the state where the public college is located.
- **Student Emancipation:** Financial Independence—students under the age of 22–24 (depending on the state regulation) must provide evidence of one year of independent living in order to be considered emancipated.

TABLE 3-1 Sample of Nineteen State Residency Guidelines

State	Domicile	Voter Registration	Residency of Parents	Student Emancipation	Required State Driver's License	State Income or State Earnings Information
Alabama	Yes	Yes	Yes	Yes	Yes	Yes
Arizona	Yes	Yes	Yes	Yes	Yes	Yes
California	Yes	Yes	Yes	Yes	Yes	Yes
Colorado	Yes	Yes	Yes	Yes	Yes	Yes
Delaware	Yes	Yes	Yes	Yes	Yes	Yes
Florida	Yes	Yes	Yes	?	Yes	Yes
Georgia	Yes	Yes	Yes	Yes	Yes	Yes
Illinois	Yes	Yes	Yes	Yes	Yes	Yes
Indiana	Yes	Yes	Yes	Yes	Yes	Yes
Massachusetts	Yes	?	Yes	?	Yes	Yes
Michigan	Yes	Yes	?	?	Yes	Yes
Minnesota	Yes	Yes	Yes	Yes	?	Yes
New York	Yes	Yes	Yes	Yes	Yes	Yes
North Carolina	Yes	Yes	Yes	Yes	?	Yes
Ohio	Yes	Yes	?	?	Yes	Yes
Oregon	Yes	Yes	?	?	Yes	Yes
Pennsylvania	Yes	Yes	Yes	Yes	Yes	Yes
Texas	Yes	Yes	Yes	Yes	Yes	?
Washington	Yes	Yes	Yes	Yes	Yes	Yes

Question mark indicates that it was unclear whether the state required the criterion for state residency.
Source: Prepared by Anthony J. Bellia, August 2005 and subject to change.

- **State Driver's License:** Student has a valid driver's license in the state where the public college is located.

- **Residency of the Parents:** In some states, the legal residency of the parent is the residency of the student.

- **Residency Classification:** Many states have a policy that a student must reside in the state for twelve consecutive months as of the first day of classes in the semester or session for which the classification is sought.

- **State Income Tax or State Earning Information:** Student has filed a state income tax form or can provide proof of employment in the state where the public college is located.

Note: Some states may modify these definitions according to their state laws governing state residency for college tuition at public institutions.

Student Financial Aid Programs

The FASFA covers the following kinds of financial aid: Federal Pell Grant, Federal Supplemental Educational Opportunity Grant, Federal Work Study, Federal Perkins Loan, and Federal Stafford Loan (subsidized and unsubsidized) programs. With the exception of unsubsidized Stafford Loans, these programs are *need-based*. That is, when determining eligibility for funds from these programs, your expected family contribution as calculated through the FAFSA process is considered.

Federal Student Aid

The dollar values listed for the following federal student aid programs are for academic year 2006–2007.

- **Federal Pell Grant** is gift aid from the federal government. The current range of the grant is $400–4,050. This grant is for undergraduates pursuing a first baccalaureate degree. Pell Grants may be used at any accredited college/ university in the United States.

Dean's Tips

- The Deficit Reduction Act of 2005 (February 2006) established the Academic Competitiveness Grant and National Science and Mathematic Access to Retain Talents Grant (SMART) programs for undergraduate students effective July 1, 2006.

- Academic Competitiveness Grant for first-year students is $750 and $1,300 for second-year awards.

- The National Science and Mathematic Access to Retain Talents Grant (SMART) is $4,000 for third- and fourth-year students.
- Award recipients must be U.S. citizen, be Pell eligible, attend full-time, and meet other eligibility requirements, e.g., complete a rigorous course of study.
- Check with your school counselor to determine if your academic coursework meets the rigorous standards established by the state, local education agency, or school.

- **Federal Supplemental Educational Opportunity Grant** is gift aid from the federal government. Preference is given to Pell Grant recipients with exceptional financial need, i.e., those with the lowest EFC. The size of the award is from $100–$4,000 annually for undergraduate study. The actual award is determined by the college.
- **Federal Work-Study (FWS) Program** provides part-time jobs for undergraduate and graduate students. Students must demonstrate financial need. Also, they must earn at least the current minimum wage, and they may work on or in an eligible off-campus organization. This program is administered by schools participating in the program.

Dean's Tips

- If you are offered FWS, investigate all the particulars regarding job placement, and the number of hours you will need to work in order to earn the full amount of the award.
- If you are not offered FWS, check for non-need based institutional work programs, food service jobs, bookstore jobs, or jobs paid from a departmental line.
- If you have a choice between a part-time job at a local business or an FWS position, keep in mind the convenience often associated with the FWS job on campus.

- **Federal Perkins Loan** is a fixed low-interest loan of 5% for both undergraduate and graduate students who demonstrate financial need. The college is the lender and determines the actual annual loan amounts. Currently, students can borrow up to $4,000 for each year of undergraduate study and $6,000 for graduate study. The aggregate loan amount is $20,000 for undergraduate and $20,000 for graduate study for a total of $40,000. There is a six-month grace period. There are deferment provisions and teacher cancellation provisions (which allow a reduction in loan principal for certain eligible teachers). Finally, no interest is charged as long as the student is enrolled in college at least half time.

- **Federal Stafford Loans (Direct and FFEL)** As stated earlier, students must complete a FAFSA to apply for a Federal Stafford Student Loan. Colleges and universities will use the FAFSA to determine eligibility for the loan. This means the Stafford loan will be a subsidized loan if you demonstrate financial need or an unsubsidized loan if you do not demonstrate financial need at a particular college. Stafford loans are probably the most common, single form of Federal Student Aid. In addition, the U.S. Department of Education administers the Federal Family Education Loan (FFEL) and the William D. Ford Direct Loan Program. The main difference between the two loan programs is as follows: Students will receive FFEL funds from private lenders (such as banks, credit unions, and other lenders) who participate in this program. Direct Loans are funded through the federal government directly to the school.

Eligibility rules and loan amounts are identical under both programs but the repayment plans are somewhat different. Refer to Chart 3-2 for additional information.

Dean's Tip

The Deficit Reduction Act of 2005 (February 2006) made significant changes to the Stafford Loan Program and other student aid provisions. Check the latest federal student aid publications for additional information. At the time of this publication, the Deficit Reduction Act was still being analyzed. Many of the changes have been included in this publication.

- **Federal Stafford Loans** may be *subsidized* or *unsubsidized*. A subsidized loan is awarded based on financial need. This means you are not charged interest before repayment occurs or during authorized periods of deferment. The federal government pays the interest for the student. An unsubsidized loan is not awarded on the basis of need. Students are charged interest from the time the loan is disbursed until it is paid in full. The interest rate effective July 1, 2006 in the repayment period is fixed at 6.8%. Note that it is possible for a student to have partial eligibility for both a subsidized and unsubsidized loan in an award year. These loans have fees up to 4%. Also, there are delayed repayment and deferment provisions. Table 3-2 provides a summary of information on Federal Stafford Loans.

Special Note on Loans: Loans, unlike grants or work-study, must be repaid. They are serious financial obligations similar to a car loan or a home mortgage. Check the www.ed.gov website for more detailed descriptions of the Federal Student Aid Programs. Also, check the Appendix for a sample Federal Stafford/Perkins Loan interview summary sheet.

Dean's Tip

Know your loans. In some instances, Federal Perkins Loans can be fully forgiven. Federal Family Education Loans (Stafford) and William D. Ford Direct Loans may also qualify for partial forgiveness.

TABLE 3-2 Federal Stafford Loans Maximum Annual Loan Limits for Subsidized and Unsubsidized, Direct, and FFEL Loans Academic Year 2006–2007

	Dependent Undergraduate Student	Independent Undergraduate Student	Graduate and Professional Student
First Year	$2,625	$6,625—No more than $2,625 of this amount may be in subsidized loans.	$18,500 for each year of study—No more than $8,500 of the annual amount may be in subsidized loans.
Second Year	$3,500	$7,500—No more than $3,500 of this amount may be in subsidized loans.	$18,500 for each year of study—No more than $8,500 of the annual amount may be in subsidized loans.
Third and Fourth Years (each)	$5,500	$10,500—No more than $5,500 of this amount may be in subsidized loans.	$18,500 for each year of study—No more than $8,500 of the annual amount may be in subsidized loans.
Maximum Total Debt from Stafford Loans When You Graduate	$23,000	$46,000—No more than $23,000 of this amount may be in subsidized loans.	$138,500—No more than $65,500 of this amount may be in subsidized loans. The graduate debt limit includes Stafford Loans received for undergraduate study.

For periods of study shorter than an academic year, the amounts you can borrow will be less than those listed. Remember that you might receive less if you receive other forms of financial aid that's used to cover a portion of your cost of attendance.
Source: "The Student Aid Guide, 2005–2006," page 21, U.S. Department of Education.

Dean's Tips

The Deficit Reduction Act of 2005 (February 2006) will make changes to the Federal Family Education Loan Program (FFELP) on July 1, 2007.

- First-year annual loan limit will increase from $2,625 to $3,500.
- Second-year annual loan will increase from $3,500 to $4,500.
- Aggregate loan limits will remain the same.
- Graduate and professional students may borrow additional unsubsidized loans: Loan limits increase from $10,000 to $12,000 annually.
- Graduate loan limits increase from $5,000 to $7,000 for coursework needed to enroll in a graduate program or necessary to obtain a required credential to become an elementary or secondary teacher.
- Authorizes loan deferments of up to three years for borrowers on active duty during a war, military operation, or natural emergency, as well as for National Guard personnel serving in a similar fashion. This loan deferment applies to Perkins, Direct, and FFELP loans.

State Aid Programs

Many states provide generous state grant programs. You need to determine the application process and timetable. In some states, for example, New York, the application process begins with the filing the FAFSA and listing an in-state (private or public) college in step six on the FAFSA. Also, you need to find out if the state grant or scholarship is portable to another state. Some state agencies have reciprocity with other states. Finally, deadline dates are important. If you submit an aid application too late, in many cases you will lose funding from the state program. Moreover, at the institutional level, the college may have awarded all of its money if you are late. Institutions' resources are limited and they typically do not save them for late applicants.

Apply Early

Check colleges, state agencies, refer to Table 3-3, private scholarship foundations, websites, college catalogs, and/or call the aid office for deadlines and required supplemental aid applications.

TABLE 3-3   Sources of Information About State Grant, Scholarship, and Loan Programs

Alabama
Alabama Commission on
   Higher Education
P.O. Box 302000
100 North Union Street
Montgomery, AL 36130-2000
334 242-1998; www.ache.state.al.us

Alaska
Alaska Commission on
   Postsecondary Education
3030 Vintage Boulevard
Juneau, AK 99801-7109
800 441-2962; www.state.ak.us/acpe

Arizona
Arizona Department of Education
1535 W. Jefferson Street
Phoenix, AZ 85007
800 352-4558; www.ade.state.az.us

Arkansas
Department of Higher Education
114 East Capitol
Little Rock, AR 72201
501 371-2000; www.arkansashighered.com

California
California Student Aid Commission
P.O. Box 419027
Rancho Cordova, CA 95741-9026
888 224-7268; www.csac.ca.gov

Colorado
Department of Education
201 East Colfax Avenue
Denver, CO 80203
303 866-6600; www.cde.state.co.us

Connecticut
Department of Higher Education
61 Woodland Street
Hartford, CT 06105
860 947-1800; www.ctdhe.org

Delaware
Delaware Higher Education Commission
820 North French Street
Fourth Floor
Wilmington, DE 19801
800 292-7935; www.doe.state.de.us/high-ed

District of Columbia
State Education Office
1350 Pennsylvania Avenue, NW
Washington, DC 20004
202 698-2400; www.seo.dc.gov

Florida
Florida Department of Education
Office of Student Financial Assistance
1940 N. Monroe Street, Suite 70
Tallahassee, FL 32303-4759
850 487-1785; www.firn.edu/doe

Georgia
Georgia Student Finance Authority
2082 East Exchange Place
Suite 100
Tucker, GA 30084
800 505-4732; www.gsfc.org

Hawaii
Hawaii Department of Education
P.O. Box 2360
Honolulu, HI 96804
808 586-3230; www.doe.k12.hi.us

Idaho
Office of the State Board of Education
P.O. Box 83720
650 West State Street
Boise, ID 83720
208 332-6800; www.sde.state.id.us

Illinois
Illinois Student Assistance Commission
1755 Lake Cook Road
Deerfield, IL 60015-5209
800 899-4722; www.collegezone.com

TABLE 3-3 Sources of Information About State Grant, Scholarship, and Loan Programs (*Continued*)

Indiana
State Student Assistance Commission
  of Indiana
150 W. Market Street
Suite 500
Indianapolis, IN 46204
888 528-4719; www.ai.org/ssaci

Iowa
Iowa College Student Aid Commission
200 Tenth Street
Fourth Floor
Des Moines; IA 50309-2036
515 242-3344; www.iowacollegeaid.org

Kansas
Board of Regents
1000 SW Jackson Street
Suite 520
Topeka, KS 66612-1368
785 296-3421; www.kansasregents.org

Kentucky
KHEAA Student Aid Branch
1050 U.S. 127 South
P.O. Box 798
Frankfort, KY 40602
800 928-8926; www.kheaa.com

Louisiana
Office of Student Financial
  Assistance for Louisiana
Scholarship/Grant Division
P.O. Box 91202
Baton Rouge, LA 70821-9202
800 259-5626; www.osfa.state.la.us

Maine
Finance Authority of Maine
Maine Education Assistance Division
P.O. Box 949
5 Community Drive
Augusta, ME 04332
800 228-3734; www.famemaine.com

Maryland
Maryland Higher Education Commission
State Scholarship Administration
839 Bestgate Road
Suite 400
Annapolis, MD 21401-1781
800 974-0203; www.mhec.state.md.us

Massachusetts
Board of Higher Education
454 Broadway, Suite 200
Revere, MA 02151-3034
617-727-9420; www.mass.edu

Michigan
Michigan Higher Education
  Assistance Authority
Office of Scholarships and Grants
P.O. Box 30462
Lansing, MI 48909-7547
517 373-3394; www.michigan.gov/
  misstudentaid

Minnesota
Minnesota Higher Education
  Services Office
1450 Energy Park Drive
Suite 350
St. Paul, MN 55108-5227
651 642-0533; www.mheso.state.mn.us

Mississippi
Mississippi Office of State Student
  Financial Aid
3825 Ridgewood Road
Jackson, MS 39211-6453
800 327-2980; www.mde.k12.ms.us

Missouri
Missouri Department of Higher Education
3515 Amazonas Drive
Jefferson City, MO 65109-5717
572 751-2361; www.dhe.mo.gov

(*Continued*)

TABLE 3-3   Sources of Information About State Grant, Scholarship, and Loan Programs (*Continued*)

Montana
Montana Board of Regents
P.O. Box 203101
2500 Broadway
Helena, MT 59620-3101
406 444-6570; www.montana.edu/
   wwwbor

Nebraska
Nebraska Coordination Commission
   for Postsecondary Education
P.O. Box 95005
Lincoln, NE 68509-5005
402 471-2847; www.ccpe.state.ne.us

Nevada
Nevada Department of Education
Attn. Wendy Skibinski
700 East 5th Street
Carson City Main Location
Carson City, NV 89701
775 687-9200; www.wskibinski@doe.nv.gov

New Hampshire
New Hampshire Postsecondary
   Education Commission
3 Barrell Court
Suite 300
Concord, NH 03301-8543
603 271-2555; www.state.nh.us/postsecondary

New Jersey
New Jersey Higher Education Student
   Assistance Authority
4 Quakerbridge Plaza
P.O. Box 540
Trenton, NJ 08625
800 792-8670; www.hesaa.org

New Mexico
Commission on Higher Education
1068 Cerillos Road
Santa Fe, NM 87505
505 476-6500; www.nmche.org

New York
Higher Education Services Corporation
Student Information
99 Washington Avenue
Albany, NY 12255
888 697-4372; www.hesc.state.ny.us

North Carolina
North Carolina State Education
   Assistance Authority
P.O. Box 14103
Research Triangle Park, NC 27709-3663
919 549-8614; www.ncseaa.edu

North Dakota
North Dakota University System
600 East Boulevard
Dept. 215
Bismarck, ND 58505
701 328-2960; www.ndus.nodak.edu

Ohio
Ohio Board of Regents
P.O. Box 182542
Columbus, OH 43218
888 833-1133; www.regents.state.oh.us/sqs

Oklahoma
Oklahoma State Regents for
   Higher Education
Tuition Aid Grant Program
655 Research Parkway
Suite 200
Oklahoma City, OK 73104
405 225-9100; www.okhighered.org

Oregon
Oregon Student Assistance Commission
Valley River Office Park
1500 Valley River Drive
Suite 100
Eugene, OR 97401
800 452-8807; www.ossc.state.or.us

TABLE 3-3 Sources of Information About State Grant, Scholarship, and Loan Programs (*Continued*)

Pennsylvania Pennsylvania Higher Education Assistance Agency 1200 N. 7th Street Harrisburg, PA 17102 800 692-7392; www.pheaa.org	**Texas** Texas Higher Education Coordinating Board Division of Student Services P.O. Box 12788, Capital Station Austin, TX 78711 512 427-6101; www.collegefortexas.com

Puerto Rico
Departmento de Educacion
P.O. Box 190759
San Juan, PR 00919-0759
787 759-2000; www.de.gobeirno.pr
	Utah
	Utah Higher Education Assistance
	  Authority
	Board of Regents Building,
	  The Gateway
	60 South 400 West
	Salt Lake City, UT 84101-1284
	801 321-7200; www.uheaa.org

Rhode Island Rhode Island Higher Education Assistance Authority 560 Jefferson Boulevard Warwick, RI 02886 401 736-1100; www.riheaa.org	**Vermont** Vermont Student Assistance Corporation P.O. Box 2000 Winooski, VT 05404-2601 802 655-9602; www.vsac.org
South Carolina South Carolina Tuition Grants Commission 1333 Main Street Suite 200 Columbia, SC 29201 803 737-2260; www.che400. state.sc.us	**Virginia** State Council of Higher Education 101 North 14th Street Richmond, VA 23219 804 225-2600; www.schev.edu
South Dakota Department of Education 700 Governors Drive Pierre, SD 57501-2291 605 773-3448; www.state.ed. us/thec	**Washington** Washington State Higher Education Coordination Board 917 Lakeridge Way P.O. Box 43430 Olympia, WA 98504-3430 360 753-7800; www.hecb.wa.gov

Tennessee
Tennessee Student Assistance
Corporation
404 James Robertson Parkway,
  Suite 1950
Nashville, TN 37243-0820
615 741-3605; www.state.tn.us/tsac
	West Virginia
	West Virginia Higher Education
	  Policy Commission
	Central Office, Higher Education
	  Grant Program
	1018 Kanawha Boulevard East
	Suite 700
	Charleston, WV 25301-2800
	304 558-2101; www.hepc.wvnet.edu

(*Continued*)

TABLE 3-3   Sources of Information About State Grant, Scholarship, and Loan Programs (*Continued*)

Wisconsin	**Guam**
Wisconsin Higher Educational Aids Board	University of Guam
131 West Wilson	Student Financial Aid Office
Suite 902	303 University Station
Madison, WI 53707	UOG Station
608 267-2206; www.heab.state.wi.us	Mangilao, GU 96923
Wyoming	671 735-2287; www.uog.edu
Wyoming State Department	**Virgin Islands**
of Education	Financial Aid Office, Virgin Islands
2300 Capitol Avenue	Board of Education
Hathaway Building, 2d Floor	P.O. Box 11900
Cheyenne, WY 82002	St. Thomas, VI 00801
307 777-7673; www.k12.wy.us	340 774-4546

Other Ways to Save Tuition Dollars at Public Colleges

Four higher education associations provide out-of-state students within specific state boundaries the opportunity to take courses at public institutions and some regions also allow enrollment at private colleges at reduced prices.

New England Regional Student Program (RSP)

This program grants students from New England states a tuition break when they pursue certain majors that are not available in their home states at public colleges and universities in other New England states. The participating New England states are Connecticut, Maine, Massachusetts, New Hampshire, Rhode Island, and Vermont. You must be a resident of one of these states in order to participate in this program.

The RSP is available at 78 public colleges and universities in New England. It is available at two- and four-year public colleges and universities offering Associate, Bachelor's, Master's, Certificates of Advanced Graduate Study, Doctoral, and First Professional Degrees. Each year, the 78 participating public colleges approve additional majors. There are more than 700 academic programs offered to out-of-state New England residents at reduced tuition. This reduced tuition break is not based on financial need. The RSP program is not a financial aid or scholarship program; it is a tuition reduction program.

Application Procedure

"No additional application is required. A participating college application form usually includes a question regarding the RSP. If not, you should write clearly on the application that you are applying through the New England Regional Student Program and declare an RSP program as your intended major. Applicants who are accepted into eligible programs will be notified by the institution where they applied for admission whether or not they have been granted RSP status" (from www.nebhe.org/apply_for_ rsp.html; August 11, 2005).

For more information contact:

New England Regional Student Program
New England Board of Higher Education
45 Temple Place
Boston, MA 02111
Tel. 617-357-9620
Email: tuitionbreak@nebhe.org

Academic Common Market

This tuition-saving program is for students from sixteen Southern Regional Education Board (SREB) states. They are Alabama, Arkansas, Delaware, Florida, Georgia, Kentucky, Louisiana, Maryland, Mississippi, North Carolina, Oklahoma, South Carolina, Tennessee, Texas, Virginia, and West Virginia.

The Academic Common Market allows eligible students to take hundreds of undergraduate and graduate programs at out-of-state public institutions if the program of study is not offered by a public institution in the student's home state. There are more than 1,400 programs available to eligible out-of-state students at in-state tuition cost. If the student is accepted into the program, the student does not have to pay out-of-state tuition.

Additional Information

Students interested in this program should check the SREB website (www.sreb.org). Each participating state has a coordinator for this program.

Students should contact the state coordinator in their home state for more information about eligible programs to determine their eligibility to participate in this program because the application process varies from state to state. Some states participate in the Academic Common Market only at the graduate level. These states are Florida, North Carolina, and Texas.

This program is also available for selected distance-learning programs. Check with your state coordinator for more information about eligible programs. If the program in which you are interested is an eligible program, you will pay in-state tuition if accepted into the program.

Midwest Student Exchange Program

The Midwest Student Exchange Program (MSEP) (www.mhec.org) is a special educational opportunity for students from six Midwestern states to study out-of-state at reduced tuition at over 125 public and private colleges and universities. The six participating states are Kansas, Michigan, Minnesota, Missouri, Nebraska, and North Dakota.

What Is the Tuition Reduction?

If you reside in one of the participating states and plan to enroll in a participating college in another state, you are eligible to receive a tuition reduction. The tuition reduction is different for public and private colleges. At participating two- or four-year public colleges and universities you will pay no more than 150% of the in-state resident tuition rate. This reduced cost is still lower than the out-of-state nonresident tuition. At participating private colleges the tuition reduction is at least 10% off the tuition cost.

How Do I Apply for This Tuition Reduction?

You should apply for admission at a participating MSEP institution. Also, you must prominently mark on the admission application that you are applying as an MSEP student.
Note: All admission and eligibility decisions are made separately by each participating college.

For More Information

You should contact your high school counselor or the college's admissions office. Also, you may contact an individual state's student exchange coordinator. The following web address will get you into the Midwestern Higher Education website, and the contact information for individual state coordinators is listed there. Also, you can download the "Midwest Student Exchange Program, 2005–2006 Bulletin" at this website: www.mhec.org/studentaccess_ studentexhchange.html.

Western Interstate Commission for Higher Education

The Western Interstate Commission for Higher Education offers students in fifteen participating states an opportunity for undergraduate study in receiving states at reduced out-of-state tuition rates. The actual tuition rate is 150% of the receiving institution's regular resident tuition rate at public colleges and universities. This program is called the Western Undergraduate Exchange Program (WUE).

Participating States

The fifteen receiving states are Alaska,* Arizona, California, Colorado, Hawaii,** Idaho, Montana, Nevada, New Mexico,* North Dakota,* Oregon, South Dakota,* Utah, Washington,* and Wyoming.*

Programs of Study

Almost all undergraduate fields are available. You need to check with the participating schools to determine their policy for admission and availability of programs. Some colleges allow students open accessibility to their curriculum on a first-come, first-serve basis, and some offer only certain programs.

Student Eligibility

Must be a resident of one of the participating states. California residents should check certain restrictions in some states. Also, the use of SAT/ACT scores and high school GPA are reviewed by some colleges and universities.

Application Procedures

Apply directly to an institution and mark WUE prominently on the admissions application. WUE does not have a general application.

For more information:

> Email: info-sep@wiche.edu
> Or mail to:
> Student Exchange Programs
> Western Interstate Commission for Higher Education
> P.O. Box 9752
> Boulder, Colorado 80301-9572
> Tel. 303-541-0214

---

*State also accepts students from California
**Residents of Hawaii may enroll as WUE students in four-year programs only.

Graduate/Professional Study

There are also graduate- and professional-level programs at reasonable cost. Check the following website for participating colleges, application procedures, eligible programs, residency requirements, and part-time study eligibility:

graduate schools: www.wiche.edu/sep/wrgp

professional schools: www.wiche.edu/sep/psep

Dean's Tips

Look for scholarship and grant aid from colleges, universities, and proprietary schools.

Institutional Aid Programs

- Each college may have its own procedures and it is your responsibility to know this.
- Institutions may require their own financial aid application or additional form. such as the CSS/Profile Form.
- Institutions may offer both merit and need-based aid programs.
- Schools will set eligibility criteria for merit and need-based aid.
- The college's financial aid budget is not bottomless. You should apply early.
- Apply for institutional aid, even if you think you are ineligible. Let the college give you an aid package or loan alternatives based on your financial situation.
- Always tell the colleges in writing about changes in family circumstances, e.g., loss of job, separation/divorce, or death in the family.

College-Sponsored Aid Programs

When applying for financial aid, it is important to keep in mind not only need-based aid, but merit-based aid as well. Many colleges are willing to reward students for their academic ability, athletics, special talent, and/or community service. Merit scholarships (non-need based aid) are usually four-year commitments that colleges make regardless of the parents' ability to pay. A college may have a special application process for this kind of aid and may require that the student maintain or satisfy certain conditions (refer to the Appendix for sample college scholarship/financial aid literature).

Merit aid is competitive in nature and recipients are chosen because of their outstanding record or achievement in whatever criteria are used for selection. Students and parents need to check individual college catalogs, college websites, and/or call the financial aid office to determine if a specific college offers merit aid programs, the application process, and deadline dates. Also, ask how the scholarship is renewed annually to ensure continued eligibility.

Athletic Money

If participating in college as a student athlete is part of your game plan, you need to know that the NCAA and the NAIA have certain rules that a student must follow. Let's first define the abbreviations NCAA and NAIA.

The National Collegiate Athletic Association (NCAA) is the governing body for students who participate in Divisions I, II, and III levels at the collegiate level (www.ncaa.org). The NAIA is the National Association of Intercollegiate Athletics (www.naia.org). Both of these athletic organizations have their own regulations that member institutions and student athletes must follow in order to participate in athletic competition at the collegiate level.

National Collegiate Athletic Association (NCAA)

Let's first outline some of the general guidelines concerning the NCAA. As you continue to investigate the possibilities of athletic funding to assist you in paying for college, you need to keep the following in mind:

- You need to know your athletic capabilities and set realistic goals and expectations.
- You should begin to prepare your resume, videotape, etc., as early as your freshman year of high school.
- Ask your high school coach for assistance.
- When you visit colleges, talk to the coach about athletic scholarships. Coaches will award student athletic scholarships, not the student financial aid office.
- Learn the admission and financial aid process at colleges and universities that interest you.
- Make sure that you understand the NCAA student eligibility regulations for Division I and II schools. Write or call for a copy of the book, *The Guide for College Board Student Athletes*. The telephone number for one free copy of the guide is 1-800-638-3731. You can also download a copy of the book from www.ncaaclearinghouse.net/ncaa/student/index_student.html.

Address:

NCAA
700 W. Washington Street
P.O. Box 6222
Indianapolis, Indiana 46206-6222
Phone: 317-917-6222
Fax: 317-917-6888

- The NCAA clearinghouse website is an excellent source for the following information:
  - Registered student login
  - List of approved courses*
  - Registration for high school students
  - Registration for foreign students

For the Classes of 2006 and 2007: Divisions I and II

Your eligibility will be determined under the new rule. That means that you must have a minimum of 14 core courses to be eligible to practice, play, and receive athletic financial aid at a Division I or Division II school. Also, you must graduate from high school with a minimum grade point average in the 14 core courses and have a qualifying SAT or ACT test score.

14 Required Core Courses

- Four years of English

- Two years of mathematics (Algebra 1 or higher level)

- Two years of natural or physical science (including one year of lab science if offered by your high school)

- One extra year of English, mathematics, or natural/physical science or non-doctrinal religion or philosophy

- Two years of social science

- Three years of additional core courses (from any of these categories or foreign language, nondoctrinal religion, or philosophy)

Approved Courses for the Class of 2008—Division I Only (16 Core Courses):
If you plan to enter a Division I college on or after August 1, 2008 you will need to present sixteen core courses in the following breakdown:

- Four years of English

- Three years of mathematics (Algebra 1 or higher level)

*The NCAA has recently changed the initial eligibility requirements (approved core courses) for Division I and II schools. Those new requirements are listed next.

- Two years of natural or physical science (including one year of lab science if offered by your high school)
- One extra year of English, mathematics, or natural/physical science
- Two years of social science
- Four years of additional core courses (from any of these categories or foreign language, nondoctrinal religion or philosophy)[*]

Home-Schooled Students: According to the NCAA, students who received any portion of their high school education at home (grades 9–12) must register with the NCAA Initial Eligibility Clearinghouse. The NCAA Clearinghouse will analyze the student's academic record and advise the student of any academic deficiencies so that the student can adjust his/her course of study prior to high school graduation.

For more information concerning the NCAA procedures for home-schooled students, check with the NCAA Clearinghouse at the following:

NCAA Clearinghouse
Attn: Home School Education
301 Act Drive
Iowa City, Iowa 52243-4043
Domestic: 1-877-262-1492
Web address: www.ncaaclearinghouse.net

Transfer Students: There are specific rules governing transfer students. You should obtain a copy of "Transfer Guide, 2005-6, Division I, II, III" from the NCAA Clearinghouse. This guide outlines eligibility requirements for students transferring from either a two- or four-year college or university.

Scholarship Information: The availability and the amount of an athletic scholarship will depend on the division, and whether the student is a qualifier, partial-qualifier, or nonqualifier.

In Division I or Division II, a full qualifier is eligible to receive financial aid, which includes tuition, fees, books, room, and board. Please note that there is no guarantee of a four-year scholarship in Divisions I, II, or III. Scholarships are renewed annually for an academic year.

Division I Partial Qualifier:

- Full or partial scholarships for tuition, fees, room and board, and books.

[*]NCAA website: "Guide for College-Bound Student-Athletes" August 11, 2005.

Nonqualifier

- Student may receive need-based financial aid that is unrelated to athletics.

Division II Partial Qualifier

- Student may receive need-based financial aid that is unrelated to athletics.

Division III

- Student may receive need-based financial aid that is unrelated to athletics. Division III schools offer only academic scholarships not athletic scholarships.

Other Aid: You should contact the college's financial aid office to determine eligibility for other aid such as the Federal Pell Grant. If you receive any outside aid, you should notify the financial aid office to avoid any NCAA violations.

National Association of Intercollegiate Athletics (NAIA)

The NAIA is an athletic association for over 280 colleges and universities in Canada and the United States. These colleges provide a rewarding athletic experience for student athletes.

- More than 90% of NAIA institutions offer athletic scholarships.
- Eligibility to participate is less burdensome than the NCAA. There is no clearinghouse.
- Write or email for a copy of the *Guide for the College Board Student Athlete* at www.naia.org/local/collegeboard.html. This booklet will explain eligibility regulations, financial assistance policies, recruitment policies, and what to ask an institution.
- There is flexibility to transfer between NAIA institutions without missing a season of eligibility. Obtain *A Guide for Students Transferring from Two-Year Institutions* at www.naia.org/local/ transferguide.html.

Scholarship Opportunities at NAIA Schools

- Institutional assistance is administered by the college. Financial aid may include the actual cost of tuition, fees, books and supplies, and room and board. You should contact the college's financial aid office to determine application procedures and financial aid policies.
- Scholarships are usually for one year.

- Full-ride scholarships will include tuition, fees, books and supplies, and room and board.

- Partial scholarships will cover only a portion of the college costs.

For more information contact the NAIA:

NAIA
23500 W. 105ᵗʰ Street
P.O. box 1325
Olathie, Kansas 66061
Telephone #: 913-791-0044
Web: www.naia.org

Military Financial Assistance Opportunities

If you are interested in pursuing a military career or have already served in the United States Military, there are scholarships, loans, and monthly benefits available to you. There is also a program to pay off existing student loans. The military also offers numerous opportunities to take college credit while on active duty.

However, according to the *Chronicle of Higher Education*, some "officials at the Department of Veteran Affairs are warning potential enlistees that money for tuition should not be the motivation for joining the armed forces."* "The average cost of $14,640 tuition, books, fees, and living expenses at a four-year public residential college"* is covered by 60% or $9036, which is the current annual benefit. Also, you will need money to live on and there is no allowance for spouse or children, unless the veteran is severely disabled. As you consider the military, keep these facts or concerns in mind.

The following programs will provide financial assistance if you are in the military:

- Montgomery GI Bill for Active Duty

- Montgomery GI Bill for Reserve Duty

- Tuition Assistance Top-up

- ROTC

- U. S. Military Academics

- Loan Repayment Programs

*"Chronicle of Higher Education," May 13, 2005, pages 31 and 32.

- College Fund Program
- Educational Assistance through most states' websites

Let's take a look at these programs.

Montgomery GI Bill (MGIB)

The MGIB is available to individuals who make a three-year, full-time duty commitment. You contribute $120.00 per month for 12 months through payroll deductions. You will receive $935.00 per month for full-time study, for up to 36 months, or up to a total of $36,144 in educational benefits toward your college education. If you contribute an additional $600, your benefits will increase by an additional $5,400 for a total of $41,544. The MGIB benefits may be used for degree programs, certificate programs, flight training, correspondence courses, and on-the-job training. Also, the MGIB benefits are good for up to ten years from the date of your last discharge or release from active duty. Check the website (www.gibill.va.gov) for more information.

Montgomery GI Bill for Selected Reserve Training (MGIR-SR)

These benefits are available to those who enrolled in the Selected Reserve Program of the Army, Navy, Air Force, Coast Guard, Marine Corps, Army, and Air National Guard.

The MGIR-SR benefits can be used for degree programs, certificate programs, corresponding courses, on-the-job training, and flight training, among others. In some cases, remedial or refresher courses may be approved. The benefits are reduced in comparison to benefits for full-time active duty, and you may receive up to 36 months of educational benefits. Check the website (www.gibill.va.gov/education) for more information.

Tuition Assistance Top-Up Benefit

This benefit, signed into law on October 30, 2000, is an amendment to the MGIB. If your service does not pay for 100% of tuition and fees, the amount of the benefit can be equal to the difference between the total cost of a college course and the amount of tuition assistance paid by the military for the course.

Eligibility Requirements

- Eligible for MGIB active duty benefits
- Approved by a military department
- Served at least two full years on active duty

- **Exclusion:** this program is not available currently to individuals who are eligible for MGIB selective service program

The application form and the addresses for the four education processing centers located in Atlanta, Buffalo, Muskogee (OK), and St. Louis are available at www.gibill.va.gov.

Reserve Officer Training Corps (ROTC)

ROTC is available for high school graduates who want to become officers after college graduation in the Army, Marine Corps, Navy, or Air Force.

Scholarships are available to those who qualify for them. Make sure that you check the application requirements and due dates. They differ for each service. ROTC scholarships are competitive and colleges consider the following:

- High school academic record
- ACT/SAT scores
- Personal interview
- Letters of recommendation
- Extra curricular activities
- Physical fitness

ROTC scholarships may be for four-year, full tuition, fees, books, and a tax-free monthly stipend. There are also two- and three-year partial scholarships.

Note: Some colleges also include free room and board for ROTC students as an extra incentive to enroll you.

Health-Related Programs

Also, check for health-related or nursing ROTC programs. The Army and Navy offer nursing ROTC programs.

Check individual college websites to determine if they can participate in any of the ROTC programs. Also, type in the words "ROTC Scholarships" and it will connect you with numerous websites offering additional information.

United States Military Academies

The five United States military academies—the U.S. Military Academy, the U.S. Naval Academy, the U.S. Air Force Academy, the U.S. Coast Guard, and the U.S. Merchant Marine Academy—are simply outstanding educational institutions and the price is right. They offer a free and excellent educational experience, which includes tuition, books, room and board, medical and dental care, and a monthly stipend. Your commitment is a minimum service obligation of five years. You enter the service as a junior officer.

Facts to Consider

- Candidates must be citizens of the United States at the time of enrollment (except foreign students admitted by agreement between the U.S. and another country).

- Appointment to a service academy is extremely competitive. You will need a political nomination to all academies, except the Coast Guard.

- The military academies consider the following factors: high school academic performance, standardized test scores (ACT/SAT), extra-curricular activities (athletic/nonathletic and community service), and physical fitness.

Check the websites for the five service academies for application procedures and timetables:

Military Academy Websites, Telephone Numbers, and Addresses

Army—www.usma.edu or 1-845-938-4011
U.S. Military Academy
West Point, New York 10996

Navy and Marines—www.usna.edu or 1-410-293-4361
U.S. Naval Academy
121 Blake Road
Annapolis, MD 21402-5000

Air Force—www.usafa.af.mil or 719-333-1110
The U.S. Air Force Academy
2304 Cadet Drive
Suite 200
USAF Academy, CO 80840-5025

Coast Guard—www.cga.edu or 1-800-883-8724 or 1-860-444-8444
U.S. Coast Guard Academy
31 Mohegan Avenue
New London, CT 06320-8103

Merchant Marine—www.usmma.edu or 1-866-546-4778 (Financial Aid Information)
U.S. Merchant Marine Academy
300 Steamboat Road
Kingsport, NY 11024

College Loan Repayment Programs

The cost of a college education worries many students, specifically the future indebtness. The armed forces (except the Coast Guard) have loan repayment programs, that can help you manage your college debt. The Army, Navy, and Air Force offer loan repayment programs as a special enlistment incentive. The criteria for participation in these programs are very specific, and they vary for the three services. You will need to understand the provisions before you sign up for this program. For example, "a federal law prohibits the GI Bill and the College Loan Program for the same enlistment program. This means, a student who enlists and receives the college loan repayment program would not be eligible for the Montgomery GI Bill (MGIB), and therefore, not eligible for the Army College Fund" (www.military.about.com). The Army and Navy will repay loans up to $65,000, and the U.S. Air Force up to $10,000. Alternative loans through private lenders do not qualify for the college loan repayment program from the Army.

Check the following website for more information: www.military.com/resources/resourcescontent.

College Fund Program

The College Fund program is an enlistment benefit that adds to the MGIB. You must meet the eligibility criteria for the MGIB because these two programs are tied together. Also, each branch of the service has its own eligibility criteria.

The Army and Navy College Fund, when combined with MGIB, allows benefits up to $50,000 toward college education. The Marine Corps and Coast Guard allow additional benefits to enlistees up to $30,000 when combined with the GI Bill. Check with armed forces recruiters for more information and make sure that you fully understand the terms to obtain this benefit. The Air Force doesn't have a College Fund program.

Check the following website for more information: www.usmilitary.com.

State Educational Assistance

Many states offer educational assistance to veterans who are state residents. Benefits vary from state to state, as do the qualifications. Some financial assistance programs include full tuition at state schools for veterans, deferment of tuition at state schools until federal GI Bill benefits are received, and partial tuition benefits, to name a few assistance programs. You need to contact your state agency for more information about state veteran benefits.

Check the following website for more information: www.military.com/education/content?file=state_benefits.htm, including an outline of benefits according to ten different regions within the United States.

As we have discussed, there are militaryrelated educational benefits from the federal and state governments. Also, some colleges will enhance ROTC scholarships to enroll more ROTC students. For more information, access the websites given, and access the website for the Department of Veteran Affairs at www.va.gov. You can obtain additional information from your local VA office.

Rotary International Scholarships

The world community is becoming smaller and smaller as technological advances continue to expand. For many students, the opportunity to learn and live in another country is an exciting way to enrich a college education.

Since 1947, the Rotary Foundation (www.rotary.org) has funded a scholarship program called the Ambassadorial Scholarship. This program is for both undergraduate and graduate students.

Ambassadorial Scholarships

As you will find on the website **(www.rotary.org** and type in **"Ambassadorial Scholarships")** there are three types of Ambassadorial Scholarships offered:

- **One-Year Academic Ambassadorial Scholarships:** This program is the most common scholarship offered by Rotary International. It provides money for the opportunity to study in another country. Specifically, it helps cover the cost of the following expenses:
  - Round-trip transportation
  - Tuition, fees, room, and board expenses
  - Other educational expenses
- The maximum dollar value according to the latest data is $26,000 U.S. or its equivalent. This dollar value is subject to change. Check with the local Rotary International chapter for more details.
- **Multiyear Ambassadorial Scholarships:** These scholarships provide an opportunity to study at other foreign colleges for two years in a specific program. The scholarship amount is $13,000 U.S. or its equivalent per year. This money is applied toward the cost of a degree program.
- **Cultural Ambassadorial Scholarships:** This program is geared for intensive study of another language and culture. Program length is either three or six

months. The dollar value of this scholarship ranges from $12,000 to $19,000 U.S. depending on the length of the course. Applications for this program are considered for study in Arabic, English, French, German, Hebrew, Italian, Japanese, Korean, Chinese, Polish, Portuguese, Russian, Spanish, Swahili, and Swedish. This is the latest listing as of August 2005. You should check to see if there are any additions or deletions to this listing.

Note: You must check with your local Rotary chapter to determine availability of these three scholarships. Some Rotary clubs may offer one type of scholarship or none at all.

Application Procedure

- Check with your local Rotary club for the application procedure and deadlines, which may vary for club and Rotary district. For example, for 2008–2009 awards, club deadlines may be as early as March 2007 or as late as July 2007. If your hometown does not have a Rotary club, check the Rotary website (www.rotary.org) and click on "club locator," which will enable you to search for a club by city name. Also, check the local telephone directory for the address and name telephone number of the local Rotary club.

Finally, the Rotary website has specific information concerning the terms of the three scholarship programs. Make sure that you understand the language requirement for study in another country if that language is not your native language.

Aid for Students with Disabilities

A question students and parents have asked over the years is: Are there special scholarships for students with disabilities? Generally speaking, there are limited scholarships available to student with disabilities. Parents of students with disabilities should begin a scholarship search as early as the sophomore year in high school. In addition to your secondary school's guidance office, the following resources will assist your search for scholarship money.

Where to Look

HEALTH, The National Clearing House on Post-Secondary Education for Students with Disabilities, is an excellent source for students with disabilities:

HEALTH, Resource Center
The George Washington University
2121 K Street, NW Suite 220

Washington, DC 20037
800-544-3284 (V/TTY); 202-993-0940 (V/TTY);
202-993-0908 (Fax)
Website: www.health.gwu.edu
Email: askhealth@gwu.edu

The U.S. Department of Education Office of Post-Secondary Education (OPE) offers numerous booklets and an excellent website to search for financial aid programs (www.health.gwu.edu). Please note that the primary source of student aid for students with disabilities is the same as students without disabilities. Consequently, you need to pursue scholarships available for criteria other than disability.

A publication of the HEALTH Resource Center, *Financial Aid for Students with Disabilities*, provides information on numerous topics that would interest individuals with disabilities and their parents, e.g., educational support services, vocational-technical training schools, transition to college and educational support services, and policies and procedures in many American colleges.

Other disability-related scholarship information is available at the following websites:

- www.fastaid.com/
- www.scholarship-page.com/
- www.free-4u.com/

General Information

Bank of America ADA Abilities Scholarship Program
Center for Scholarship Administration, Inc.
PO Box 1465
Taylors, SC 29687-0031
864-268-3363
www.scholarshipprograms.org/fsp_bankofamerica.html

Foundation for Science and Disability, Inc.
Richard Mankin, Grants Committee Chair
503 NW 89 Street
Gainesville, FL 32607-1400

Lions Club International
(Check with your local chapter)
www.lionsclubs.org/

Stanley E. Jackson Scholarship Award for Students with Disabilities
Foundation for Exceptional Children
1920 Association Drive
Reston, VA 22091
703-264-3507

Health Impairments

Hemophilia Federation of America
102 B Westmark Boulevard
Lafayette, LA 70506
800-230-9797
www.hemophiliafed.org/

Parke Davis Epilepsy Scholarship Award
c/o IntraMed
1622 Broadway, 25th Floor
New York, NY 10019
800-292-7373

Hearing Loss/Deafness

Alexander Graham Bell Association for the Deaf
3417 Volta Place NW
Washington, DC 20007
202-337-5221
www.agbell.org/financialaid.cfm

Minnie Pearl Scholarship Program
EAR Foundation
2000 Church Street, Box 111
Nashville, TN 37236
800-545-HEAR

Stokoe Scholarship
National Association of the Deaf
814 Thayer Avenue
Silver Spring, MD 20910
301-587-1788
301-587-1789 (TTY)
www.nad.org/

Learning Disabilities

Ann Ford Scholarship Program
National Center for Learning Disabilities
381 Park Avenue South, Suite 1401
New York, NY 10016
888-575-7373
www.ld.org/

Learning Through Listening Award
Recording for the Blind and Dyslexic
20 Roszel Road
Princeton, NJ 08540
609-453-0606
www.rfbd.org/

Mobility Impairments

ChairScholars Foundation
16101 Carencia Lane
Odessa, FL 33556
813-920-2737
www.chairscholars.org/

Spina Bifida Association of America
4590 MacArthur Boulevard NW, Suite 250
Washington, DC 20007
800-621-3141
www.sbaa.org/

Venture Clubs of America
2 Penn Center Plaza, #1000
Philadelphia, PA 19102-1883
215-557-9300

Visual Impairments

American Council of the Blind
1155 15th Street NW, Suite 720
Washington, DC 20005
202-467-5081
www.acb.org/

American Foundation for the Blind
11 Penn Plaza, Suite 300
New York, NY 10001
800-232-5463
www.afb.org/

Association for Education and Rehabilitation of the Blind
    and Visually Impaired
4600 Duke Street, #430
P.O. Box 22397
Alexandria, VA 22304
703-823-9690

Other Sources of Funds

Social Security: Supplemental Security Income (SSI)

SSI is a federal income supplement program that pays monthly benefits to individuals with low incomes, and blind and disabled people. This program provides cash to meet basic needs for food, clothing, and shelter. For more information consult the website (www.ssa.gov.disability), which is available in English and Spanish.

State Agencies

State Vocational Rehabilitation offices assist people with disabilities to prepare for, obtain, and keep a job. These services may include the following:

- assessment services
- counseling and advisement
- independent living
- numerous other support services

Contact Information: Check your local telephone book under "Vocational Rehabilitation" in the state government listings. You can also consult the Web by simply typing in "state vocational rehabilitation services," which will allow you to explore numerous websites.

College Planning Calendar, Middle School to High School Senior Year

In this section, we suggest some timetables to keep in mind as you begin to plan for the college years ahead.

Middle School

- Take the time to develop good study skills.
- Talk to a school counselor or teacher about taking challenging courses in math, English, foreign language, social studies, and science.
- Begin to save for college from your allowance and gifts. Parents should begin a savings plan.
- In seventh grade, visit high schools with strong academic (college preparation) programs.
- Be active both at school and in your community.
- Begin to talk to neighbors, relatives, and your parent's friends about careers.
- If you have an older sibling who is visiting colleges with your parents, ask if you can join them.

Grade 9: Freshman Year

- If you don't already have one, apply online for a Social Security number (www.ssa.gov).
- Ask your school counselor about taking an aptitude or skills assessment test.
- Review career information in areas that interest you.
- Begin to take challenging courses in high school to prepare you for college. Colleges are looking for students who have taken challenging courses.
- Discuss career opportunities with your parents, school counselors, relatives, and your parent's friends.
- Parents should complete the "Calculate your EFC" worksheet in Chapter 4 to determine the EFC. Also, check out the EFC calculating websites: www.collegeboard.com, www.act.org.fane, or www.finaid.org. At this time, parents may want to consider some aid strategy tips outlined in Chapter 1.
- Begin to volunteer in your community in order to obtain work experience for future employment opportunities in high school.
- Get involved in extracurricular activities both in school and in the community.
- If you have an older sibling who is visiting colleges with your parents, ask if you can join them.

Grade 10: Sophomore Year

- Begin to look at scholarship search material.

- Take the PSAT or PLAN as a practice examination. Check with the school counselor for dates and cost.

- Continue to take appropriate courses for college admission and high school graduation requirements and college admission.

- Parents should complete the "Calculate your EFC" worksheet on websites www.collegeboard.com, www.act.org.fane, or www.finaid.org, or the worksheet in Chapter 4. Compare this worksheet with the one completed last year to determine any changes in the expected family contribution. You may want to consider the aid strategy tips outlined in Chapter 1.

- Continue to talk to parents, relatives, and people in your community about different careers.

- Ask your school counselor if the guidance office has special software for career searches. Some software packages are Discover, My Road, Career Cruising, and Guidance Direct.

- Begin to look at different colleges using their websites. For more detailed information contact the colleges for catalogs, and departmental material.

- If you have an older sibling who is visiting colleges with your parents, ask if you can join them.

Grade 11: Junior Year—Fall/Winter

- Continue to take appropriate courses for high school graduation requirements and college admission. Discuss AP courses with your school counselor. Many colleges look for AP courses and in the long run they may shorten your time in college.

- Parents should calculate the expected family contribution at websites www.collegeboard.com, www.act.org.fane, or www.finaid.org or use the worksheet in Chapter 4. Compare this worksheet with the one completed last year to determine any changes in the expected family contribution. You may want to consider the aid strategy tips outlined in Chapter 1.

- Begin to apply for outside grants and scholarships. Check the various websites listed in Chapter 9 and reference material in the school counselor's office.

- Continue your college search and begin to narrow down the list.

- Begin to check college websites and catalogs for payment options.

- Ask the colleges if they will provide an estimator of financial aid based on your high school record and current family financial situation.

- It is not too early to draft a plan on how the family plans to pay for college expenses. Normally, parents pay for college from savings, current income, and future income.

- Continue to think about career choices.
- Begin to attend college fairs, college nights, and financial aid seminars in your community.
- Talk to college representatives when they visit your high school.
- Take the PSAT, which establishes eligibility for the National Merit Scholarship Program, National Hispanic Scholars Awards Program, and the National Achievement Scholarship Program for Outstanding Black Students.

Grade 11: Junior Year—Spring

- Begin to visit colleges. Make sure that you visit the college when students are on campus so that you can talk to them. Make sure that you make an appointment with both the admissions and financial aid offices.
- If you are interested in attending a military academy, check with school counselors about the timetable and application process.
- Take the SAT or ACT. Check with your school counselor for timetable and cost.
- Make sure that you understand the admission requirements for the colleges on your "short list." If the colleges require portfolios, writing samples, audition tapes, or a personal interview, you should begin to prepare the material.
- Begin to prepare a resume.

Summer before Grade 12: Senior Year

- Visit colleges as part of any family vacation.
- Get a job and save a substantial portion of your earnings.
- Begin to request admission and financial aid application material.
- Continue to apply for private and outside scholarships. (Note the deadline dates.)

Grade 12: Senior Year—Fall (September to December)

- Continue to visit colleges, attend open houses, college fairs, and college days.
- Meet with college representatives when they visit your school or sponsor an event in your community.
- Request admission and financial aid applications from colleges on your short list.
- Continue to take the appropriate high school courses for graduation requirements and college admission.

- Continue to apply for private and outside grants and scholarships. (Note the deadline dates.)

- Submit the college admissions application according to the college's timetable. Make a folder for each college and keep a record of material submitted to the college.

- Ask the financial aid office if they will provide an estimate of student aid based on your high school record and current family financial situation.

- Register in October to receive the CSS Financial Aid Profile form, if any of your prospective colleges require it. Submit the Profile according to the college's timetable.

- Take the SAT/ACT if you plan to attend college after your senior year, or discuss with your school counselor if you should retake the SAT/ACT.

- Obtain a PIN for parent and applicant for completion of the FAFSA in January.

Dean's Tip

Apply for aid even if you think that you won't qualify for it.

Grade 12: Senior Year—Winter (January to March)

- Submit the FAFSA online or mail after January 1 of your senior year but before February 15. If the college requires the FAFSA submitted any earlier, follow its timetable.

- Submit any supplemental financial aid forms to colleges based on their timetables.

- Continue to apply for private and outside grants and scholarships. (Note the deadline dates.)

- After you submit the FAFSA, you will receive an SAR, which will have an EFC listed on it. This EFC is the amount that colleges will use to determine your eligibility for federal student aid and often, but not always, the amount they expect the family to contribute toward college. If the SAR has mistakes, you should correct the mistakes online immediately. You will then receive a corrected SAR.

- Males 18 years or older must register for the Selective Service to receive federal student aid. To register, complete the appropriate box on the FAFSA or register at your local post office.

- Apply for state financial aid according to the state's timetable and application procedure.

- Promptly submit and respond to colleges all requests for additional information including the family's most recent federal tax forms (if requested).

Grade 12: Senior Year—Spring (April to May)

- Review financial aid award letters with your parents. If you do not understand any award or conditions for renewing an award, contact the financial aid office.
- Compare all college award letters. Check for the amount of grants, loans, work study, and unmet need. Make sure that you understand how much your family is expected to pay for your college education at each college. Use the websites listed in Chapter 5 to compare packages.
- If you need more money to attend a particular college, contact the financial aid office.
- As you narrow down your list, notify the colleges that have accepted you that you do not plan to enroll there.
- Accept the financial aid award and submit the required tuition deposit to your final college selection. Some colleges assign dormitory rooms based on date of tuition deposit.
- Note: You have to reapply for aid annually.

Summer Before College

- Find a job and save for college expenses.
- Register and attend summer orientation. Try to get into an early session for a better selection of courses and time slots.
- Send your final high school transcripts.
- If appropriate, finalize student loan applications with the student aid office.
- Select the right meal plan.
- Make sure that all paperwork is completed for any state aid.
- Notify the student aid office of any outside scholarships or grants you have or will receive.
- If you were awarded a work-study position, check with the aid office for job placement information.
- If appropriate, sign the necessary promissory notes for student loans.
- If you are residing on campus, contact your future roommates and coordinate what to bring to college. (Dorm rooms are usually small.)
- Make travel plans. If appropriate, book fares early for best prices.

- Don't forget to set up a bank account near or on campus.
- Arrange to pay the fall tuition and fees bill according to the college's timetable.
- Establish a budget for your freshman year. Review it with your parents.
- Have fun during the summer.

You are ready for college. Enjoy it and study hard.

Summary: Financial Aid Applications

The following is a suggested financial aid application timetable for your senior year of high school.

November/December

Pick up an FAFSA at your high school counselor's office, local or regional library, or at a local college. Begin to review the FAFSA (though you cannot mail it in until on or after January 1). However, many students now choose to submit the FAFSA online at www.fasfa.ed.gov). If you are planning to file online, obtain a PIN at www.pin.edu.gov in November/December. The PIN is needed for an electronic signature. Also, contact colleges to determine if they require a supplemental form and, if so, note the deadline for submitting these forms. Some colleges will require the CSS/Profile form. Register online at www.collegeboard.com in October/ November and follow the college's timetable. Both the FAFSA and CSS/Profile are available in Spanish.

January/February

In early January, you should begin to complete the FAFSA and mail it or submit it online by February 15. Make sure that this timetable is acceptable to the colleges receiving it. It is imperative that the income data submitted on the FASFA be accurate. Aid administrators strongly encourage parents of all aid applicants to complete their federal tax returns early enough to meet college deadlines. If you are applying for aid for academic year 2007–2008, the income information submitted on the FASFA must be for calendar year 2006 (January 1, 2006 to December 31, 2006). However, if completing the tax return this early is impossible, it is acceptable to realistically estimate your 2006 calendar year income on the FAFSA. You may want to use your 2005 federal income tax return as a guide when answering the questions for calendar year 2006. Try to be as accurate in your estimate as possible. You will have an opportunity to correct your data once the return is filed. Remember, it is not necessary to submit your tax returns to the IRS before submitting the FAFSA or being accepted at a college.

You need to submit an FAFSA to the aid office so that the aid office can compile an aid package for you. Remember that there is scholarship money available regardless of your family income in the form of merit scholarships. Be careful of making the assumption that you will automatically become a state resident after living one year in another state. Finally, following the college planning calendar will assist you in navigating the financial aid process more easily and more effectively.

Test Yourself

True or False

1. I can use the Free Application for Federal Student Aid to apply for most types of financial aid.
2. PELL Grants and Stafford Student Loans may be used at accredited colleges throughout the United States.
3. Most private colleges offer Merit Scholarships (no-need aid).
4. If students receive grants from more than one source, they must choose only one grant or scholarship.
5. Students can receive financial aid only as entering freshmen if they have a "B" average or better.
6. Both student and one parent should apply for a PIN number in November or December of the student's senior year.
7. The FAFSA is used by some states to apply for state grants and scholarships.
8. If a student is selected for verification by the U.S. Department of Education, the student is ineligible for federal student aid.
9. All private colleges require the CSS/Profile form for institutional money.
10. If you attend an out-of-state public college, you are automatically eligible for the in-state tuition cost.
11. Applicants must submit an FAFSA to determine eligibility for a subsidized Stafford Loan.

Test Yourself

Fill in the Blanks

1. Scholarships and grants are forms of _____ aid.
2. Seniors should submit an FAFSA online after _____ but before _____.
3. The PIN acts as the _____ signature for both the _____ and _____.
4. Some private colleges will require a supplemental form called the _____ _____ _____ for college money in addition to the FAFSA.

5. The maximum Pell grant is $_____$ and the minimum award is $_____$.

6. A federal unsubsidized loan is not awarded on the basis of $_____$.

7. Students should apply for student aid $_____$.

8. SAR means $_____$ $_____$ $_____$, which includes the expected family contribution.

9. Colleges are required to verify $_____$ percentage of the applicant pool. However, some colleges verify $_____$ to $_____$% of their new students.

Your Share of the Cost of a College Education

Do I Need to Read This Chapter?

You and your parents' first question regarding financial aid is typically, "How much will I have to pay?" You need to read this chapter if you need to learn about

➡ Calculating parental and student contributions with worksheets

➡ Simplified need analysis formula for low-income families

➡ The criteria for a student to become financially independent

➡ The definition of "parent" on the FAFSA

➡ Explaining special financial circumstances to the student financial aid office

➡ The definition of "unmet need"

Federal Methodology

In Chapter 3, we learned that colleges must use the Free Application for Federal Student Aid (FAFSA) to determine eligibility for federal student aid programs. The information submitted on the FAFSA is used in an analysis called Federal Methodology (FM). This methodology is a formula created by Congress to determine the Expected Family Contribution (EFC). It uses family income and assets to compute the EFC (Parent Contribution or the PC). The EFC will also include a contribution from the student's income and a contribution from student assets (Student Contribution or the SC). Under the Federal Methodology, parental assets are assessed at up to 5.6% and students assets are assessed at up to 35%. (The 35% assessment rate decreases to 20% as of July 1, 2007.) Also, the PC is divided by the number of dependent children concurrently in college at least half time. For example, if the PC is calculated at $4,000, with two children in college, the federal PC is $2,000 per child, even if one child is attending a high-priced college and the other child is attending a community college with substantially lower tuition.

The FM does not necessarily assume that the expected family contribution will come out of present income. Families often meet the expected family contribution from current income, savings, and loans. In some cases, families are surprised by their EFC, and they will inform the financial aid office that the EFC is simply too high in relation to other family expenses.

Institutional Methodology

Some colleges use a need analysis formula called Institutional Methodology (IM). Since 1954, the College Board, in cooperation with member institutions, has developed and maintained an institutional Need Analysis Formula. This formula is used to determine eligibility for both institutional and private foundation funds, not federal student financial aid. Many colleges request undergraduate students to complete the CSS/Financial Aid Profile annually.

For additional information on Institutional Methodology, check www.collegeboard.com/parents. Click on "Financial Aid Calculation," then click on "Pick a Formula," and follow the directions.

Finally, each institution has its own policy to determine financial eligibility for institutional funds, so financial eligibility may vary among institutions using IM.

Quick Review

Family Contribution

- The EFC is calculated by a mandated federal government formula called Federal Methodology. The EFC is determined once you submit an FAFSA.

- The EFC will consist of a contribution from parents' income and assets, student assets, and a student contribution from income. Because the EFC is recalculated annually, you must reapply annually.

- The Federal EFC will remain the same at all colleges for federal student financial aid. This includes determining eligibility for Federal Stafford Student Loans.

- The FM is also used by many institutions, but not all, to determine the student's eligibility for institutional (not federal) student aid.

Calculating the Expected Family Contribution Under Federal Methodology

Let's explore the evaluation process to better understand how the EFC is calculated under FM.

Principles of Need Analysis

According to the National Association of Student Financial Aid Administrators, the following are principles of need analysis:

- To the extent they are able, parents have primary responsibility to pay for their dependent children's education.

- Students also have a responsibility to contribute to their educational costs.

- Families should be evaluated in their present financial condition.

- A family's ability to pay for educational costs must be evaluated in an equitable and consistent manner, recognizing that special circumstances can and do affect its ability to pay.[*]

---

[*]National Association of Student Financial Aid Administrators, (NASFAA). Copyright 2004. Printed with permission.

Calculating the Expected Family Contribution

The purpose of this section is to help you determine whether you might be eligible for financial aid—grants, loans, and student employment.

Almost all colleges and other organizations that award financial aid believe that the primary responsibility for paying for a college education rests with the parents and student, according to each family's means. Determining how much a family could be expected to pay is a fairly complicated process called *need analysis*. The three worksheets and six tables in this section provide additional information about the federal need analysis system for academic year 2006–2007. They are used to analyze the information submitted by parents and students on the FAFSA.

By completing these worksheets, you can get some idea of what you and your family might be expected to contribute toward your college expenses. Once your family contribution is estimated, your need for financial aid is calculated by subtracting the EFC from the total cost of the college you wish to attend. Most financial aid is awarded on the basis of financial need.

As you do your computations, remember that the simple outline presented here cannot provide the exact determination of financial need that a college or aid program will make. The figures you arrive at will be useful for planning purposes, but they will be only a rough estimate of your family's financial strength and need for financial aid. The need analysis performed once you have completed the FAFSA will be based on more detailed and specific information. In addition, actual aid decisions are made by individual institutions and scholarship programs. Financial aid administrators can, and often do, adjust the figures when they consider your specific family circumstances.

The important point is that if your estimates show that you cannot meet your total educational costs with your available resources, you should apply for aid. Just as you should not simply assume that you will qualify for a certain amount of aid, you shouldn't assume that you will not qualify at all. Financial aid doesn't just happen to people. To be considered for aid, you must apply for it. Ask each institution you are considering about its application procedures, and give yourself the best chance by applying early and correctly. If you have any concern about paying for college, you need to follow through with this process.

The worksheets in Tables 4-1 through 4-3 contain material related to federal student aid programs. They provide examples of the expected parent, student, and total family contributions for fictional families with different financial profiles. The worksheets have spaces for you to fill in your family's financial information. These worksheets and examples have not been reviewed or approved

TABLE 4-1 Parents' Expected Contribution

	Andrea 4-member family; both parents work; age of older parent is 55	Beth 1-parent family; untaxed income only; some assets; age of parent is 43	Carlos 6-member family; income from a business; 3 children; 2 in college; age of older parent is 45	Your Example
A. 2005 Income				
1. Father's yearly wages, salaries, tips, and other compensation.	$37,040	$0	$54,590	
2. Mother's yearly wages, salaries, tips, and other compensation.	33,688	0	32,340	
3. All other income of mother and father (dividends, interest, social security, pensions, welfare, child support, etc.). Include 401(K) or 403(B) contributions.	1,500	27,430	3,850	
4. IRS-allowable adjustments to income (interest penalties, alimony paid, etc.). Do not include IRA/Keogh payments.	0	0	0	
B. Total Income (add 1, 2, 3, and subtract 4)	**$72,228**	**$27,430**	**$90,780**	
5. U.S. income tax parents expect to pay on their 2005 income (not amount withheld from paycheck). If negative, enter zero.	$8,945	$0	$11,822	
6. Social Security (FICA) tax (see Table 4-4). If negative, enter zero. Multiply .0765 × lines 1 & 2.	5,411	0	6,650	
7. State and other taxes (see Table 4-5). If negative, enter zero. Multiply Total Income (B) by appropriate tax rate.	NY State 5,056	Alabama 822	Tennessee 0	

(Continued)

TABLE 4-1   Parents' Expected Contribution (*Continued*)

	Andrea 4-member family; both parents work; age of older parent is 55	Beth 1-parent family; untaxed income only; some assets; age of parent is 43	Carlos 6-member family; income from a business; 3 children; 2 in college; age of older parent is 45	Your Example
8. Employment allowance. If 2-parent family and both parents work, allow 35% of lower salary to a maximum of $3,000. If 1-parent family allow 35% of salary to a maximum of $3,000. No allowance for a 2-parent family in which 1 parent works (enter zero).	3,000	0	3,000	
9. Income Protection Allowance (see Table 4-6).	22,200	14,430	30,640	
C. Total Allowances Against Income (add 5, 6, 7, 8, and 9).	44,612	15,252	52,112	
D. Available Income (subtract C from B).	27,616	12,178	38,668	
Assets *				
10. Cash, savings, and checking accounts	$7,000	$9,200	$6,355	
11. Other net worth of your parents' investments, including real estate. Do not include the family home. (Net worth means current value minus debt.)	0	0	0	
12. Business or farm net worth. (Figure total value minus indebtedness and then take percentage shown in Table 4-7.) Do not include a "family owned" farm. (If negative, enter zero.)	0	0	$60,120	
13. Other investments (current net value).	$30,000	0	0	
E. Total Assets (add 10, 11, 12 and 13).	$37,000	$9,200	$66,475	

TABLE 4-1   Parents' Expected Contribution (*Continued*)

	Andrea 4-member family; both parents work; age of older parent is 55	Beth 1-parent family; untaxed income only; some assets; age of parent is 43	Carlos 6-member family; income from a business; 3 children; 2 in college; age of older parent is 45	Your Example
Deductions				
F. **Education Savings Asset Protection Allowance** (see Table 4-8).	$57,500	$19,200	$44,300	
G. **Remaining Assets** (subtract F from E).	−20,500	−10,000	22,175	
H. **Income supplement from** assets (multiply G by 12%, if G is negative, enter $0).	0	0	2,667	
I. **Adjusted Available** Income (add D and H).	27,616	12,178	36,001	
J. **Parents' Expected Contribution** (multiply I by taxation rate amount given in Table 4-9).	$7,774	$2,679	$11,715	
K. **Parents Expected Contribution if More Than One Child is in College** (divide J by number of children in college at least half-time— exclude parents).	—	—	$5,857	

*When you complete the actual FAFSA, asset information is reported "as of today," which means the day you complete the form.

**Federal need analysis provisions provide a "simple needs test" treatment for families with total Adjusted Gross Income or earned income of $49,999 or less, who file a 1040A or 1040EZ federal income tax return, or do not file taxes.

When the "simple needs test" is applied, there is no contribution from assets. A further explanation of the "simple needs test" is provided later in this chapter.

TABLE 4-2   Student's Expected Contribution

	Andrea Some Savings ($1,700)	Beth No assets, but part-time employment	Carlos Savings: $2,142	Your Example
L. Student's 2005 Income				
14. Student's yearly wages, salaries, tips, and other compensation.	$3,000	$3,180	$3,800	
15. Spouse's yearly wages, salaries, tips, and other compensation.	0	0	0	
16. All other income of student (dividends, interest, untaxed income, and benefits).	0	0	0	
M. Total Income (add 14, 15, and 16).	$3,000	$3,180	$3,800	
Allowances				
17. U.S. income tax student (and spouse) expect to pay on income (not amount withheld from paychecks). If negative, enter zero.	$0	$0	$0	
18. Social Security (FICA) tax (see Table 4-4). Multiply .0765% by line 14.	230	243	291	
19. State and other taxes (see Table 4-5). Multiply Total Income (M) by appropriate tax rate.	NY State 150	Alabama 64	Tennessee 0	
20. Income Protection Allowance (see Table 4-6).	2,550	2,857	2,841	
N. Total Allowances Against Student's Income (add 17, 18, 19, and 20).	2,930	2,857	2,841	
O. Available Income (Subtract N from M). Resources	$70	$323	$959	
21. Contribution from income (line O × 50%, if negative, enter 0).	$35	$161	$479	
22. Contribution from assets (multiply the total value of savings and other assets—such as stocks and bonds—by 35%).	595	0	750	
P. Total Student Resources (add 21 and 22).	$630	$161	$1,229	

TABLE 4-3 Total Family Contribution

	Andrea Some savings $1,700	Beth No assets, but part-time employment	Carlos Savings $2,145	Your Family
J. Parents' Expected Family Contribution (use figure K instead of J if there is more than one family member in college).	$7,774	$2679	$5,857	
P. Student's Expected Contribution from Resources	630	161	1,229	
Q. Total Family Contribution (add J and P).	$8,404	$2,840	$7,086	

by the U.S. Department of Education. Tables 4-4 through 4-9 will assist you in estimating your expected family contribution by providing tax and related information. The worksheets are printed with permission of the Canisius College, Buffalo, New York, Student Financial Aid Office, August, 2005. The tables, which apply to award year 2006–2007, are based on charts in *Federal Register, Vol 70, No. 101 FR 30425/Thursday, May 26, 2005* and NASFAA Announcement dated July 18, 2005.

The allowance for state and other taxes protects a portion of the parents' and students' income from being considered available for postsecondary educational expenses. Table 4-5 reflects allowances for parents of dependent students; independent students with dependents other than a spouse; dependent students; and independent students without dependents other than a spouse.

TABLE 4-4 Social Security (FICA) Tax

Income Range	FICA Calculation
$1 to $90,000	7.65% of income earned by each wage earner
$90,001 or more	$6,885 + 1.45% of income above $90,000 earned by each wage earner

Calculate separately the Social Security Tax of father, mother, and student.
Source: Federal Register/Vol. 70, No. 101/Thursday, May 26, 2005, pages 30425–30429.

TABLE 4-5 Allowances for State and Other Taxes

| | Parents of Dependents; Independents with Dependents Other than a Spouse | | Dependents; Independents without Dependents Other than a Spouse |
| | Percent of Total Income | Percent of Total Income | Percent of Total Income |
State	$0–14,999	$15,000 or more	All
Alabama	3%	2%	2%
Alaska	2%	1%	0%
American Samoa	3%	2%	2%
Arizona	4%	3%	2%
Arkansas	3%	2%	3%
California	7%	6%	5%
Canada	3%	2%	2%
Colorado	4%	3%	3%
Connecticut	7%	6%	4%
Delaware	4%	3%	3%
District of Columbia	7%	6%	6%
Federated States of Micronesia	3%	2%	2%
Florida	2%	1%	0%
Georgia	5%	4%	3%
Guam	3%	2%	2%
Hawaii	4%	3%	4%
Idaho	5%	4%	3%
Illinois	5%	4%	2%
Indiana	4%	3%	3%
Iowa	5%	4%	3%
Kansas	5%	4%	3%
Kentucky	5%	4%	4%
Louisiana	2%	1%	2%
Maine	6%	5%	4%
Marshall Islands	3%	2%	2%
Maryland	7%	6%	5%
Massachusetts	6%	5%	4%
Mexico	3%	2%	2%
Michigan	5%	4%	3%
Minnesota	6%	5%	4%
Mississippi	3%	2%	2%
Missouri	4%	3%	3%
Montana	5%	4%	3%

TABLE 4-5   Allowances for State and Other Taxes (*Continued*)

| State | Parents of Dependents; Independents with Dependents Other than a Spouse | | Dependents; Independents without Dependents Other than a Spouse |
	Percent of Total Income	Percent of Total Income	Percent of Total Income
	$0–14,999	$15,000 or more	All
Nebraska	5%	4%	3%
Nevada	2%	1%	1%
New Hampshire	4%	3%	1%
New Jersey	8%	7%	4%
New Mexico	4%	3%	3%
New York	8%	7%	5%
North Carolina	6%	5%	4%
North Dakota	2%	1%	1%
Northern Mariana Islands	3%	2%	2%
Ohio	6%	5%	4%
Oklahoma	4%	3%	3%
Oregon	7%	6%	5%
Palau	3%	2%	2%
Pennsylvania	5%	4%	3%
Puerto Rico	3%	2%	2%
Rhode Island	7%	6%	4%
South Carolina	5%	4%	3%
South Dakota	1%	0%	0%
Tennessee	1%	0%	0%
Texas	2%	1%	0%
Utah	5%	4%	4%
Vermont	6%	5%	3%
Virgin Islands	3%	2%	2%
Virginia	5%	4%	3%
Washington	2%	1%	0%
West Virginia	3%	2%	2%
Wisconsin	7%	6%	4%
Wyoming	1%	0%	0%
Wisconsin	7%	6%	4%
Wyoming	1%	0%	0%

Multiply parents' total income (EFC Formula Worksheet in Table 4-1, line 7) by the appropriate rate from Table 4-5 to get the "state and other tax allowance." Use the parents' state of legal residence.

TABLE 4-6 Income Protection Allowances (IPA)

Family Size (Include Students)	Number In College				
	1	2	3	4	5
2	$14,430	$11,960	......	......	......
3	$17,970	$15,520	$13,050	......	......
4	$22,200	$19,730	$17,270	$14,800	......
5	$26,190	$23,720	$21,270	$18,800	$16,340
6	$30,640	$28,170	$25,710	$23,240	$20,790

For each additional family member add $3,460.
For each additional college student subtract $2,460.

The Income Protection Allowance (IPA) is the amount of living expenses associated with the maintenance of an individual or family that may be offset against the family's income. It varies by family size. The income protection allowance for the dependent student is $2,550. For award year 2006–2007, the income protection allowances for parents of dependent students and independent students with dependents other than a spouse, as shown in Table 4-6.

The IPA for single independent students and independent students without dependents other than a spouse for award year 2006–2007 is given in the following table:

Marital Status	Number in College	IPA
Single	1	$5,790
Married	2	$5,790
Married	1	$9,260

A portion of the full net value of a farm or business is excluded from the calculation of an expected contribution since (1) the income produced from these assets is already assessed in another part of the formula; and (2) the formula protects a portion of the value of assets. The portion of these assets included in the contribution calculation is computed according to the schedule shown in Table 4-7. This schedule is used for parents of dependent students; independent students without dependents other than a spouse; and independent students with dependents other than a spouse.

The Education Savings and Asset Protection Allowance protects a portion of net worth (assets less debts) from being considered available for postsecondary educational expenses. There are three asset protection allowance tables: one for parents of dependent students; one for independent students without

TABLE 4-7   Business and Farm Net Worth Adjustment

If the Net Worth of a business or farm is-	Then the adjusted net worth is-
Less than $1	$0
$1 to $105,000	$0 + 40% of NW
$105,001 to $310,000	$42,000 + 50% of NW over $105,000
$310,001 to $515,000	$144,500 + 60% of NW over $310,000
$515,000 or more	$267,500 + 100% of NW over $515,000

TABLE 4-8   Education Savings and Asset Protection Allowance

	Parents of Dependent Students	
	And...	
	there are two parents	there is one parent
If the age of the older parent is...	then the education savings and asset protection allowance is...	
25 or less	0	0
26	2,600	1,200
27	5,200	2,400
28	7,800	3,600
29	10,500	4,800
30	13,100	6,000
31	15,700	7,200
32	18,300	8,400
33	20,900	9,600
34	23,500	10,800
35	26,100	12,000
36	28,700	13,200
37	31,400	14,400
38	34,000	15,600
39	36,600	16,800
40	39,200	18,000
41	40,200	18,400
42	41,200	18,800
43	42,200	19,200
44	43,200	19,700
45	44,300	20,100
46	45,400	20,600
47	46,600	21,000
	(*Continued*)	

TABLE 4-8 Education Savings and Asset Protection Allowance (*Continued*)

	Parents of Dependent Students	
	And...	
	there are two parents	**there is one parent**
If the age of the older parent is...	then the education savings and asset protection allowance is...	
48	47,700	21,500
49	48,900	22,100
50	50,100	22,600
51	51,600	23,000
52	52,900	23,600
53	54,500	24,100
54	55,800	24,800
55	57,500	25,400
56	58,900	26,000
57	60,600	26,600
58	62,400	27,400
59	64,200	28,000
60	66,100	28,800
61	68,000	29,500
62	70,000	30,300
63	72,300	31,100
64	74,400	32,000
65 or older	76,900	32,900

	Independent Students without Dependents Other than a Spouse	
	And they are...	
	Married	**Single**
If the age of the student is...	then the education savings and asset protection allowance is...	
25 or less	0	0
26	2,600	1,200
27	5,200	2,400
28	7,800	3,600
29	10,500	4,800
30	13,100	6,000
31	15,700	7,200
32	18,300	8,400
33	20,900	9,600
34	23,500	10,800
35	26,100	12,000

TABLE 4-8 Education Savings and Asset Protection Allowance (*Continued*)

36	28,700	13,200
37	31,400	14,400
38	34,000	15,600
39	36,600	16,800
40	39,200	18,000
41	40,200	18,400
42	41,200	18,800
43	42,200	19,200
44	43,200	19,700
45	44,300	20,100
46	45,400	20,600
47	46,600	21,000
48	47,700	21,500
49	48,900	22,100
50	50,100	22,600
51	51,600	23,000
52	52,900	23,600
53	54,500	24,100
54	55,800	24,800
55	57,500	25,400
56	58,900	26,000
57	60,600	26,600
58	62,400	27,400
59	64,200	28,000
60	66,100	28,800
61	68,000	29,500
62	70,000	30,300
63	72,300	31,100
64	74,400	32,000
65 and older	76,900	32,900

Independent Students with Dependents Other than a Spouse

	And they are...	
	Married	**Single**
If the age of the student is	then the education savings and asset protection allowance is...	
25 or less	0	0
26	2,600	1,200
27	5,200	2,400
28	7,800	3,600
29	10,500	4,800
		(*Continued*)

TABLE 4-8   Education Savings and Asset Protection Allowance (*Continued*)

Independent Students with Dependents Other than a Spouse		
	And they are...	
	Married	Single
If the age of the student is	then the education savings and asset protection allowance is...	
30	13,100	6,000
31	15,700	7,200
32	18,300	8,400
33	20,900	9,600
34	23,500	10,800
35	26,100	12,000
36	28,700	13,200
37	31,400	14,400
38	34,000	15,600
39	36,600	16,800
40	39,200	18,000
41	40,200	18,400
42	41,200	18,800
43	42,200	19,200
44	43,200	19,700
45	44,300	20,100
46	45,400	20,600
47	46,600	21,000
48	47,700	21,500
49	48,900	22,100
50	50,100	22,600
51	51,600	23,000
52	52,900	23,600
53	54,500	24,100
54	55,800	24,800
55	57,500	25,400
56	58,900	26,000
57	60,600	26,600
58	62,400	27,400
59	64,200	28,000
60	66,100	28,800
61	68,000	29,500
62	70,000	30,300
63	72,300	31,100
64	74,400	32,000
65 and older	76,900	32,900

TABLE 4-9   Assessment Schedules and Rates

If AAI is...	Then the contribution is...
Less than –$3,409	–$750
–$3,409 to $12,900	22% of AAI
$12,901 to $16,200	$2,838 +25% of AAI over $12,900.
$16,201 to $19,500	$3,663 +29% of AAI over $16,200.
$19,501 to $22,800	$4,620 +34% of AAI over $19,500.
$22,801 to $26,100	$5,742 +40% of AAI over $22,800.
$26,101 or more	$7,062 +47% of AAI over $26,100.

dependents other than a spouse; and one for independent students with dependents other than a spouse.

Two schedules are used to determine the EFC toward educational expenses from family financial resources. For dependent students, the EFC is derived from an assessment of the parents' Adjusted Available Income (AAI). For independent students with dependents other than a spouse, the EFC is derived from an assessment of the family's AAI. The AAI represents a measure of a family's financial strength, which considers both income and assets.

The parents' contribution for a dependent student is computed according to the schedule shown in Table 4-9.

The contribution for an independent student with dependents other than a spouse is computed according to the following schedule:

If AAI is...	Then the contribution is...
Less than –$3,409	–$750
–$3,409 to $12,900	22% of AAI
$12,901 to $16,200	$2,838 +25% of AAI over $12,900.
$16,201 to $19,500	$3,663 +29% of AAI over $16,200.
$19,501 to $22,800	$4,620 +34% of AAI over $19,500.
$22,801 to $26,100	$5,742 +40% of AAI over $22,800.
$26,101 or more	$7,062 +47% of AAI over $26,100.

Employment Expense Allowance

The Employment Expense Allowance for employment-related expenses, which is used for the parents of dependent students and for married independent students, recognizes additional expenses incurred by working spouses and single-parent households. The allowance is based upon the marginal differences in costs for a two-worker family for meals away from home, apparel and upkeep, transportation, and housekeeping services.

The Employment Expense Allowance for parents of dependent students, married independent students without dependents other than a spouse, and independent students with dependents other than a spouse is the lesser of $3,100 or 35% of earned income.

Financial Need Calculation

The college aid administrator will subtract the family's expected contribution (as calculated through the FAFSA) from the institution's cost of attendance to determine the student's financial need. Institutional policy and availability of funds will determine the level of financial need that can be met through financial aid. The actual financial need for a given student will vary, as it will be a result of each institution's costs. The following is a worksheet to determine financial need:

Financial Need Calculation				
Name of Institution:	_____	_____	_____	_____
Cost of Attendance:	$_____	$_____	$_____	$_____
Family Expected Contribution:	−_____	−_____	−_____	−_____
Your Financial Need:	$	$	$	$

Financial need may be funded through federal, state, institutional, and all other student financial aid programs. Many colleges may not fund 100% of financial need; the need that a college does not fund is called *unmet need*.

Simplified Need Analysis Formula

Dependent Students

As a part of the processing system, the federal government allows the central processor and postsecondary institutions to calculate a simplified EFC for students who meet certain income and tax filing requirements. Family assets are *not* used in the simplified EFC calculations. The general rule is that if a family's total parental adjusted gross income is $49,999 or less and the family does not file a Federal Form1040, the family assets will not be considered in calculating the EFC. These families usually file a Form1040EZ or 1040A. An exception to the 1040 filing rule is when a family files a Federal 1040 and is eligible to file either a 1040A or 1040EZ but files a Form1040 only to claim a Hope or Lifetime Learning Tax Credit. This family is still eligible for the simplified needs test. If a family does not file a tax return, they are eligible for the simple needs test if the income shown on the 2005 W-2 forms of both parents (plus any other earnings from work not included on the W-2's) is $49,999 or less.

Dean's Tip

The Deficit Reduction Act of 2005 (February 2006) expanded the eligibility for the Simplified Needs Test (effective July 1, 2006) for students and parents who receive benefits from a means-tested federal benefit program. The term means-tested applies to mandatory spending programs of the federal government in which eligibility for the program benefits are determined on the basis of income or resources of the applicant or family seeking the benefits. The following are some of the programs: Food Stamps, School Lunch, Supplemental Social Security Income, Special Nutrition Program for Women, Infants and Children, Temporary Assistance for Needy Families (TANF), and other programs.

Independent Students

The criteria for the simplified EFC formula for independent students is similar to the dependent student criteria.

Dean's Tip

The Deficit Reduction Act of 2005 (February 2006) expanded the automatic zero eligibility income cap from $15,000 to $20,000 on July 1, 2006.

Who Automatically Qualifies for a Zero EFC?

Some students will automatically qualify for a zero EFC. A dependent student for 2006–2007 award year automatically qualifies for a zero EFC if all the following criteria are met:

1. The student's parents filed or are eligible to file a 2005 IRS Form 1040A or 1040EZ (they are not required to file a 2005 Form 1040), or the parents are not required to file any income tax return; and

2. The student filed or is eligible to file a 2005 IRS Form 1040A or 1040EZ (he or she is not required to file a 2005 Form 1040), or he or she is not required to file any income tax return; and

3. The 2005 income of the student's parents from one of the following two sources below is $20,000 or less:
   - For tax filers, the parents' adjusted gross income from 2005 From 1040A or 1040EZ is $20,000 or less, or

   For nontax filers, the income shown on the 2005 W-2 forms of both parents (plus any other earnings from work not included on the W-2s) is $20,000 or less."*

Dean's Tip

If the award year is for 2006–2007, or any part of it, the base calendar year for the tax forms is 2005. The base year is the calendar year preceding the award year.

Independent Students

The criteria for the automatic zero for independent students is similar to the dependent student criteria.

Who Is Considered a Parent?

Definitions

The definition of a *parent* for student financial aid can be confusing. The following should be considered when completing the FAFSA:

- If the parents are divorced, the income and assets of the custodial parent (the parent with whom the child lives more than half the time during the prior calendar year) must be reported on the FAFSA. If the custodial parent is remarried, the income and assets of the stepparent must be reported as well. The federal need analysis methodology does not include the income and assets of the noncustodial parent, except for child support paid to the custodial parent.

- A stepparent is treated in the same manner as a biological parent if the stepparent is married, as of the date of completing the FAFSA.

- Prenuptial agreements: According to the 2005–2006 *Federal Student Aid Handbook*, the Federal Need Analysis System does not recognize prenuptial agreements.

*EFC Formula, 2006–2007, U.S. Department of Education and The Deficit Reduction Act of 2005 (February 2006).

- Legal guardians are not considered to be a student's parents.

- Foster parents are not considered to be a student's parents.

- Grandparents (or aunts or uncles), nonparent relatives, or nonrelatives are not considered to be the student's parents even if the student is living with them, unless they have adopted the student.

Dean's Tip

If the student's parents are divorced or separated, the federal formula will look at only one parent. However, a school may use both parents' information in awarding of its institutional funds.

Non-Custodial Parent

It is important to note that some colleges and scholarship programs may require the non-custodial parent to submit income and asset information. This information will not affect eligibility for federal aid but might be used for awarding institutional aid or for assessing eligibility for an outside scholarship. This information may be collected on a form called the Non-Custodial Parent Statement, or the college may have its own form for non-custodial parents.

Home Schoolers and Federal Student Aid

Many parents have decided to educate their children at home and these students are enrolling in both public and private colleges and universities throughout the country. Generally speaking, these students are eligible to participate in federal student aid programs. (Refer to the Appendix for a list of programs.)

Question 25 on the FAFSA asks, will the student have a high school diploma or GED before you begin the 2006-2007 school year? Many homeschoolers will not have a high school diploma or GED but they are still eligible to receive Title IV student aid. According to the "High School Counselors' Handbook, 2004–2005, Federal Student Aid," page 44, written by the U.S. Department of Education, "home schooled students should answer yes to question 25 if (a) he or she will have completed a home-study program recognized by his or her home state, or (b) state law does not require a home schooled student to obtain appropriate credential, and the student has completed in the home a secondary education that qualifies as an exemption from the compulsory attendance requirements under state law."

Source: "High School Counselors' Handbook," 2004–2005.

Independent versus Dependent Status

For purposes of student aid, students are classified as either *dependent* or *independent*. In general, all single undergraduates are considered dependent. At one point, students qualified as independent by moving out of their parents' home and by parents not claiming them as dependents on their income tax form. As a result, they qualified for a significant amount of aid. Today, some parents think that they can do the same for their child. They cannot. The federal government changed the regulation when it was discovered that too many parents were exploiting the rules in order to avoid financial responsibility for their children's college bills. The rules are much tougher today and only in unusual and well-documented cases will an aid professional consider a student independent.

A student must meet one of the following criteria to be considered independent for student aid for academic year 2006–2007:

- Is twenty-four or older by December 31, 2006 (was born before January 1, 1983);
- Is married;
- Is working on a Master's or Doctorate program during the school year 2006–2007;
- Is a veteran of the U.S. armed forces;
- Has a legal dependent, other than spouse; for which the applicant provides at least 50% support to that child;
- Is a ward/dependent of the court, or was a ward/dependent of the court until age 18; or
- Is an active duty member of the armed forces for purposes other than training.

According to the U.S. Department of Education, "In unusual cases, an aid administrator can determine that a student who doesn't meet these criteria should still be treated as an independent student. The financial aid administrator can change your dependency status from dependent to independent based on adequate documentation of your special circumstances that you must provide. But, the aid administrator will not automatically do this. The decision is based on the aid administrator's judgment and is final—you can't appeal the decision to us."[*]

If you think that you qualify as an independent student, you should contact the financial aid offices at the colleges on your short list.

Special Circumstances

Student Financial Aid Administrators can also make adjustments to the information used to calculate the EFC. The following are examples of adjustments that the financial aid administrator can make with proper documentation. Please note that the financial aid administrator's decision is final and cannot be appealed to the Department of Education.

- Cost of attendance, to take into account special circumstances (e.g., cost related to a student's disability)
- Unusual medical or dental expenses
- Significant change in employment status or a serious concern about the amount that you and your family are expected to contribute
- Elementary or secondary school tuition
- Divorce, separation, or death of a parent or spouse after the application was filed

If you think that you have any other special circumstances, you should contact the financial aid administrators at the colleges on your short list or, if you are enrolled in the college, the aid administrator at your college.

If you took the time to calculate your estimated expected family contribution, you now have an estimation calculation of your share of the cost of your child's education. Also, you have some guidance when requesting the aid administrator to make adjustments to your information on the FAFSA.

Test Yourself

True or False
1. Colleges expect students to contribute toward their own educational expenses.
2. If you or a parent receives Social Security benefits, you cannot receive financial aid.
3. Once a parental contribution has been determined, it will increase when the cost of the college increases.

[*]"The Student Guide," 2005–2006, U.S. Department of Education, page 9.

4. Undergraduate students who are over 22 years of age are automatically classified as independent for federal student aid.
5. Family income is the only factor considered when federal and institutional aid is awarded.
6. Students from families with the same amount of income will be eligible for the same amount of aid.
7. Federal Methodology is used by many institutions to award institutional (not federal) student aid.
8. Financial need will vary from college to college due to college costs.
9. The federal EFC is the same for all colleges and universities.
10. Families with adjusted gross incomes of $49,999 or less may be eligible for the simplified need analysis formula.

Test Yourself

Fill in the Blanks

1. Legal guardians are _____ considered to be a student's parents for federal student aid.

2. Undergraduate married students are considered _____ for federal student aid.

3. Subtracting the family contribution from the college's cost of attendance will result in the student's _____.

4. In the Federal Methodology, student assets to determine contribution from assets will decrease from _____% to _____% on July 1, 2007.

5. The expected family contribution is _____ by the number of _____ in college at least half time.

6. Federal Methodology is used to determine the family's _____ _____ _____.

7. In a divorce/separation, some colleges may require a _____ _____ form for institutional money. This form is _____ required for federal student aid.

8. The Simplified Needs Analysis Formula will not consider family _____.

9. _____ _____ is when a college does not fund 100% of financial need.

10. A family will automatically qualify for a zero EFC if the parents' base year adjusted gross income is less than _____.

Refer to the Appendix for correct answers.

Student Financial Aid Office and Award Notification Process

Do I Need to Read This Chapter?

You need to read this chapter if you need to learn about

➡ The role of the student financial aid office

➡ The award letter process

➡ Reviewing and comparing award letters

➡ Appealing the aid offer

➡ Private scholarships: their impact on an aid package

The Role of the College Student Financial Aid Office

We have now addressed the importance of seeking student financial aid and how to apply for it. Once you have applied for financial aid, the Student Financial Aid Office at the college takes over. All colleges have a Student Financial Aid Office. One of the primary functions of this office is to assist students, parents, and school counselors in understanding the financial aid application process and the various student aid programs, as well as how to finance college costs. In seeking assistance from a Financial Aid Office, please remember that your family is not the only one mailing aid applications, making phone inquiries, etc. Depending on the size of the college, the Financial Aid Office may receive hundreds or even thousands of applications. You can assist the Financial Aid Office in its efforts to process your application efficiently by ensuring that all of your correspondence accurately provides your Social Security number, or student ID number, date of birth, full name with middle initial, and a complete mailing address. Errors or omissions will delay the processing of your application—sometimes significantly.

Dean's Tip

You must realize that during times of heavy volume you may not hear from the Financial Aid Office until the next day or so. Please have patience.

As you prepare to deal with the Student Financial Aid Office, please remember the following:

- Know the application deadline dates for each college, and apply in advance of those dates.

- Complete the forms accurately and completely.

- Respond in a timely fashion to requests from the Student Financial Aid Office for additional information.

- If you plan to visit the college, please make an appointment to speak with the Financial Aid representative as well as an admission representative.

- Finally, make a folder for each college to which you apply, and keep all correspondence received from and sent to the college in this folder

Dean's Tips

Role of the Financial Aid Office

- Advises students and parents on student aid programs.
- Determines final eligibility for federal and institutional need-based aid.
- Provides a student aid package.
- Sends a financial aid award letter that details types, amounts, and conditions of aid.
- Sets disbursement procedures for institutional, federal, and state student aid.
- Provides alternatives, if needed, for helping to meet expenses.

Dean's Tips

What Happens After You Submit the Financial Aid Forms?

- They are processed by appropriate agencies.
- Your results are shared with the colleges listed on the forms.
- Each college receives the results and evaluates them.
- The Financial Aid Office may make further inquiries of you. Respond to any such request in a timely fashion.
- College awards financial aid to you.
- Financial aid award letters are mailed to you from March to April/May.
- You and your parents evaluate the financial aid package. They either accept, decline, or seek clarification.

Award Letter Notification

Determining Student Financial Need

Once the FAFSA has been processed, each college that you have indicated on the FAFSA will receive the results. The Student Financial Aid Office staff will roll up their sleeves and begin the review process.

Each student is assigned a Cost of Attendance budget: either a commuter (living at home) budget or a residential budget. The EFC is subtracted from the appropriate budget and the student's financial need is determined according to the following formula:

$$\frac{\text{Cost of Attendance} - \text{Expected Family Contribution (EFC)}}{\text{Financial Need}}$$

College Awarding (Packaging) Student Aid

Once your financial need is calculated, the Student Financial Aid Office will develop a comprehensive student aid package that may include need-based federal and state grants, merit scholarships, loans, and work-study employment. Each college will have its own aid packaging policies, resources, and timetable for mailing aid award letters. Consequently, when the aid award letters begin arriving in early March to April, you need to review them carefully because they may all be different. Some colleges may request a decision within two weeks of receipt of the award letter but you can request an extension to May 1, which is the National Candidate Reply date.

Let's walk through a sample aid package:

$23,200	Commuter budget (living at home)
–8,000	Expected family contribution
$15,200	Financial need
–$2,200	State Grant
13,000	Remaining Financial Need

There are many options for an institution to help meet the remaining need. In addition to its resources, the options will depend on the college's philosophy concerning the amount of grant, loan, and work study as a percentage of the need. Also, the student's academic profile may influence the aid packages. The college's packaging options may include the following:

- Institutional aid (merit scholarship and/or grant funding)
- State Aid Programs
- Federal Stafford Loan
- Federal Pell Grant
- Federal Supplemental Grant
- Federal Academic Competitiveness Grants
- Federal Perkins Loan
- Federal Work Study

- Institutional Loan
- Some unmet financial need (increases the family's responsibility)

Students who do not demonstrate financial need can borrow through the unsubsidized Stafford Loan program. Parents can also use the Federal Parent Loan for Undergraduate Students (FPLUS) if there is a remaining balance to be paid. Both loans currently have low interest rates. Some institutions may also refer applicants to alternative financing opportunities.

Reviewing the Award Letter

Once you receive your award letters, you should review them carefully to determine if it is financially feasible to attend the college of your choice. Remember the concept of *net cost*. A family is now at the point to compare net cost among colleges. Remember, educational cost minus aid equals net cost, e.g., the amount for which the family is responsible.

Financial aid award offers can vary significantly from college to college. When reviewing aid offers, consider both the amount of your family contribution and the amount offered in self-help aid, e.g., loans and work programs. Do not forget about unmet need, as it may mean that you or your parent(s) will have to secure additional resources, e.g., from the FPLUS or perhaps an alternative loan source. If an institutional grant is offered, it is important to ask how it can be renewed. Also, what are the criteria to renew merit scholarships? What percentage of these awards is renewed each year? If the college's literature or website does not answer your questions, call, write, or visit the Student Financial Aid Office.

You also need to evaluate the aid package—compare how much in loans and how much in free money (scholarships and grants) each college is offering. There are free online services called "Compare Your Financial Aid Awards" at www.collegeboard.com and www.NASFAA.org to assist you in understanding the aid packages from different colleges. Use Table 5-1 to compare financial aid packages.

Dean's Tip

Review the two sample award letters in the Appendix. These award letters are for two different students, with different financial profiles.

TABLE 5-1   Comparing College Financial Aid Award Letters

	College A	College B	College C
Step 1: List the name of each college. A: Total cost of attendance (COA)[1]	_____ $	_____ $	_____ $
Step 2: List all the student aid each college has listed in its award letter.[2] Grants/scholarships			
• State grants/scholarships			
• College grants/scholarships			
• Federal Pell grant			
• Federal SEOG			
• Other grant/scholarships			
Total grants/scholarships			
Loans			
• Federal Stafford			
• Federal Perkins			
• Other loans			
Total loans			
Work Opportunities			
B. Total aid (grant, loans, work)[2]			
C. A – B = Net Cost to family[3]	$	$	$
Cost of Attendance[1] –	$	$	$
Total Aid[2]	—	—	—
Net Cost to Family[3]	$	$	$

[1]Cost of Attendance may be on the college's award letter or the information accompanying the award letter. If not, check the college's website.
[2]You should calculate for each college the percentage of the aid package that is grant, loan, and work. Then make a comparison among the colleges.
[3]Net cost to the family is the difference between the college's cost of attendance and aid offered by the college. This net cost is the amount a family will pay from current savings, current income, and loans.
Source: Prepared by Anthony J. Bellia.

> **Note:** In each aid package, you need to determine if the grants and or scholar-ships are four-year commitments. If not, be sure to ask each college for the criteria to renew them.

> While you are reviewing and comparing the different aid packages, it is imperative that you respond to each college's deadline date. If you don't respond by

the deadline, there is a risk that a college may withdraw its offer. Responding to an aid letter does not officially commit you to attend that college. You need to know that most colleges subscribe to a National Candidate Reply date of May 1 for tuition, room, and board deposits. Many colleges will give a reasonable extension beyond May 1. You need to check with each college for its extension policy.

In responding to the award letter, you have some choices:

- Accept the aid package as presented by the college.
- Accept portions of the aid package and decline others.
- Decline the aid package entirely.
- Ask for a revision in the composition of the aid package (less loan money/ more grant money).
- Appeal the decision if you feel that additional aid is needed.

Dean's Tips

- Determine the out-of-pocket costs for the year. Compare the direct costs and the billable aid on the award letter. Keep in mind that student employment forms of assistance will not be credited to the bill.
- When comparing aid offers, separate gift aid from self-help.

Dean's Tips

Comparing Awards

- Is there a Parent Loan (PLUS) in the body of the award, which makes the package appear larger than another college's award letter?
- Are grants or scholarships tied to any conditions, e.g., residency?
- Remember to compare commuter to commuter aid packages and resident to resident (i.e., on campus housing) aid packages.
- If you applied as a resident, but decide the award is not good enough for the resident cost but great for a commuter, your aid package could change once you change to a commuter status.

- -

Quick Review

Two Categories of Aid

- Merit-based
- Need-based

- -

Case Studies: How Aid Packages Will Differ

Let's assume that three colleges all have the same college cost; consequently, a student should have the same financial need at all three colleges. However, each college has a different packaging policy and enrollment goals. The following three examples will illustrate how the aid packages may differ.

	College A	College B	College C
Budget	$23,200	$23,200	$23,200
E.F.C.	–8,000	–8,000	–8,000
Financial Need	$15,200	$15,200	$15,200
State Grant	–2,200	–2,200	–2,200
Remaining Need	$13,000	$13,000	$13,000
Merit Scholarship	–10,500	–7,500	–5,000
Remaining Need	$2,500	$5,500	$8,000
Stafford	–2,500	–2,625	–2,625
Remaining Need	0*	$ 2,875	$5,375
Federal Work Study		–2,200	–2,400
Remaining Need		$675*	$2,975
Perkins Loan			–1,500
Unmet Need			$1,475*
FPLUS			–9,475

*Unmet need or family responsibility.
Source: Prepared by Anthony J. Bellia.

Observations:

- **College A** has met 100% of the financial need of $15,200.
- **College B** left $675 unmet need.

- **College C** has left $1,475 in unmet need, but included a $9,475 parent loan. The parent loan was sufficient to replace the $1,475 unmet need and $8,000 parental contribution.

Note: Colleges A and B could have included a Parent PLUS loan on the award letter, but the college's packaging policy did not include the PLUS loan.

- Also, note that all three colleges awarded merit scholarships but in significantly different amounts, $10,500, $7,500, and $5,000, respectively.
- College A could award only a $2,500 Federal Subsidized Stafford Loan to avoid overfunding the student's financial need.

These examples illustrate that colleges will have different aid packaging policies, and that you must analyze aid packages carefully; the information materials included with a financial aid decision will provide important details that will help you better understand the institution's policies. For example, the University of Notre Dame explains its packaging policy as follows:

How Is University Financial Aid Awarded?

By filing the Free Application for Federal Student Aid (FAFSA) and the CSS PRO-FILE Application, a Notre Dame student is considered for all sources of assistance administered by the University of Notre Dame's Office of Financial Aid. Scholarships are based upon both demonstrated financial need and academic performance.

A "self-help" component including student loan and campus employment programs typically serves as the foundation of a financial aid package prior to scholarship consideration. The amount of self-help will generally grow annually, based on several factors including increases in cost, annually determined financial need, and self-help limits of loan and work programs. Currently, Stafford Loan annual maximums are $2,625 for freshmen, $3,500 for sophomores, and $5,500 for juniors and seniors.

Source: Printed with permission from The University of Notre Dame, Office of Student Financial Services, August, 2005.

Fictional Case Study 1

Curtis Domer is a high school senior from Kenmore, New York. Since Curtis is a male student, his name has been forwarded to Selective Services as requested on the FAFSA. Curtis is a bright student attending an independent Catholic high school. His high school average in a college preparatory curriculum is 96%, SAT's 710 Verbal, 690 Math, and 740 on the writing section for a total of 2140 out of 2400 based on the new SAT maximum score.

Curtis lives with his mother, age 45, and three siblings. His parents are divorced and the family's adjusted gross income is $31,259. He works part-time and his adjusted gross income (AGI) is $3,464. The family has modest assets of $2,000 in the bank, $1,200 in investments, and net worth of a small business of $5,000. The family did not pay federal taxes. Curtis is the first family member to attend college and is a New York State resident.

Since he is a bright student, Curtis has received numerous, unsolicited admissions and financial aid mailings. Some colleges have offered academic merit scholarships based solely on his scholastic ability. Curtis has applied as a resident student to six colleges, and he was accepted at five schools. It is early April and student aid packages are being received and reviewed by both Curtis and his mother. Let's review three of his aid packages.

	A	B	C
	Private 4-year College	In-state 4-year public College	Out-of-state Public 4-year College
Cost of Attendance	$34,200	$15,000	$34,300*
EFC	−700	−700	−700**
Financial Need	$33,500	$14,300	$33,600

Student Aid Packages			
	A	B	C
TAP (State Grant)	4,400	3,900	Nonportable
Pell	3,300	3,300	3,300
Institutional Merit Scholarship	15,000	3,000	14,000
Stafford Loan	2,625	2,625	2,625
Federal Work Study	2,200	1,475	2,200
Institutional Grant	0	0	6,800
Perkins Loan	1,500	0	2,000
Total	$29,025	$14,300	$30,925
Unmet Need	$4,475	$0	$2,675

*Includes $18,805 additional out-of-state tuition for nonresidency.
**Based on 2005–2006 Federal Methodology.
Source: Prepared by Anthony J. Bellia.

Observations:

- The unmet need is added to the EFC, which is $700, so the family responsibility under packages A, B, and C is $5,175, $700 (the same), and $3,375, respectively.

- This family might consider appealing these aid packages in order to reduce the unmet need.

- The family should check to see whether the in-state grants and scholarships are portable to other states.

- Since Pell is a federal entitlement grant, it would be the same at all three colleges.

- Each aid package is different concerning the percentage of loans, work, and free money (scholarships and grants).

- Money from private scholarships should reduce the unmet need, and consequently the remaining family responsibility.

- All schools offered at least one loan and two schools included two loans in the aid package.

- Institutional gift aid is $15,000, $3,000, and $20,800, respectively.

- Curtis was selected for federal verification, as indicated by the asterisk after the EFC on the SAR, so he must follow the federal procedures for verification.

Fictional Case Study 2

Sally Griffin is an outstanding softball pitcher and wants to attend a Division I school on an athletic scholarship. She lives in California but wants to attend college in the South or Southwest.

Sally is a good student with an 86% high school average and SATV of 570, SATM of 590, and 500 on the writing section for a total of 1660. According to NCAA regulations she is a full qualifier for Division I athletic scholarships.

Sally lives with her mother and father and one brother. Sally will be the only family member to attend college. Both parents are employed. Father's income is $45,305, Mother's is $28,700, and the family adjusted gross income is $74,005. The family paid $6,084 in actual federal taxes. Father is age 51. The parents have $500 in the bank and no investments. The parents filed a Form1040. Sally did not file because she didn't work. Sally has no savings. Sally's FAFSA was not selected for federal verification. Sally has applied to eight schools and was accepted by six of them.

The parents are concerned about the college costs because Sally has applied to some expensive private institutions that have Division I softball.

Let's review three aid packages that Sally received beginning in March of her senior year.

	A	B	C
	Private 4-year College	Public 4-year School	Public 4-year School
Cost of Attendance	$26,650	$19,200	$20,500
EFC	–10,750*	–10,750*	–10,750*
Financial Need	$15,900	$8,450	$9,750
Student Aid Packages			
	A	B	C
Pell	0	0	0
Merit Scholarship	0	2,000	0
Athletic Scholarship	10,000 (partial)	0	7,000 (partial)
Stafford Loan	2,625	2,625	2,625
Federal Work Study	2,200	2,000	0
Institutional Grant	0	1,000	0
Perkins Loan	500	0	0
Total	$15,325	$7,625	$9,625
Unmet Need	$575	$825	$125

Based on 2005–2006 Federal Methodology.
Source: Analysis prepared by Anthony J. Bellia.

Observations:

- Sally was ineligible for a Pell grant, as the EFC was too high for this federal grant.

- Two schools offered partial athletic scholarship in different amounts.

- One school offered a merit scholarship; two did not offer such a scholarship.

- School A offered $10,000 in free money, School B offered $3,000 in free money, and School C offered $7,000 in free money.

- Unmet needs were modest due to high expected family contribution and moderately priced colleges.

- All colleges had a loan component and two colleges had work-study.

- Sally, due to family income, was ineligible for a California State Grant. If she were eligible, Sally should check to see if the California grant is portable to another state.

Fictional Case Study 3

Renee Byron has always wanted to be an elementary school teacher. She plans to attend a smaller school with an excellent teacher preparation program. She lives in Texas and wants to go to college within 4–5 hours of home. Renee has a 90% high school average at a large public high school. Her SAT scores are 680V, 710M, and 650 on the writing part for a total of 2040.

Renee's parents are married and she has one younger brother. The family adjusted gross income is $102,055, and both parents work. Renee works part-time for a fast food chain and she earned $1,393. Renee's parents have $3,000 in their savings account and $1,000 in investments. Renee's father is 52.

Renee has applied to five schools in Texas. She was accepted at four colleges. Renee wants the experience of living on-campus but she has also applied to a local public college as a backup school to which she could commute. Let's review three of the four aid packages that Renee received in late March. Two colleges requested a decision from her within two weeks.

	A	B	C
	Public 4-Year College	**Private 4-Year College**	**Public 4-Year School**
Cost of Attendance	$13,900	$28,250	$10,200 (commuter)
EFC	–22,800*	–17,200**	–22,800*
Financial Need	$0	$11,050	$0
Student Aid Packages			
	A	**B**	**C**
Pell	0	0	0
Merit Scholarship	0	8,000	0
Institutional Grant	0	3,000	0
Stafford Subsidized	0	0	0
Stafford Unsubsidized	2,625	2,625	2,625
PLUS	11,275	14,625	7,575
Total	$13,900	$28,250	$10,200

*Based on 2005–2006 Federal and Institutional Methodology.
**Private college is using Institutional Methodology for awarding its own private money.
Source: Analysis prepared by Anthony J. Bellia.

Observations:

- If the family needs more than two weeks to respond, they should request an extension to May 1, which is the National Candidate Reply Date.
- Renee is ineligible for a Pell grant because EFC is too high.
- Renee was not selected for verification.
- Renee did not demonstrate financial need at the two public schools.
- The private college used Institutional Methodology to award its own money. Renee's financial need based on institutional methodology was $11,050 and the private school awarded $11,000 in gift aid (merit scholarship and grant money).
- All schools offered a PLUS loan in different amounts. At all colleges, the combination of institutional aid, the unsubsidized Stafford Loan, and PLUS loan cannot exceed the cost of attendance.
- The unsubsidized Stafford Loan is the same amount at all schools.
- Merit scholarship could be a four-year commitment, but Renee needs to verify the school's policy on renewing merit scholarships.
- Renee has to reapply annually for the institutional grant. However, the college did state that most likely the $3,000 will be a minimum amount if family finances remain the same.
- Renee should check to see if she is eligible for any aid from the state of Texas.

"Let's Make a Deal": Appealing the Aid Package

The last point in the award letter process is what I call "Let's make a deal," or negotiating with the Financial Aid Office. Financial Aid Offices do not use this term; they prefer to discuss adjustments in aid packages as an appeal procedure. Most colleges will consider adjusting an aid package if they are given legitimate documentation. If the initial aid package is insufficient to attend the college, you should contact the aid office. Certainly, simply asking for more money will not automatically get you more money. You have to make a case for additional aid and your case should be based on documented financial circumstances.

Dean's Tip

Do not hesitate to ask for a review of any unusual circumstances affecting your financial situation.

The following are some reasons for making an appeal:

- The remaining amount of the family responsibility is more than you expected and you simply can't afford to provide that much money.
- The composition of the aid package and the amount of unmet need in the aid package has left you in a very difficult bind.
- Data is incorrect on the aid application or has changed significantly since original data was submitted.
- There is an unusual financial situation in your family. Be sure to organize material that you want to present to the office—e.g., medical bills, receipts, etc.

A few colleges may have an appeal policy that includes meeting or matching aid offers from other colleges.

When you visit or call the aid office, make sure that you have your documentation ready to support your appeal (e.g., final Form 1040, medical expenses, significant loss of employment, award letters from other colleges, divorce or separation, death of a spouse, etc.).

The success of an appeal with a college will depend on numerous factors, e.g., the academic qualifications of the student, how competitive the college is in attracting new students, and the willingness and ability of the college to provide more institutional aid dollars. In some cases, a personal visit to the aid office may be necessary if telephone calls or letters do not solve the problem.

Dean's Tip

When you submit an appeal to the Financial Aid Office, ask when you will receive a response. If the answer is "not before the school's candidate reply date," which is usually May 1, ask for an extension beyond that date.

How Outside Private Scholarships Affect the Aid Package

During the summer, as you prepare for the beginning of the Fall semester, an outside agency awards you a $2,500 scholarship. A family celebration is planned because the $2,500 will make paying the tuition a lot easier. But wait, it may not be that simple. The $2,500 may impact the financial aid package that you have received. According to federal law, financial aid offices cannot exceed financial need if federal aid is part of the aid package. This includes subsidized Stafford and Perkins Loans, Federal Work-Study Programs, and Federal Supplemental Opportunity Grants.

Once you receive notification of an outside scholarship, the Student Aid Office must be notified. Colleges have different ways of dealing with the $2,500 outside scholarship. The following two examples will illustrate this point:

- If you have an unmet need of $2,500 or more, the college may simply apply the $2,500 toward the unmet need. This is good news because the aid package has been enriched by $2,500 and out-of-pocket costs have been reduced by $2,500.

- If the financial need has been met, the college may reduce a federal loan by $2,500 and replace it with the $2,500 outside scholarship. The dollar value of the aid package will remain the same, but the good news is that you have borrowed less money for the year. You need to check with the college to determine their policy concerning the treatment of outside scholarships. There are other options that a college may use. For example, the University of Notre Dame, a highly selective, private institution, which meets full financial need of its students, offers the following example in a flier entitled "Frequently Asked Questions."

How Will the Receipt of an Outside Scholarship Affect My Financial Aid Package?

Many Notre Dame students receive scholarships/grants from private organizations. The receipt of any scholarship/grant not listed on the Financial Aid Award Letter must be reported to the Office of Financial Aid as soon as the student is notified of the award. Please indicate the name of the award for the 2005/2006 academic year, and whether the award is renewable in future years. Awards are divided evenly and credited to the student's University account equally between the fall and spring semesters unless otherwise noted by the organization.

As a guide, if a student receives a scholarship/grant beyond that which is noted on the Financial Aid Award Letter, the financial aid award may be revised adjusting other assistance in the following order:

- Perkins Loan (if applicable);
- Federal Work-Study;

- Subsidized Stafford Loan;
- University Scholarship

For example:

Initial Financial Aid Award		Revised Financial Aid Award	
		$5000	Private Scholarship
$2625	Stafford Loan	2,625	Stafford Loan
4,000	Perkins Loan	0	Perkins Loan
2,300	Work-Study	1,300	Work-Study
10,000	University Schol.	10,000	University Schol.
$18,925	Total	$18,925	Total

Source: Printed with permission from The University of Notre Dame, Office of Student Financial Services, August 2005.
Printed with permission from The University of Notre Dame, Office of Student Financial Services, August 2005.

Post-Enrollment Activity With The Financial Aid Office

Once you have started college, many things can happen. Family finances may change. For example, additional children may begin college, there may be a death in the family, unemployment may occur in the family, investment income may be lost, parents may separate or divorce, etc. You should never hesitate to contact the Financial Aid Office to explain unusual circumstances or difficulty you are experiencing in paying the direct expenses at a college. Keep the lines of communication open. The college does not want you to leave, and the Financial Aid Office may be able to adjust a financial aid package.

Dean's Tips

- Write down your questions before calling the Financial Aid Office and be sure to make notes when you get your answers, such as the appropriate time you can expect paperwork, Federal Perkins and Federal Stafford master promissory note, work study information, etc. Also, note the date, time, and name of the person with whom you talked. That way you will have a time frame for a follow-up phone call.

- Information overload: You will receive a lot of information at one time. If you don't understand and need clarification on some issue, don't be afraid to call the Financial Aid Office again. Your final selection of an institution is a major decision and colleges will want to help you.

- Look into the refund policy at the school you have choosen. Be sure to arrive at campus with money in your pocket, as some schools do not begin issuing refunds until after the drop/add period has concluded.

Finally, once you've done all of this—and you're actually in college with an adequate financial aid package—don't think you can sit back and relax. Many types of aid don't renew themselves automatically; you must submit the FAFSA and supplemental forms (CSS/Profile or Institutional Aid Application) every year by the published deadline. And at many colleges the renewal of merit scholarships is tied to grades and/or some other condition(s). You need to determine the minimum grade point average to renew the scholarship. In some cases, if the student does well—or very well—additional scholarship money may be available.

With today's uncertain economy and with college costs continuing to increase 5–7% or more each year, financial aid has to be considered a team effort. This "partnership" could include parents, students, school, government, and private organizations. So start early, research the actual cost of the college in which you are interested, apply for aid on a timely basis, talk to the financial aid professionals at the college of your choice, and don't get discouraged.

Here the focus was on the roles of the student aid office and the need for effective communication with that office. Also, you should be aware of the importance of carefully reviewing and comparing aid offers. Don't be afraid to appeal the aid decision.

True or False
1. It won't make any difference if my application for financial aid is a little late.
2. I may be offered different amounts of financial aid by different colleges.
3. A financial aid "package" may consist of grants, loans, and a job.
4. If I'm offered aid for my freshman year, I can count on automatically receiving the same amount every year.
5. Student aid packaging policies are the same for all colleges.
6. Students may ask for an extension to May 1 which is the national candidate reply date.

7. Some colleges will allow a student to appeal an aid package if another college has given a better one.

8. All grants are two- or four-year commitments based on the type of institution.

9. Student financial aid offices will determine an applicant's eligibility for need-based aid, including loans.

10. All colleges listed on the FAFSA will receive the results from the central processor.

Test Yourself

Fill in the Blanks

1. Even students who do not demonstrate financial need can borrow through the Stafford _____ Loan program.

2. Parent loans will make the aid package appear _____ than an aid package without one.

3. Financial aid offers can vary _____ from college to college.

4. Parents should compare net cost when comparing aid packages from different _____.

5. Appealing an award letter can be done in person, on the _____, in _____, or electronically.

6. When comparing aid packages, make sure that you compare total _____ _____, _____ , and _____ opportunities.

7. All colleges have a student _____ _____ office.

8. Sometimes the student's academic profile may _____ the aid package.

9. Unmet need will increase the _____ _____ _____.

10. You should always ask what the criteria are to renew _____ scholarships.

11 Outside private scholarships may _____ the financial aid package that the student has received.

Refer to the Appendix for correct answers.

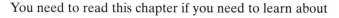

Student Debt: An Investment in Your Future

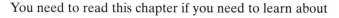

You need to read this chapter if you need to learn about

→ College as an investment with a return

→ What constitutes "reasonable debt"

→ Tips and questions to consider when borrowing

→ Different loan repayment plans

→ Calculating estimated loan repayments

→ Alternative loan programs

→ Website and telephone numbers for private lenders

Investment with a Return

Obviously, college is an expensive proposition and borrowing a substantial amount of money is a serious consideration. However, college is the gateway to an economically brighter future. Many students are understandably reluctant to borrow money to attend college. They are fearful that they will be unable to repay the loans. However, this reluctance to borrow should be carefully considered. There is a small percentage of parents who have saved sufficient funds to pay in full for the expenses required for their children's college education. Consequently, students and their parents often find it necessary to consider borrowing through various federal and private loan programs to pay college expenses. The good news is that there are many reasonable ways and means to do this.

Key to this discussion is the need to view a college education as an investment, which it truly will be for the vast majority who receive it. The following income data, released by the U.S. Census Bureau on March 28, 2005, for calendar year 2003, illustrates this point more fully.

All College Graduates

- College graduates, regardless of race or gender, will earn on average $51,000—nearly twice the $28,000 earned by someone with a high school diploma or general education diploma (GED).

Women's Earning Power

- Women with a college degree on average earned $38,000, compared to $22,000 for women with a high school diploma or an equivalent degree.

Male College Graduates

- All males with a college degree on average earned $63,000, compared to $33,000 for men with just high school diplomas.
- Also, the net worth of college graduates in 2003 was $364,000, in comparison to $109,000 for a high school graduate or equivalent.[*]

This Census data is evidence of the financial return of a college degree. High school students need to realize that borrowing money to attend college is a serious consideration, but it is often a necessity in order to invest in their future.

---

[*]U.S. Census Bureau, March 28, 2005.

Dean's Tip

Before borrowing, review a projected budget and income estimation chart for your chosen field. You may find that your projected income and expenses will not support the amount of money you need to borrow. Check reference books in the school counselor's office or college placement office.

What Is Reasonable Debt?

Recent studies indicate that students are serious about repaying their loan obligations. Here are some facts about student loans:

- Student loans have low interest rates.
- Favorable tax laws allow borrowers to deduct interest on student loans.
- Usually, there is no penalty for prepayment of the principal.
- Student loans have deferment, postponement, and loan consolidation provisions that allow borrowers more time to repay loans.
- Loan repayment periods may range from 10–30 years depending on the principal amount borrowed and the repayment plan.
- Some loan programs such as the Federal Perkins and Federal Stafford Loans have forgiveness provisions for certain occupations; e.g., special education, science, and mathematics teachers.
- The average student loan cumulative debt in fiscal year 2004 was as follows:

Four-year public college	$15,982
Four-year private college	$18,206
Two-year public college	$8,004
Proprietary (private for profit) college	$8,157

Source: U.S. Department of Education, 2004 National Secondary Student Aid Study. Data System, May 2005. Figures include debt from Federal Stafford subsidized and unsubsidized and Educational Perkins Loans.

- According to a U.S. Department of Education press release dated September 14, 2004: The average national student loan default rate for Federal Family Education Loan (FFEL) and Direct Loan programs was 5.2% for fiscal year 2003.

- Median debt burden for student loans in fiscal year 2000 for bachelor's degree recipients after graduation was approximately the same as the debt burden for bachelor's degree recipients for fiscal year 1992–1993. The debt burden has not increased due to higher incomes and increased scholarship and grant money offered by colleges and universities.* College graduates typically are able to manage the higher indebtedness to attend college due to higher salaries and the different repayment plans available to them.

Tips for Borrowing

- Borrow what you actually need and only after all other resources have been exhausted. Avoid borrowing for nonessential items.

- Apply for private scholarships and check out all grant programs, e.g., state-funded programs and institutional programs.

- Make sure that you notify the lending institution of any address change. Usually, the first payment is late due to the lender mailing the first bill to your old college address or parents' home. This can adversely affect your back-end benefits.

- Choose a lender carefully. Lenders will offer incentives or benefits that will affect interest rates and can substantially determine how much you will pay over the life of the loan (i.e., principal plus interest = total loan cost).

- Some lenders may be very aggressive...be careful with those using heavy pressure.

- Consider using auto-debit to repay student loans. Students who make late payments or miss payments may lose repayment incentives from FFELP lenders.

- When choosing a FFELP lender, be sure what repayment incentives are available. Lenders offer a variety of incentives. Be cautious of incentives that are linked to a certain number of on-time payments. Many students miss a payment and do not qualify for the benefit.

- Federally backed loans can help create a good credit rating.

Incentives from Lenders

- **Back end prices:** Some lenders will reduce the interest rate by one-quarter of one percent (25 basis points) when the borrower agrees to have payments made electronically through a checking account (ACH payments).

- **On-time payments:** Some lenders will give a 2–3% reduction in interest rates if the borrower makes the first 36 or 48 consecutive payments on time.

---

*"Debt Burden: A Comparison of 1992–1993 and 1999–2000 Bachelor's Degree Recipients a Year after Graduating." Department of Education's National Center for Education Statistics website.

- **Cash back program:** Some lenders will give a rebate of 3.3–3.5% of the original Stafford Loan amount if the borrower makes the first 24–36 consecutive payments on time.
- **Principal reduction:** Some lenders have initiated a 3% reduction on the principal amount of the Stafford Loan after 12 consecutive on-time payments.

Note: These percentages and number payments are frequently changed by lenders, so check with individual lenders concerning these offers.

According to an article written by Ely Portillo, Knight Ridder, Buffalo News dated August 3, 2005, "Actually, 19 out of 20 student borrowers don't, according to the banks," make on-time payments. Also, "Only about 5% of students earned loan rebates or interest cuts. That's true even after the lender reduced the required number of on-time payments from 48 to 24."

Loan Repayment Plans

Borrowers can select from several repayment plans to assist them in repaying their loans. **Caution:** Borrowers should always factor in the total cost of the loan when considering a repayment plan. Remember that principal plus interest equals the total loan cost.

Standard Repayment Loan Plan

Most students will use this plan. Payment are always the same. The borrower pays the level principal and interest throughout the loan repayment period.

The *advantage* of using this plan is that payments will end in ten years. The *disadvantage* of this plan is that these payments will consume a larger part of a borrower's income when they are just beginning a new career.

Graduated Repayment Plan

This plan allows a borrower to reduce payments in the early years of repayment, after which, usually every two years, the payments gradually will increase. This loan is still repaid within the standard ten-year period. The *advantage* to this payment plan is that the borrower's income will likely increase accordingly. A *disadvantage* to this plan is that the borrower will pay more interest over the life of the loan.

Loan Consolidation Plan

This plan allows a borrower to combine all eligible loans into a single monthly payment currently at a fixed rate. The *advantage* is that the borrower will have more time to pay off the loan. A *disadvantage* is the longer repayment period may result in paying a lot more interest over the life of the loan. Not all loans may be consolidated. You must check with your lender to understand eligibility.

Income Sensitive Plan

This plan allows a borrower to make loan payments according to monthly gross income. Borrower must reapply annually in order to establish the monthly payments, which are adjusted to reflect changes in income. The *advantage* is longer repayment period of up to 25 years. A *disadvantage* is the longer the life of the loan, the more interest the borrower will pay.

The Extended Repayment Plan

This plan allows a borrower who needs lower payments to extend the repayment time. The standard ten-year period may be extended anywhere from twelve to thirty years depending on the loan principal amount. One *advantage* is a longer repayment period with lower monthly payments. A *disadvantage* is that the borrower will pay a lot more interest because the repayment period is longer.

Other Financial Terms

There are some additional financial terms that you need to understand before you select a loan program. These terms, which are defined in the Glossary, are as follows: automatic debit payment, loan cancellation provisions, deferments, and forbearance.

Two other financial terms associated specifically with the Federal Stafford Loan are *subsidized* and *unsubsidized*. Simply, when the Federal Stafford Loan is subsidized, the student has demonstrated financial need and the federal government will pay the interest while he/she remains enrolled in college at least on a half-time basis. If a student is awarded an unsubsidized Federal Stafford loan, the student does not demonstrate financial need for the loan and the borrower is responsible for the interest while in college. The following is a simple illustration of this concept.

$17,000	Cost of Attendance	$17,000
−10,000	Estimated Family Contribution	−18,000
$7,000	Financial Need	0 Need**
−4,000	Scholarship or Grant	
$3,000*	Remaining Need	

*First year Federal Stafford Loan borrower is eligible for a $2,625 subsidized loan.
**Since this student does not demonstrate financial need, a first-time borrower may borrow a $2,625 unsubsidized Federal Stafford Loan.

Dean's Tips

- First-year loan limits will increase from $2,625 to $3,500 on July 1, 2007 (academic year 2007–2008).
- Second-year loan limits will increase from $3,500 to $4,500 on July 1, 2007 (academic year 2007–2008).

Finally, when you are considering a repayment plan, remember to consider the total cost of the loan. Also, consider up-front fees, sometimes called *origination fees* and insurance fees, which may add up to 4% of the principal amount of the loan. These fees are deducted prior to loan disbursement to the college.

Dean's Tips

- The Deficit Reduction Act of 2005 (February 2006) will incrementally reduce or phase out origination fees for both Direct loans and FFELP loans. Beginning on July 1, 2006 over the next five years the Direct loan will decrease the origination fees from 3% to 1% in July 1, 2010, and the FFELP loan will phase out the origination fee from 2% to 0% in July 2010.
- The reduction of origination fees means that students will receive more money to pay for educational expenses.

Calculating Estimated Loan Repayments

To assist you in your planning, the following websites will allow you to calculate estimated loan payments based on different loan principal amounts and interest rates:

- www.collegeboard.com
- www.finaid.org/calculators/

Table 6-1 provides monthly payments according to different interest rates and loan amounts.

Alternative Loan Programs

After reviewing the college's financial aid package, you may still need additional money to pay college expenses. At this time, you may want to consider an alternative

TABLE 6-1 Your Estimated Monthly Loan Payment

Your Monthly Payment on a Ten-Year Education Loan							
Loan Amount	3%	4%	5%	6%	7%	8%	9%
$10,000	$96.95	$101.25	$106.07	$111.02	$116.11	$121.33	$126.68
12,500	120.70	126.56	132.58	138.78	145.14	151.66	158.34
15,000	144.84	151.87	159.10	166.53	174.16	182.00	190.01
17,500	168.98	177.18	185.61	194.29	203.19	212.32	221.68
20,000	193.12	202.49	212.13	222.04	232.22	242.66	253.35
25,000	241.46	253.11	265.16	277.55	290.27	303.32	316.69
30,000	289.68	303.74	318.20	333.06	348.33	363.98	380.03

Your Monthly Payment on a 15-Year Education Loan							
Loan Amount	3%	4%	5%	6%	7%	8%	9%
$15,000	$103.59	$110.95	$118.62	$126.58	$134.82	$143.35	$152.14
20,000	138.12	147.94	158.16	168.77	179.77	191.13	202.85
25,000	172.65	184.92	197.70	210.96	224.71	238.91	253.57
30,000	207.17	221.91	237.24	253.16	269.65	286.70	304.28
35,000	241.70	258.89	276.78	295.35	314.59	334.48	355.00
40,000	276.23	295.88	316.32	337.54	359.53	382.26	405.71

Your Monthly Payment on a 20-Year Education Loan							
Loan Amount	3%	4%	5%	6%	7%	8%	9%
$25,000	$138.65	$151.50	$164.99	$179.11	$193.82	$209.11	$224.93
30,000	166.38	181.79	197.99	214.93	232.59	250.93	269.92
35,000	194.11	212.09	230.98	250.75	271.35	292.75	314.90
40,000	221.84	242.39	263.98	286.57	310.12	334.58	359.89
45,000	249.57	272.69	296.98	322.39	348.88	376.40	404.88
50,000	277.30	302.99	329.98	358.22	387.65	418.22	449.86

Source: Prepared by Anthony J. Bellia, July 2005.

loan. These loans from private lenders are available to supplement a student's financial aid package. Make sure that you have researched all student aid possibilities before you borrow from an alternative loan program. These loan programs are usually more expensive than federal government guaranteed loans.

There are numerous private lenders involved in the student loan industry. Student loans are a profitable business for private lenders, and attracting potential student borrowers is a competitive business. Students and their parents need to understand the services that private lenders will offer them. The fees associated with their loan programs attempt to be competitive. An excellent website to learn more about private lenders is www.studentloanhut.com/private_ student_loan. html. This website is a gateway to a wealth of information on private lender companies. The site describes different student loan programs, state agencies offering student loans, charts that allow you to compare loan programs, and a directory with links to numerous websites providing loan program information.

Dean's Tip

While some lenders may be willing to bundle the payment of a private loan with a Stafford Loan it provided, it cannot formally consolidate these two programs as federal consolidation loans. Private consolidation loans are available, but are often costly and may cause the borrower to lose deferment options.

As you begin researching the various loan programs, you may want to consider the following questions:

- What is the minimum and maximum I can borrow?
- How long does it take to get the money?
- Does the lender offer pre-approval over the phone or Internet?
- What is the interest rate?
- Will the interest rate stay the same or how often does it change?
- Is there a cap on how much this rate can increase?
- What is the length of the repayment period?
- How much will this loan cost me over the repayment period (i.e., principal plus interest plus fees is the total cost of the loan)?
- Can I combine payment of this loan with other student loans (e.g.,Federal Stafford)?
- Will I need a cosigner?
- If there is a cosigner, is that person's obligation permanent?
- What criteria are used to determine if a person is creditworthy?
- Is there a penalty for prepayment of principal?
- Does the loan have deferment and forbearance provisions?
- Do I make payments while I am in school?

- What if I go back to school after making payments for a period of time?
- When is my first payment due?
- Does the lender reward borrowers that make consecutive on-time payments?
- Are the interest rates competitive with other alternative loan programs?
- Are there origination fees?
- Are the fees comparable to other alternative loan programs?
- What if I have employment problems?
- Can the borrower of an alternative loan be released if the borrower dies?

Remember the higher the loan fee, the more expensive the loan.

Some additional factors to consider when comparing student loans are origination and guarantee fees, loan repayment terms, minimum and maximum loan amounts, and interest reduction programs such as automatic debit payments and consecutive on-time payments. Finally, you need to ask lenders if you can save money or reduce the interest rate by adding a cosigner to your loan. If yes, ask if there is a cosigner release option. This means that the cosigner is released from the loan obligation after the borrower has made a designated number of on-time payments and has a clean credit record. Some lenders will release cosigners after 24, 36, or 48 consecutive, on-time payments. Table 6-2 compares features of some of the most popular student loans:

Websites and Telephone Numbers for the Private Student Loan Lenders

1. Citibank: www.studentloan.com; 1-800-967-2400
2. Key Bank: www.keybank.com/educate/alternative; 1-800-539-5363
3. Nellie Mae: www.nelliemae.com; 1-800-634-9308
4. Sallie Mae: www.salliemae.com; 1-800-695-3317*
5. Teri Loans: www.teri.org; 1-800-255-8374
6. Wachovia Education Loan: www.educaid.com; 1-800-955-8805
7. Wells Fargo: www.wellsfargo.com/student; 1-800-658-3567*

Check with lending institutions in your area and also your state agency listed in Chapter 3.

*Available in Spanish.

TABLE 6-2 2005–2006 Alternative Loan Comparison*

Loan Program	Wachovia Education Loan	Key Alternative Loan Key Bank	CitiAssit Loan Citibank	Sallie Mae Signature Loan through Bank One	TERRI Alternative Loan	Nellie Mae Excel Loan	Wells Fargo Collegiate Loan
Minimum Loan Amount	$500	$500	NONE	NONE	$500	$500	$1,000
Annual Loan Limit	Cost minus Financial Aid or $45,000	Cost minus Financial Aid	Cost minus Financial Aid	Cost minus Financial Aid	Cost minus Financial Aid	Cost minus Financial Aid	Cost minus Financial Aid
Aggregate Loan Limit	No Aggregate Limit	$100,000 $120,000 Graduate	$75,000 Undergraduate	$100,000	NONE	$50,000	$120,000
Length of Repayment	Generally up to 20 years	10–20 years	Up to 12 years	15–25 years	Up to 25 years	Up to 20 years	Up to 12 years
Cosigner Requirements	Must meet credit and income requirements, if not cosigner is required.	Usually requires a cosigner	May require a cosigner	Cosigner generally required, must meet credit criteria	NONE–must be credit worthy and currently employed	May require cosigner	May require cosigner
Who May Borrow	Graduate or undergraduate	Student with a credit worthy cosigner. At least half-time. Degree seeking.	Graduate or undergraduate	Age 18 or older. Enrolled at least half-time.	Enrolled at least half-time and degree seeking	Enrolled at least half-time in a degree program	Enrolled at least half-time
Deferment	Yes, if enrolled at least half-time up to 60 months	Yes, if enrolled at least half-time	Yes, if enrolled at least half-time	Yes, if enrolled at least half-time	Deferment until 45 days out of school	Yes, if enrolled at least half-time	Deferred until 6 months out of school

TABLE 6-2 2005–2006 Alternative Loan Comparison* (*Continued*)

Loan Program	Wachovia Education Loan	Key Alternative Loan Key Bank	CitiAssit Loan CitiBank	Sallie Mae Signature Loan through Bank One	TERRI Alternative Loan	Nellie Mae Excel Loan	Wells Fargo Collegiate Loan
Interest Rate and Fees	Prime + 0% Fees: 0-8%	3-month LIBOR rate + 3.3% Fees: None	Prime + 4% No Fees	Prime + 0-6% Fees: 0-3% depending on credit rating	Prime Fees: 0-10.5% depending on credit rating	91day T-bill + 2.25% Fees: 0-6%	Prime + 0-6% Fees: 0%
Phone Numbers	1-800-955-8805	1-800-539-5363	1-800-967-2400	1-800-695-3317	1-800-255-8374	1-800-353-3357	1-800-658-3567
Internet Address	www.educaid.com	www.key.com/educate/alternativ	www.studentloan.com	www.salliemae.com/signature/bankone	www.teri.org	www.nationaleducation.com	www.wellsfargo.com/student
Loan Program	Educaid Select Loan	Key Alternative Loan	CitiAssist Loan	Sallie Mae Signature Loan	TERRI Alternative Loan	Nellie Mae/Excel Loan	Wells Fargo

*Some lenders may provide "customized" versions of these private loans to students enrolled at certain colleges and universities.
Source: Prepared July 2005 by Anthony J. Bellia. Information is subject to change. Please refer to lender websites for more current and additional information on eligibility criteria.

It is no secret that the costs of a college education are continually on the rise. It is also no secret that loans are often part of a student's final financial aid package. This chapter provided a word of encouragement to those hesitant about incurring debt for an education, perhaps even to the point of forgoing college altogether. A college education is an investment in your future. It is an investment in your ability not only to earn money in the future, but also to flourish in the pursuit of the worthy ends of human life itself.

True or False

1. Fees for alternative loans may vary from 0% to a higher percentage depending on student loan lenders.
2. College graduates will earn nearly twice the amount that a high school graduate will earn.
3. There is no earning difference for women according to race.
4. The default rate for student borrowers is less than 5.5%.
5. Students should borrow through an alternative loan program only if the combination of student aid, parental support, and student earnings is insufficient to pay college expenses.
6. The total amount a borrower will repay will always remain the same regardless of the length of the repayment period.
7. All lending institutions offer the same incentives if you borrow from them.
8. A standard repayment plan is when a borrower makes different monthly payments throughout the repayment period.
9. Alternative loans are typically more expensive than federal government guaranteed loans.
10. A cosigner is responsible to repay a student loan if the borrower is unable to repay the loan.

Fill in the Blanks

1. College graduates will earn $_____ in comparison to $_____ for a high school graduate.
2. The average student default for fiscal year 2003 was _____.
3. Some lenders will give interest reductions if a borrower agrees to

   _____ _____ _____.

4. _____ _____ _____ allows a borrower to establish a monthly payment as a percentage of monthly gross income.
5. The longer the loan repayment period the _____ interest the borrower will pay over the life of the loan.

6. When students combined two or more eligible loans into a single monthly payment loans, this is called _____ _____.

7. Alternative loans should be used only to _____ a student financial aid awards and family contribution.

8. The average loan indebtedness for a student is attending a four-year public college is $_____ and $_____ for a four-year private college.

9. The five repayment plans are _____, _____, _____, _____, and _____.

10. Alternative loan programs will usually allow a student to borrow the _____ minus _____ _____.

CHAPTER 7

Controlling the Cost of a College Education

Do I Need to Read This Chapter?

You need to read this chapter if you need to learn about

➡ Reducing college costs

➡ The credit card trap

➡ The cell phone trap

➡ Meal plans

➡ Preventing identity theft

➡ Purchasing books and supplies

➡ Three-year degree programs

➡ Other cost-saving tips

In many cases, students leaving home for the first time are inexperienced in managing money, and it is their first taste of financial independence. This chapter will give some tips on cash management and how to cut college costs.

The easiest part of calculating college cost is when the semester bill is received at home. It will include the tuition and room and board (if living on campus). In addition, some colleges may list the college fees as one comprehensive list and others list the fees separately (e.g., technology fees or health fees).

Once you know the fixed charge from the college, you are in a position to control other college-related expenses during the year.

Dean's Tips

- You should establish an annual budget with your parents and then break it down into semesters. You should also analyze cash flow or where the money is coming from. Will your parents mail or deposit money bi-weekly, monthly, or via a lump sum at the beginning of the semester? Also, if you have a job on campus, ask the financial aid office if you will be paid bi-weekly or monthly.

- If the college has a course in the freshman year or during orientation on money management, it wouldn't hurt to take it.

There are a number of controllable expenses that can have a significant impact on the cost of your college education.

Cell Phones

- Shop around for competitive prices and a realistic plan.
- Make sure that the cell provider has service near your college.
- Consider tying into a family plan that allows unlimited calling among family plan members. Usually cell phones are cheaper than using a college phone service.
- Check into the phone plan provided by the college to determine cost and other phone-related services.
- Another option to save money on phone calls is obtaining a toll-free number for calling home. Check out the following website to compare phone rates:

www.lowermybills.com. This website will allow you to search by price and minutes per month.

Credit Cards

The advice given here about obtaining and using a credit card may seem overly cautious, protective, but abuse or overuse of a credit card is a very dangerous pitfall. Such abuse may lead to a bad credit record that will cause serious problems later in your life, e.g., when attempting to rent an apartment or buy an automobile. It can also limit your ability to obtain an alternative loan in the event that your family chooses that option to finance a portion of the tuition bill.

Stay clear of card companies that come to college campuses offering free water bottles, T-shirts, or other promotional gimmicks.

- Select one credit card before you leave home and discuss it with your parents. You might also ask to tie the credit card to your parents' account. This will help prevent late payments, and your parents can monitor expenditures.
- Establish a modest limit, maybe $500–$600.
- Look for a low interest rate and no annual fee.
- Establish rules for use of the credit card, e.g., using it only in an emergency.
- Avoid online charging.
- Pay your credit card bills on time to avoid late charges (some companies charge from $25–$45 for a late payment), and pay it off in full each month to avoid paying interest.

This advice should also be considered if you want to become more independent and learn how to manage your life in a responsible fashion.

The key to having a credit card is to be responsible and exercise restraint. Finally, avoid excess credit card use for consumable goods like coffee, pizza, and cigarettes.

Dean's Tip

Students are usually solicited for credit cards during the college years. Be sure you are aware of the risks associated with this type of debt.

Leave the Car at Home

This simple decision could save your family literally hundreds and even thousands of dollars. If you are considering purchasing a car, ask the question: Why do I need a car? Yes, it may be convenient, but is it really a necessity? At many colleges, students who bring cars pay a parking fee from approximately $60–$100 annually, and in reality the parking fee is simply a hunting pass to find a parking space. There will also be additional costs for gas, oil charges, maintenance, insurance, and repairs. In an urban setting, public transit is usually available at a reasonable price. Also, many colleges provide shuttle services to shopping malls, downtown areas, and local entertainment centers, such as ski resorts and movie theatres. Check to see what services are provided by the college or university.

If you must bring a car to campus, make sure that you notify your insurance agent in order to avoid the possibility of no coverage if you have a claim. Also, premiums may either increase or decrease depending on your on-campus or off-campus address.

Purchasing School Supplies

This is an area where you can really save some money. You should attempt to purchase used textbooks when they are available. Used textbooks are not discounted deeply, but the prices are lower. Try to buy them during freshman orientation after you have registered for your classes. Check the Internet for websites dealing with used books. Some useful websites are eBay, eCampus.com, bookbyte.com, barnesandnoble.com, and efollet.com. Also, some colleges are allowing online textbook exchanges where students can sell their used books and browse for others.

For dorm room items, check the college bulletin boards to purchase used refrigerators, desk lamps, and small appliances. And in this age of computers, be wary. This is an area where, according to many ITS experts, students spend too much money. These experts think that a basic computer is sufficient to handle college course work. You should check with the college to determine if they have any special arrangement with computer suppliers for computers, printers, and other computer supplies. Also, many colleges have wireless connections, so make sure your computer has this capability.

Finally, shop early at discount stores for the best values in basic school supplies.

Dean's Tip

Shop around for books. You may be able to find less expensive books online or at used bookstores. Be careful to get the correct editions.

Selecting the Right Meal Plan

Generally, freshmen gain about 10–15 pounds during the first year of college. Colleges will promote a full meal plan. However, many students simply do not need three meals a day, seven days a week, provided by the college. You should determine if you need a smaller meal plan, e.g., 14 meals a week or even a smaller one. Don't pay the extra money for something that you won't use. Many student residences have kitchen facilities, and you may want to purchase a basic meal plan to make sure that at least one meal a day is a balanced one. Also, meal plans may be adjusted at the end of each semester depending on the college policy.

Travel to and from College

Generally, most students in the United States attend a college within five to six hours of home. Consequently, this advice will pertain to these students. Most colleges offer car pooling opportunities to reduce expenses. Some colleges will provide bus service at a reduced cost to selected cities along a major thruway or toll road. Also, check into bus and rail service to reduce traveling cost when going home for long weekends or semester breaks. If you have to fly home, make sure that you book your airlines well in advance to maximize your savings.

Checking Accounts

You should consider applying for a checking account at a bank near the college. These lending institutions have experience with students who have low monthly balances and in most cases steadily declining balances from the beginning of the academic year. Look for an account with no monthly service fee, no minimum balance, and no or nominal fees for use of an ATM machine. If the bank offers no fee for a certain number of monthly checks, you need to determine if the number of free checks is reasonable and you can transact your business within these limits.

Consider signing up for overdraft protection to avoid penalties for bounced checks. You should also consider linking your checking account with your parents' credit card to cover any potential overdrafts.

Preventing Identity Theft

During college, you may reside in close living quarters while on campus. Safeguard your social security number, monthly bank statements, computer passwords, drivers' license number, credit card numbers, and other personal identification numbers and records. You may want to consider keeping a small safe in your room.

Dean's Tips

- Don't discard any banking statements or invoices before you destroy them.
- Don't share your social security number or credit card account number with anyone over the phone or online before you verify that the company is legitimate.
- Don't give financial or personal information over the phone or online unless you initiated the contact.
- Be wary of high pressure sales to initiate a transaction (e.g., a scholarship search).
- Don't leave your cards unattended (in, for example, a health club, or a glove compartment).

If you suspect identity theft, file a complaint with the Federal Trade Commission (FTC) at www.consumer.gov/idtheft, U.S. Department of Education at www.ed.gov/misused or 1-800-MISUSED (1-800-647-8733), or call 1-877-IDTheft (1-877-438-4338). Also contact the local police or campus security. Finally, contact the fraud departments of one of the following major credit bureaus. This alert requests creditors to contact you before allowing a credit to your existing account or if there is a request to open a new account.

- Equifax: 1-800-685-1111 or visit www.equifax.com
- Experian: 1-888-397-3742 or visit www.experian.com
- Transunion: 1-800-916-8800 or visit www.transunion.com

Three-Year BA/BS Programs

Three-year BA/BS programs are designed to allow students to achieve the end result of a four-year program in three year's time. Students may complete the requirements of a traditional four-year program, for example, over the course of eight semesters in three years, two of which must be completed during summer months. Three-year programs are rigorous. Pursuing a college degree in three years takes a highly motivated, organized student who is willing to tackle the course offering hurdles that colleges inadvertently create for students.

What Are the Benefits of Graduating in Three Years?

- Reduces college costs and student debt by substantial amounts
- Saves time
- Allows you to enter graduate or professional school one year early
- Allows you to combine an undergraduate degree with a master's degree and earn both in 4 or 5 years depending upon the length of the master's degree
- Allows you to participate in athletics, on campus programming, study abroad, and still participate in community service
- Allows you to enter the workforce early

Three-year programs are offered by fewer than 20 colleges. Check out www.naicu.edu for a complete listing. Some of the colleges that offer three-year degree programs are Bates College (Maine), Regis College (Colorado), Northern Arizona (Arizona), Guilford College (North Carolina), Hood College (Maryland), Florida State University (Florida), Harvard College (Massachusetts), Waldorf College (Iowa), and Valparaiso University (Indiana).

Advanced Placement/College Credit Courses

For many students, three-year programs are attainable because they entered college with advanced credit through a variety of means including Advanced Placement courses, International Baccalaureate degrees, the College Level Examination Program (CLEP), and college credits earned from local colleges in the student's hometown. In many cases, high school seniors are graduating with eighteen to twenty-four college credits already achieved. If students have had the ambition and motivation to take the time to earn college credit in high school, then this advanced credit should be used to reduce college costs, borrow less money, and enrich their college experience.

- You should request advanced standing based on the number of your college credits and the college's policy on providing such credits. Needless to say, each college will have its own policy on accepting advanced credit.

- With proper planning, you can graduate in less than four years. This will save money and reduce student debt.

- Some students use advanced credit to reduce the course load during the academic year. This allows more time to participate in community service projects, internships, research projects, and social organizations.

For more information on advanced placement and CLEP programs, visit the College Board website (www.collegeboard.com).

Some Other Tips

Living on campus is obviously a 24-7 experience and your lifestyle on campus will impact the total cost of your college experience. Some areas that may significantly increase college cost are the following: your social life, your fashion statement, your college major, your decision to join a club sport, and renter's insurance.

1. *Social life:* Some colleges have very elaborate fraternity and sorority chapters. If you plan to join one, look at the initiation fee. Some initiation fees exceed $1,000 per year. These initiation fees do not include meals, housing, and other special activities within the chapter.

2. *Fashion statement:* You don't have to go overboard on clothes. Many fashion experts state that basic fashion won't go out of style. During your campus visits, check out how the students are dressing. From that observation, you will have a sense of the campus fashion.

3. *College major:* Selecting a college major is a very important decision. Some majors are more expensive than others, e.g., art, music, and computer science. Don't let cost influence your selection of a major, but budget accordingly. Make sure that you ask an upperclassman about additional costs within the major.

4. *Club sports:* If you are interested in participating in a club sport, check out how much it will cost you to participate in this activity. Ask if there are dues, travel expenses, including lodging and meals, equipment costs, and additional medical insurance costs.

5. *Renter's insurance:* Finally, look into renter's insurance to cover your worldly belongings on campus or in an off-campus apartment. If you are bringing an expensive item to college, ask your insurance agent for a *rider* to cover the cost of a specific item. This coverage is usually for full replacement cost.

There are many pitfalls that lead college students to increase the costs of their college education unnecessarily. Credit cards, cell phones, extra semesters, and the like all can significantly increase the cost of attaining a college degree. In many cases, increased costs are due simply to a student's inexperience in money management. This chapter provided advice on how students can best manage their money while in college and, accordingly, control the costs of their education.

True or False

1. Students normally gain 10–15 pounds during the first year of college.
2. Generally, students in the United States attend college within 5 to 6 hours of home.
3. Identity theft is not a concern while attending college.
4. All banks charge the same fees for ATM use, monthly balance, and monthly service fee.
5. If you take your car to college, your car insurance may change due to college location.
6. Books and supplies will vary from major to major.
7. College fraternities and sororities are an inexpensive way to socialize on campus.
8. Leaving your car at home is an excellent way to reduce indirect college costs.
9. All cell phone plans are the same.
10. Club sports are fully funded by colleges.

Fill in the Blanks

1. Most colleges offer _____ _____ to reduce travel expenses to and from college.
2. Freshmen should attempt to buy _____ books to save money.
3. Student and parent(s) should establish a _____ for the year and break it down into _____.
4. Some ITS experts think that a _____ computer is sufficient to handle college course work.
5. If you suspect identity theft, contact the _____ _____ _____ or a local law enforcement agency.

Refer to the Appendix for correct answers.

Options for Paying College Expenses

You need to read this chapter if you need to learn about

➡ Loan programs to fund unmet need or supplement the parental contribution

➡ College-sponsored loan and repayment options

➡ Home equity loans / lines of credit

➡ Alternative loans: some questions you need to ask

➡ The impact of loans on the student aid formula

Loan Programs to Finance Parental Contribution and Unmet Need

Let's say the Student Financial Aid Office has reviewed your request for additional aid and even after an increase in financial aid, you still find yourself short in meeting the educational expenses for the first year. Don't panic—there are alternatives available to you for paying. In this chapter, we will discuss some financing options to help pay for any unmet financial need that the college was unable to fund, and all or part of the expected family contribution. As discussed earlier in this book, parents can pay for college from yesterday's income (savings), today's income (current income), and tomorrow's income (future earnings). In this example, let's assume that the expected family contribution is $9,000 and the unmet financial need is $3,000, leaving the family responsible for a total of $12,000 for meeting the first-year college expenses:

$12,000	Total Family Contribution
–2,500	Savings
$9,500	Amount of Family Responsibility

After contributing $2,500 from savings, the new amount of family responsibility is $9,500. This balance would be paid from current parental earnings while you are enrolled in college and/or future parental earnings after you graduate or leave college.

There are several options for meeting the $9,500 balance:

- 10 to 12 monthly installment payments through the college
- 3 or 4 monthly payments per semester through the college
- Long-term loan through the college
- Home equity line of credit
- Home equity loan
- Federal PLUS Loan
- Alternative loans through private lenders
- Other financing options:
  - Retirement fund
  - Life insurance

Before you use one of these options, you need to know that both private lenders and the federal government are interested in knowing if you are a good credit risk.

Your Credit Score

Most loans and interest rates available to parents will be based on their credit report, sometimes called a *credit score*. During your sophomore or junior year in high school, your parents should check their credit status. A credit report can be ordered from one of the following credit bureaus:

- Equifax: 1-800-685-1111 or visit www.equifax.com
- Experian: 1-888-397-3742 or visit www.experian.com
- Transunion: 1-800-916-8800 or visit www.transunion.com
- TRW: 1-800-498-0965 or www.trwcredit.com

Once you receive and review your credit report, you can act accordingly. If the credit score indicates that you may be a credit risk, you will need to implement a plan to improve your credit score. It is important to improve the credit score because lending institutions will use it to determine whether to lend you money, how much credit to allow, and what interest rate to charge you. Remember that credit decisions are made quickly and the credit score is usually the key factor.

Financing Options

When mailing the financial aid award letter and/or the tuition bill, most colleges will include literature on how to finance all or part of the expenses. There are many options to finance these expenses.

The following worksheet will assist you in calculating how much money you may want to consider borrowing once the colleges provides a student financial aid package:

Expenses:	
Tuition & Fees*	$ _____
Room and Board	_____
Books and Supplies	_____
Transportation	_____
Personal Expenses	_____
Study Abroad	_____
Handicapped (disability)	_____
Miscellaneous	_____
Total Costs	**A**$ _____
Family Contribution:	
Estimate the actual family contribution that you can contribute from:	
Current income	_____
Savings and investments (529 plans, etc)	_____

Student's contribution from:		
Income (summer earnings, off-campus part-time work and work-study)		_____
Checking account, savings, trust accounts, etc.		_____
Free Money (Scholarships and Grants) in aid package**		_____
Gifts (graduation, relatives)		_____
Student loans provided in aid package		_____
Total Student Resources		**B$** _____
Additional Money Required	**(A – B = C)**	**C$** _____

*Make sure that you use the correct tuition amount if attending an out-of-state public college/university.
**Include any scholarship or grant money from private sources if not included in the award letter.

Dean's Tip

If you can't pay your balance outright, consider the college or outside agency payment plans instead of loans or costly credit cards.

College-Sponsored Payment And Loan Programs

The first place to look for alternatives is directly from the college. Usually colleges will offer some institutional payment plans to assist students and parents in paying college expenses. Here are three sample institutional plans:

1. **Ten or Twelve Monthly Payments to the School (Beginning in July or August):** These monthly payments are not loans. They allow families to spread out the cost over the academic year. Usually, the last payment for the semester is due by the last month of the semester. These plans allow for the whole academic year to be spread over both semesters. Here are some specifics. There is usually a $50–$75 annual fee that could include life insurance. Sometimes a college will charge an additional fee for late enrollment. Also, no interest is charged on the unpaid balance. This payment plan is usually available to all full and part-time students, both undergraduate and graduate students.

The *ad antage* of this plan is that it spreads out-of-the-pocket costs over the academic year with a minimal processing fee and no interest on the unpaid balance.

The disadvantage of this plan is that late payments may result in the cancellation of this option and/or may prevent you from registering for the next enrollment period.

2. **Installment Loan to the College:** This plan usually has three monthly payments per semester. Usually there is an administrative fee depending on the amount financed. Sometimes, a default penalty is charged if the total amount is not paid in full by the due date. Generally, no interest is charged for this installment plan. Both full and part-time students are eligible to use this plan.

   The *ad antage* of this plan is that it spreads out-of-the-pocket costs over the semester with a minimal processing fee and no interest on the unpaid balance.

   The *disad antage* of this plan is that late payments may result in the cancellation of this option and/or may prevent you from registering for the next enrollment period. Some colleges will allow student/parent to make installment payments directly online if the borrower participates in one of these payment options. Check with individual colleges.

3. **College Sponsored Long-Term Loans:** Some colleges provide long-term loans to students and/or parents. Generally, these loans have a reasonable interest rate. Also, some colleges will offer loans to students who demonstrate financial need and to students with no financial need if they need to borrow in lieu of the parental contribution. Usually these loan programs use institutional resources, which may be limited. Also, the maximum loan amount will vary from college to college.

   The *ad antages* of this plan are that it has long term, low interest, no administrative fees, usually repayment begins six months after graduation or after the student leaves the college. Also, there are usually deferment provisions during periods of at least half-time study.

   The *disad antage* of this plan is that some colleges will require a co-signer.

Home Equity Lines of Credit/ Home Equity Loans

Many families are in a position to pay some or all of college expenses by borrowing against the equity in their home. The following example will illustrate how to calculate an estimated home equity line of credit:

$180,000	Present market value of home
75%*	Maximum lending level
135,000	
–60,000	Unpaid mortgage
$75,000	Available for line of credit

*Some lenders may allow you to borrow up to 85% or more depending on your credit rating.

In this illustration, the family has the potential to borrow up to $75,000 in either a home equity line of credit or loan. The differences between a home equity loan and home equity line of credit are discussed next.

Home Equity Line of Credit

The equity line of credit is flexible, lets you borrow what you need, and pay interest only on the amount actually used. The interest is usually variable rate tied to the prime rate. Also, once the principal is repaid, it may be borrowed again.

Advantages include the following:

- One time application (without having to renew or pay fees).
- Potential tax deductibility.
- Funds are available when needed.
- Funds are available to more than one sibling attending different schools.
- Only pay interest on funds actually used.
- Some lending institutions will not charge an application or closing fee.
- Repayment up to 20 or more years depending on the size of your loan.
- Various repayment plans, e.g., interest only initially, then regular repayment schedule.

The following are some conditions for getting an equity line of credit:

- Borrower must be credit worthy and have an acceptable debt to income ratio.
- Borrower must be a homeowner (home is collateral).
- Interest rate will vary with lender.
- Check with tax advisor if interest paid is tax deductible. The interest is deductible only if you itemize deductions on Form 1040.
- Usually an annual fee.

- Your home is the collateral for this loan.
- The loss of an emergency fund.

Home Equity Loan

The borrower will receive one lump sum payment and the borrower pays interest on the total principal borrowed. This loan is actually a second mortgage on the borrower's home.

Advantages to an equity loan include the following:

- A fixed interest rate.
- Predictable monthly payment for a specific repayment period.
- Allows a family to consolidate tuition for two or more children in college into one loan payment.

The considerations are the same concerns as the home equity line of credit. In summary, if you are thinking of using a home equity loan, keep the following in mind:

- Shop around for the best rate.
- Compare annual fees and closing costs.
- Compare repayment schedules.
- The Federal Trade Commission urges potential home equity borrowers to be aware of negative loan practices. Check out www.ftc.gov/bcp/conline/pubs/homes/eqscams.htm for additional information on negative loan practices.

Federal Loan

Some families are nervous about using their home as collateral to pay college expenses. Don't worry. There are other loan opportunities available to you. The federal government offers a long-term, 8.5% fixed interest loan to parents of full- and part-time dependent undergraduate students.

Dean's Tip

- The Deficit Reduction Act of 2005 (February 2006) allows graduate and professional students eligibility for PLUS loans effective July 1, 2006.
- A FAFSA is not required to apply for a PLUS loan.

Federal Plus Loan

Parents and graduate and professional students may borrow up to the cost of attendance (COA) minus any financial aid awarded (COA – other aid = maximum PLUS Loan). Colleges will determine the actual PLUS loan amount. If parents are considering a PLUS loan, they should encourage their dependent children to file a FAFSA so that the financial aid office can evaluate the applicant for all student aid possibilities including state scholarships and/or grants. (Refer to the sample Plus Loan pre-approval form in the Appendix.)

Eligibility Criteria

- U.S. citizen or eligible noncitizen.
- Parent of a full-time or a part-time undergraduate dependent student.
- Graduate and professional students.
- Generally have to pass a credit check, but will not consider income to debt ratio.
- May not be in default or owe a refund to any federal student aid program.

Advantages

- No collateral is required.
- Income and assets are not considered .
- Interest may be tax deductible. Check IRS Publication 970.
- No penalty for prepayment.

Federal Plus Interest Rates, Fees, and Repayment Schedules

- There is a fixed interest rate of 8.5%.
- There are origination and guarantee fees up to 4% of the total loan.
- Ten-year standard repayment, which begins 60 days after the final disbursement for the year. Interest is charged from the time the loan is disbursed to the school.
- There are several other repayment plans available: extended, graduated extended, and income sensitive plan (the income sensitive plan is available to FFEL PLUS borrowers). Refer to the Glossary or Chapter 6 for information on these repayment plans.
- PLUS loans can be consolidated with other federally guaranteed loans.
- Borrowers have to be credit worthy. If they don't pass the credit check, they may still receive a PLUS loan with an eligible co-signer. Some lenders offer a "second look" to assist in the resolution of minor credit report issues.

- PLUS loans have death and disability provisions.
- There are deferment and forbearance provisions.

You may wonder if it makes better sense to borrow a Federal PLUS loan than either a home equity loan or line of credit. Each family's circumstances will dictate what is appropriate for its unique situation.

Alternative Loans

As stated earlier in this chapter, parents have the opportunity to borrow money to pay for college expenses through either home equity loans, home equity lines of credit, or the Federal PLUS loan. As another option, a family may wish to have the student borrow what is still needed through an alternative loan. Before you obtain an alternative loan, you need to conduct a thorough review of private lenders. There are numerous lenders offering different student loan programs to make college expenses more manageable. There is likely to be a loan program to meet your individual needs. In Chapter 6, there is a comparative alternative loan chart for your review.

Quick Review of What You Should Look for in an Alternative Loan Program

- Does the college's financial aid office recommend the lender?
- How long has the private lender been involved in providing student loans?
- Does the lender offer special services to borrowers, for example, toll free lines, cooperative services with the college, and a service representative assigned specifically to the college?
- Does the lender provide incentives for automatic debit payments, reduced interest rates for 24, 36, or 48 consecutive, on-time monthly payments?
- Will the lender hold the loan through repayment or sell it?
- Are there origination fees? If so, how much are they?
- Does the lender offer loan pre-approval online or over the phone?
- Does the lender offer different repayment plans if you require additional time to repay the loan?
- How frequently does the lender calculate interest? The more often the interest is calculated, the larger the student debt.
- What will be the criteria for renewal of this loan in future years?
- Compare forbearance provisions offered by the various lenders and determine how much additional loan will be created if you use the forbearance option.

TABLE 8-1 Some Differences Between Federal PLUS and Private Alternative Loans

	Federal PLUS Loans	**Private Alternative Loans**
Eligible Borrowers	• Undergraduate student parents • Graduate and professional students	• Student and parents • Both undergraduate/ graduate students
Interest Rates	• 8.5% fixed rate	• Usually higher than PLUS loan, no maximum cap
Loan Amount	• Cost of attendance minus student aid = PLUS loan	• Maximum annual loan limit is set by the bank
Repayment	• Within 60 days after final loan disbursement, while the student is still enrolled in college	• Depends upon the lender
Guaranteed by Federal Government	• Yes	• No
Grace Period	• None	• Depends upon the lender
Income Contingent Repayment Plan	• No	• Depends upon the lender
Debt Forgiven if Borrower Dies	• Yes	• No

Source: Prepared by Anthony J. Bellia.

- Can the co-borrower be released from the debt obligation in the future?
- Will the borrower have a different interest rate and/or fees if no co-borrower is used?
- Also review the material in Chapter 6.

Review Table 8-1 for differences between the Federal Plus and private alternative loan programs.

Other Financing Options

For many families, the loans options described in this chapter will provide all the money needed to pay college expenses. However, for some families these options will not meet their needs, so they need to explore other borrowing opportunities, such as retirement plan loans, life insurance loans, loans against savings, loans from family members, and as a last resort, credit cards.

Retirement/IRA Plans

Qualified retirement plans and IRAs are most likely the largest cash resource available to parents. If you decide to obtain a loan from one of these sources, you need to discuss this borrowing with a qualified tax advisor or certified financial planner to determine whether there are any tax consequences. Here are some suggested questions that need to be answered before you make the decision to borrow either from a retirement plan or an IRA account.

- Does your retirement plan allow you to borrow or withdraw money to pay for college?
- Is there a limit on the amount you can borrow?
- If yes, is all or part of the distribution taxable?
- Is there a 10% early distribution penalty?
- Is the interest rate competitive with other loans?
- What are the repayment requirements? Are they more or less favorable than other loans?
- How will an IRA distribution for college expenses impact your tax liability?
- Will you qualify for an education loan interest deduction on your federal tax return?
- If you are $59\frac{1}{2}$ or younger, you need to fully understand the restrictions on your 401(K), 403(b), or 457 plans.

Life Insurance Loans

Another financing option to pay for college expenses is borrowing against the cash value of existing life insurance policies. Sometimes, you are able to secure favorable rates and repayment terms. Be sure to discuss tax consequences with a tax advisor or a certified financial planner.

Will Loans Impact the Student Aid Formula?

1. **Parental Assets:** As reviewed in Chapter 4, parental assets do not have a major impact on the Federal Need Analysis formula since they are assessed up to 5.6%. Generally speaking, the loans from retirement plans, IRA, and insurance policies will not impact the Federal Need Analysis formula.

2. **Home Equity:** The federal government does not require the reporting of the primary residence on the FAFSA. So a home equity loan or a line of credit will not impact the federal formula. For colleges that require reporting the equity of the primary residence, it will typically have some impact on institutional methodology. For example, earlier in this chapter we used the example of

a family owning a home worth $180,000 and unpaid mortgage of $60,000, which results in $120,000 in home equity. If this family borrowed $75,000 in a home equity loan, the new net worth of the house is $45,000, which will reduce the family asset contribution from the primary residence and increase financial need. Remember, this calculation may be used only for institutional funds not federal student aid.

3. **Debt:** Any debt against a nonretirement investment will impact both Federal and Institutional Methodology. This additional debt will reduce the value of reported assets on the FAFSA and increase financial need. Consumer debt (e.g., credit cards) is not considered in Federal or Institutional Methodology.

4. **Retirement Funds/Insurance Policies:** The FAFSA doesn't require the reporting of retirement funds or the cash value of insurance policies. Consequently, the loans will not impact the Federal Need Analysis formula.

A college education can be a very expensive venture but it is also a necessary expenditure. The various financing options outlined in this chapter will assist you in paying college expenses. However, these options are the last piece of the puzzle. Students should normally first submit a FAFSA annually on a timely basis and apply for maximum aid possibilities before you (the parent) explore the use of the financing options outlined in this chapter.

Many families will need to borrow to cover college expenses. The loan amount may include part or all of the expected parental contribution and any unmet need. There are numerous options to consider. These loans will have little or no impact on the federal need analysis formula, and can greatly assist families in meeting educational expenses. But, as always, caution and research must be used.

True or False

1. Parents will pay for college expenses from savings, current income, and future income.
2. Federal PLUS loans do not require a credit check.
3. A negative credit rating will affect the interest rate charged by a lender.
4. Most colleges have several payment options to assist students and parents.
5. Federal PLUS loans have a set maximum loan amount regardless of the college's cost of attendance.
6. A home equity loan has a lump sum payment and a fixed interest rate.
7. Parents should apply for alternative loans before a student submits a FAFSA form.
8. Some alternative loan lenders will give reduced interest rates for 24, 36, or 48 consecutive, on-time monthly payments.

9. Parent loans from a retirement fund will have a significant impact on the Federal Need Analysis formula.
10. All private lenders offer the same variable interest rates for alternative loan programs.

Test Yourself

Fill in the Blanks

1. Home owners can obtain either a home equity _____ or _____ _____ _____.

2. Loan interest for _____ expenses may be tax deductible.

3. Federal PLUS loans do not require any _____ to obtain this loan.

4. The fixed interest rate on a PLUS loan is _____.

5. The federal government does not require reporting the value of the _____ _____ on the FAFSA.

6. The largest cash resource available to families is usually found in _____ _____ or _____ account.

7. List three college-sponsored payment and loan programs.

8. Home equity loans may be up to _____% or more of present market value.

9. _____ _____ _____ urges potential home equity loan borrowers to be aware of negative loan practices.

10. A home equity loan is actually a _____ _____ on the borrower's home.

▼▼▼▼▼▼▼▼▼▼▼▼▼▼▼▼▼▼▼▼▼▼▼▼▼▼

Consultants, Scholarship Search Companies, and Other Resources

▼▼▼▼▼▼▼▼▼▼▼▼▼▼▼▼▼▼▼▼▼▼▼▼▼▼

Do I Need to Read This Chapter?

You need to read this chapter if you need to learn about

➡ Financial aid consultants

➡ Aids for Spanish-speaking students

➡ Scholarship search companies

➡ Financial aid source books

➡ Internet sources

Financial Aid Consultants

Many people assume that the financial aid application process is so complicated that they need to hire a financial aid consultant to help them through the process. They really don't need to. In its September 8, 2003 issue, *U.S. News and World Report* published an article entitled "Not Worth the Price, Don't Fork Over Money for Financial Aid that is Available and Free." The article described families who were attracted to seminars by misleading invitations that "their child has been selected for financial assistance, when in reality the letter was part of a mass mailing."[*] The article also explained that throughout the United States, the Federal Trade Commission is investigating scholarship search firms and financial aid consultants who claim that they can reveal secret strategies about Federal Methodology, and uncover hidden grants, lucrative scholarships, and easy loans. The FTC discovered that some companies filed forms late, incorrectly, or not at all. Also, some simply gave advice that was incorrect. An example of this continuous scrutiny by the FTC is *The 2005 Annual Report*. This report revealed some alarming data concerning complaints about scholarship-related fraud. Since 1993, the FTC has been tracking complaints involving scholarship companies. The increase in complaints went from 670 in 2003 to 4,486 in 2004. This increase may be attributed to better reporting.

Table 9-1 shows the increase nationally of scholarship-related fraud complaints.

This study also reported that there has been an increase in complaints involving financial aid consulting services.[†] Please be aware that no one can guarantee you 100% funding in paying college bills.

That being said, if you think a consulting firm may assist you, ask what credentials it has that make it qualified to serve as a financial aid consultant. Check out

TABLE 9-1   Scholarship-Related Fraud Complaints

Year	Complaints	Year	Complaints
1993–95	114	2000	380
1996	151	2001	322
1997	182	2002	517
1998	337	2003	670
1999	420	2004	4,448

[*]*U.S. News and World Report*, September 8, 2003.
[†]Website NASFAA, May 16, 2005, written by Elizabeth B. Guerance.

the backgrounds of the firms with the Better Business Bureau, state or local consumer protection agencies, or a college or school counselor before paying the consulting fee.

Dean's Tips

- Though some of you will choose to hire an outside company to do your forms, remember that it is the Free Application for Federal Student Aid. Most parents hire an outside "expert" mostly out of fear that they will make a terrible mistake that will cost them thousands of dollars in financial aid. Be assured that financial aid offices will contact you for correct information if mistakes are made.

- Parents: Don't be intimidated by the whole process. There are horror stories regarding financial aid sessions at high schools where financial aid consulting companies herd parents into a room and use scare tactics, telling them that if they don't sign up with them, that they will be losing thousands of dollars in aid for their children. The "rookie" parent will do anything at that point. Beware of these kinds of scare tactics and remember that if something appears to be too good to be true, it probably isn't.

- Call colleges and attend financial aid sessions to learn about the application process and different aid programs. Read and study the FAFSA before jumping to conclusions. Don't pay hundreds of dollars to have forms completed when you can do it yourself with a little help (see text) and perseverance.

Selling Points for Financial Aid Consulting Companies

Consultant Services

Financial aid consultants offer many services, including assisting families with completing the FAFSA, state aid forms, and institutional aid applications; assisting with scholarship searches; calculating an expected family contribution; and assisting in appealing an aid award from colleges (some also offer to complete family tax returns). For parents who are first-timers to the application process, one may say that these services are needed. Yes, these are valuable services but these services can all be obtained *free of charge*. Let's look at each service individually.

Assisting with Aid Application:

Financial aid offices will assist parents in completing aid applications. Also, many high schools and community action organizations conduct free workshops on the application process and completing the forms. The Department of Education provides a toll-free hotline, 1-800-4-FED-Aid (1-800-433-3243 or TDD 1-800-730-8913), for questions about the student aid process and specific programs, including completing the FAFSA. This hotline is operated through the Federal Student Aid Information Center. Since it is sponsored by the Department of Education, your question should be answered by individuals familiar with the federal student aid programs and procedures. Finally, the National Association of Student Financial Aid Administrators (NASFAA) has a College Goal Sunday in late January to assist parents and students with completing the FAFSA. This service is offered in thirty-five states and the District of Columbia (refer to Table 9-2). Also, College Goal Sunday now has a line-by-line FAFSA presentation for the 2006–2007 academic year available in English, Cambodian, Chinese, Korean, Russian, Spanish, and Vietnamese. To learn more, check the College Goal website (www.collegegoalsundayusa.org). As you will see, there are many organizations willing to assist you in completing the FAFSA and other aid forms as well as explaining how the application process works.

TABLE 9-2   States Participating in College Goal

Alaska	Minnesota
Arizona	Missouri
Arkansas*	Montana
Colorado*	Nevada
Delaware	New Jersey
District of Columbia	New Mexico
Florida	New York*
Georgia*	North Carolina*
Hawaii	Ohio
Illinois	Oklahoma
Indiana	Oregon*
Kansas	South Carolina*
Kentucky	South Dakota*
Maine	Tennessee
Maryland	Texas
Massachusetts	Washington*
Michigan	Wisconsin
Wyoming	

Source: Prepared by Anthony J. Bellia, March 2006
*Implementing January, 2007

Scholarship Services

This topic was addressed thoroughly in Chapter 2. Remember that the high school counselor's office, many local libraries, and community action organizations have material to assist you with scholarship searches. Also, the following websites will provide additional information:

- www.collegeboard.com
- www.ed.gov
- www.fastweb.com
- www.finaid.org
- www.wiredscholar.com
- www.nasfaa.org
- www.princetonreview.com
- www.brokescholar.com

It is worth noting that many financial aid offices will scrutinize an application more thoroughly if they know a consultant has completed it. Remember that a consultant must sign the FAFSA if they assist you in completing it.

Calculating an Expected Family Contribution (EFC)

The amount that you are expected to contribute toward your child's education, or what is called the Expected Family Contribution (EFC) is the key number used to determine your financial aid eligibility. Remember that when you take the college cost of attendance and subtract the EFC, the result is the financial need at a particular college. However, you don't need to pay a consultant to determine your EFC. There are free tools to assist you in calculating your family's EFC. You can use the worksheets in Chapter 4. Also, the following are some of the websites that provide an expected family contribution estimator worksheet:

- www.collegeboard.com
- www.act.org/fane
- www.finaid.org

Many college websites have links to other websites that will assist you in calculating your family's EFC.

Appeal to Colleges

Simply stated, you can handle the appeal. Colleges are prepared to respond to students and their parents who want to appeal their aid offer. Refer to Chapter 3 for more information on the process. Also, some colleges get turned off and upset when a consultant appeals an aid award. It is better to do it yourself.

Guidelines to Consider Before Hiring a Consultant

Despite the concerns noted earlier, you may still want to use a financial aid consultant. In choosing a consultant, consider the following guidelines:

- Ask about their qualifications.

- Ask for references.

- Determine if their fees are reasonable. Never agree to a fee based on percentage of aid that is received.

- The consultant's fee should be refundable if the forms have been completed incorrectly.

- Never sign a blank aid application form.

- You should review the aid application and sign it and mail it yourself. This way you know that no one has altered the information on the form.

- Never sign a form before January 1 that is dated January 1 or after. Remember that that FAFSA must be mailed or filed online on or after January 1, prior to the next academic year.

- Make sure that you keep copies of all forms, e.g., FAFSA, institutional aid applications, bank loan applications, and scholarship applications.

- Financial aid consultants cannot guarantee financial aid. Remember that it is the college's responsibility to award financial aid and produce the award letter, not the consultant.

- Be careful of invitations inviting you to a free financial aid seminar. The seminar is simply an opportunity for the company to sell its services.

Dean's Tip

If you decide to use a financial aid consultant, please remember that colleges award money to the students not consultants. Also, if a consultant assists you in preparing the FAFSA, make sure that the consultant signs the FAFSA as the preparer.

- Finally, you are responsible for the material submitted on the FAFSA and other aid applications. Make sure that they honestly represent your financial situation.

Negative Experiences

If you have a negative experience with a consultant or a consulting firm, the Federal Trade Commission has established a website and telephone number where you can file complaints. The telephone number is 1-877-382-4357. The website is www.ftc.gov/schlolarshipscams.

Financial Aid Source Books

The following are some suggested free student aid publications:

Affording College (2006): Published by the Commission on Independent Colleges and Universities, 17 Elk Street, P.O. Box 7289, Albany, New York, 12224-0289. A Spanish version of this publication is available.

Get A Jump: The Financial Aid Answer Book (2d ed., 2004): Published by Thomson Corporation and Petersons 2004. Website: www.petersons.com/ about.

Cash for College (2005): Published by National Association of Student Financial Aid Administrators. Website: www.nasfaa.org.

The Student Guide 2006–2007: Published by the U.S. Department of Education. Both English and Spanish versions are available at the website.www.ed.gov. This website has numerous links to many federal student aid brochures and fact sheets.

Your College Search— A Guide to Finding the College of Your Choice, 2004 edition, New York's 100+ Private Colleges and Universities: (2004): Published by Commission on Independent Colleges and Universities, 17 Elk Street, P.O. Box 7289, Albany, New York, 12224-0289. A Spanish version of this publication is available. Website: www.nycolleges.org.

Dean's Tip

Beware of scholarship scams. The time you spend with an outside agency would be better spent reviewing options with your high school guidance office, public library, financial aid office, or conducting free scholarship searches. Processing paperwork through a middleman often slows the delivery of aid.

Scholarship Search Companies: Private Scholarships

Financing a college education is similar to putting together a puzzle. One piece is money from the family. A second piece is applying for federal, state, and institutional aid programs. Finally, the last piece is money from private and outside scholarships. As you consider looking for private scholarship money, keep in mind that there are substantial private or outside scholarships available to you. Also, there are numerous websites and guidebooks that will assist you in your search for additional scholarship and grant money to pay for college expenses. However, be careful of scam artists who solicit your business. The federal government is continually prosecuting and closing down fraudulent scholarship companies, so you have to be careful that you select a legitimate organization.

The 2005 Annual Report, issued jointly to Congress by the Department of Education, Department of Justice, and the FTC "on college scholarship found that the number of scholarship-related fraud complaints and inquiries to a Federal Trade Commission database increased significantly in 2004, although the increase could be attributed to better reporting or other factors. The report also found that the nature of the complaints and inquiries had shifted from scholarship search services to financial aid consulting services."[*]

Let's start off with a positive view of scholarship search companies. Some websites that provide excellent scholarship search services are the following: www.collegeboard.com, www.fastweb.com, www.finaid.org, www.brokescholar.com, www.nasfaa.org, www.princetonreview.com, and www.wiredscholar.com. You should also check the website for your state higher education agency, which administers the state's grant and loan programs. Check the directory in Chapter 3 for the website and mailing address for your state higher education agency. These websites are also excellent tools to learn more about the college selection process, financial aid process, and colleges and universities within your state.

Individual colleges and universities are also excellent sources of possible leads for scholarship opportunities. Check with your school counselor for local organizations that award scholarships. Other possible sources of scholarships are student's employers and parents' employers. Many department stores, supermarkets, and

---

[*] Website NASFAA, May 26, 2005, written by Elizabeth B Guerance.

fast food chains offer scholarships to their employees. Many companies also offer assistance to the children of their employees.

Scholarship Assistance

The following are some places to look for scholarship assistance:

- Check for local opportunities from community or private foundations which offer scholarships.
- Check your high school library or school counselor's office for scholarship handbooks, e.g., College Board's *Scholarship Handbook.*
- Check for national organizations such as Coca-Cola Scholars Foundation, Reserve Officer Training Corps (ROTC), National Merit Scholarship Program, Robert Byrd Scholarship, and The American Legion, to name a few organizations.
- Check the websites previously mentioned in this chapter.
- Be sure to comply with all deadlines.

Your scholarship search should begin at the start of the sophomore year in high school. Some scholarships have a deadline date at the end of junior year or early in the fall of senior year. As you continue to research scholarship opportunities, you need to organize the materials that scholarship organizations may require.

Materials to Submit

The following are some materials that may be required by scholarship organizations:

- High school transcript.
- College transcript if applying while in college.
- List of community and school service activities.
- Standardized test scores. (SAT or ACT).
- Parental financial information, completing a FAFSA or CSS/Profile Form (if required).
- Parents' most recent federal tax form (1040EZ, 1040A, 1040), or verification of nonfiler status.
- Letters of recommendation from a high school teacher, a school counselor, and/or an assistant principal. The individuals writing your recommendations should know your academic achievements and/or community service activities.
- One or more essays.

Scholarship Letter Tips

According to the FastWeb website (www.fastweb.com), Feb/March 2004 high school edition, the following are five tips on how to complete the scholarship search process:

1. Be brief and to the point in asking for the needed materials— you'll have the chance to sell yourself in your application.

2. Request the materials early to leave enough time to prepare a strong application packet.

3. In your application request, tell the provider where you heard about the scholarship and explain concisely why you're eligible.

4. Provide your correct address and other contact information where you know you can be reached. Include a self-addressed stamped envelope, if applicable.

5. If you win a scholarship, be sure to thank the provider and your recommender.

It should be noted that the dollar value of many private or outside scholarships tend to be relatively modest, fifty to a couple of thousand dollars. However, these small scholarship amounts will help to pay your tuition bill, and eventually this additional money may reduce your total loan indebtedness.

How to Identify a Scholarship Scam Company

Unfortunately, there are scholarship scam companies. Be careful if the company makes or uses any of the following claims or tactics:

*   Guarantees that you will win an award.

*   Charges a fee for a matching scholarship service.

*   Claims to have an exclusive listing of scholarship information.

*   States that you have already won an award for a scholarship that you did not apply for or that you are a finalist in a contest that you did not enter.

*   Provides only a P.O. box number rather than a full address.

*   Uses pressure or scare tactics to convince customers to use its service.

*   Company request is a credit card number, checking account number, or other personal financial information to start the scholarship service process or to hold a potential scholarship for you.

*   The company says, "sit back, we'll do all the work."

If you decide to use a scholarship search company, make sure that you get their refund policy in writing before you give any money or a credit card number.

How To Report a Suspected Scam

Finally, if you suspect that a company is attempting to commit a fraud against you, report the company to one of the following organizations:

Federal Trade Commission (FTC)
Ph: 877-FTC-HELP (1-877-382-4357) or visit www.ftc.gov/scholarshipscams

Better Business Bureau (BBB)
Ph: 703-276-0100 or visit www.bbb.org

United States Department of Education Inspector General Office
Hotline at 1-800-MIS-USED (1-800-647-8733) or visit oig.hotline@ed.gov

Postal Inspection Service (USPIS)
Ph: 800-654-8896 or visit www.usps.gov/postalinspectors/fraud

When you contact one of these organizations, you should provide as much information as possible. Copy all correspondence, written and/or email, and submit for evidence. If you attended a seminar and took notes, provide them to the organization. Also, provide any material distributed at the seminar.

If you were contacted by telephone, attempt to reconstruct the telephone conversation—e.g., date, time, telephone number, and the name of the person with whom you spoke.

Internet Resources

There is a goldmine of information about the financial aid application process available on the Internet. There are useful websites that provide insight on scholarships and how to complete the FAFSA. The websites in Table 9-3 will help get you started.

Dean's Tip

Type in "college scholarship service" on *Google* or *Yahoo!* for a list of additional resources.

TABLE 9-3 Student Financial Aid Programs, Tuition Payment Plans, and College Savings Plans Websites

Academic Management Services www.amsweb.com	• Academic Management Services is a provider of integrated payment solutions for higher education and private school tuition.
Aid for Students with Disabilities www.health-resource-center.org/	• Annotated bibliography of books for disabled students: Fact sheet.
Broke Scholar www.brokescholar.com	• A scholarship engine that accesses a database of over 900,000 scholarships.
CSS (College Scholarship Service) www.collegeboard.com	• Excellent site to conduct college searches, information on SAT I, SAT II, PSAT tests, Advanced Placement tests, etc., and options on how to pay for college.
College Answer www.wiredscholar.com	• Appropriate for students, parents, and school counselors. • Thorough scholarship search engine. • Financial aid calculator. • Offers guidance about how to evaluate award letters. • Site can be viewed in Spanish.
College Connection www.careermosaic.com/cm/cc/ccl.html	• Information-rich college directory. • Career counseling advice. • Directory of available jobs. • How to post resumes.
College Fund/UNCF www.uncf.org/	• Program dedicated to African American higher education assistance. • Extensive amount of scholarship information and internships.
College Net www.collegenet.com	• Provides over 1,500 customized Internet admissions applications for both college and university programs. • Variety of scholarship searches and college resources.
College Opportunities On-line (COOL) www.nces.ed.gov/ipeds/cool	• Directly linked to approximately 7,000 U.S. colleges and universities. • Provides a search engine for students to select a college based on programs offered, location, enrollment, and degree offerings.
College is Possible www.collegeispossible.org	• Encourages both middle and high school students from underprivileged backgrounds and communities to seek higher education.

TABLE 9-3   Student Financial Aid Programs, Tuition Payment Plans, and College Savings Plans Websites (*Continued*)

College Savings Plan Network www.collegesavings.org	• Connects you to any state's college savings programs. • Tuition programs including program features, investment options, tax benefits, and more.
College View www.collegeview.com	• Geared toward students, parents, and school counselors. • Career center, financial aid information, scholarships searches, and virtual campus tours.
CollegeXpress www.collegexpress.com	• A scholarship search database of over 2 million awards.
FastAid www.fastaid.com	• One of the world's largest and oldest scholarship search databases, constantly updated. • Provides a worldwide college and graduate level scholarship directory.
Fast Web www.fastweb.com	• Offers a college search engine to match a student with his or her "dream school," matching with over 4,000 colleges. • Provides a scholarship search engine of 600,000.

Financial Aid for Students
www.ed.gov/offices/OSFAP/Students
	• Vehicle to Federal Aid information.
	• Can link to
	  • FAFSA;
	  • Publications on student aid; and
	  • Information on grants, loans, and work study programs.

The Financial Aid Information Page
www.finaid.org
	• Guide to
	  • Scholarships,
	  • Loans,
	  • Financial aid applications, and
	  • Military aid.
	• Offers personalized advice and detailed "how to" instructions to apply for financial aid.

Financial Aid Need Estimator www.act.org/fane	• Allows you to calculate your Expected Family Contribution and costs as well as your eligibility for federal financial aid.
Glossary of Financial Aid Terms www.petersons.com/resources/gloss.html	• Glossary of important and useful terms to know when talking about financial aid.
Kiplinger www.kiplinger.com	• Calculator—what will it take to save for college.

(*Continued*)

TABLE 9-3 Student Financial Aid Programs, Tuition Payment Plans, and College Savings Plans Websites (*Continued*)

National Association of Intercollegiate Athletics (NAIA) www.naia.org	• Guide to over 300 colleges for athletic eligibility and scholarship opportunities.
National Association for Student Financial Aid Administrators www.nasfaa.org	• Information on preparing for college. • Information and advice on preparing financially and academically for college. • All information is from financial aid administrators.
National Collegiate Athletic Association www.ncaa.org	• Encourages students who wish to pursue athletics during college. • Information regarding competition, eligibility, recruiting, internships, and scholarships.
New York State Higher Education Services Corp. www.hesc.com	• This site provides tips for middle and high school students, how to apply for state aid and college saving (529 plans), and financial aid calculator. • Tuition Assistance Program and Loan information.
Peterson's www.petersons.com	• Search for colleges by name, location, major, size, sports, and tuition. • Information on testing, financial aid, study abroad, etc.
Princeton Review www.princetonreview.com	• Scholarship search engine. • Online applications to over 950 colleges. • Provides information about testing strategies, admissions, and financial aid.
Savings for college (529 plans) www.savingforcollege.com	• Internet guide to 529 plans, Coverdell (ESA), and college planning resources. Lists all state and private college 529 plans.
Scholarships.com www.scholarships.com	• Provides information regarding financial aid and educational loans. • After creating a personal profile students can search for scholarships according to their own criteria.
Scholarships 101 www.scholarships101.com	• Provides a scholarship search engine of over 8,000 funding sources with more than 600,000 individual awards.
Scholarship Scams www.ftc.gov/bcp/conline/ edcams/scholarship/index.html	• Powered by the Federal Trade Commission. • Provides advice and tips to help parents and students avoid scholarship scams.

TABLE 9-3 Student Financial Aid Programs, Tuition Payment Plans, and College Savings Plans Websites (*Continued*)

Student Financial Assistance www.ed.gov/offices/OPE/Students/ index.html	• This site is from the U.S. Department of Education. Has information for students and institutions. Many good links to additional sites.
Students www.students.gov	• A comprehensive website providing answers to students' question on education, careers, government, and more.
Veterans and Dependents: Federal Benefits www.va.gov	• Information about the benefits you are eligible for with Veterans Administration Programs. • Provides detailed program descriptions as well as applications.
U.S. Department of Education www.ed.gov	• Informative site for both students and parents: site includes information on preparing for college, how to apply for aid, and how to pay for college.
U.S. News & World Report www.usnews.com	• Database: for America's Best Colleges Ranking. • Provides information regarding graduate school, careers, admissions, and financial aid.
Ways in Mentor www.waysinmentor.org	• Information database for higher education opportunities in the Southern states. • Created by the Southern Regional Education Board.
Wiredscholar.com www.wiredscholar.com	• Provides advice for completing the admissions and financial aid processes. • Site available in Spanish.

Financial Aid Resources in Spanish

If Spanish is your first language, there are many opportunities to learn about student financial aid. This section will list some websites, printed publications, and aid applications available in Spanish.

Websites

• www.nasafaa.org/publications : link to Citibank website—Provides information on preparing for college both financially and academically. Written by Student Aid professionals.

- www.ed.gov—Informative federal site for both students and parents, including information on preparing for college, how to apply for aid, and how to pay for college.

- www.collegeboard.com—Excellent site to conduct college searches and to discover options on how to pay for college.

- www.hesc.com—This New York State site provides tips for middle and high school students, how to apply for state aid and college saving (529 plans), and a financial aid calculator.

- www.newyorkcolleges.org—Guide to colleges in New York City and New York State

- www.collegeanswer.com/index.jsp—This website connects to Sallie Mae's college answer section.

- www.wiredscholar.com—Provides advice on admission and financial aid practices.

- mapping_your_future.org/—This is a public service project of the financial aid industry.

- www.thesalliemaefund.org/preparing/index/html—This website provides information on preparing for college, selecting a college, and about applying, paying, deciding on, and financing a college education.

- www.citibank.com—The CitiBank website contains information on college planning, financial aid process, and education loan options.

- www.collegezone.com—This website is sponsored by the Illinois Student Assistance Corporation.

- www.studentloannet.com/foryou/—Bank One outlines the college financial aid and loan programs.

- www.nelliemae.com/espanol/—The Nellie Mae website outlines private and federal loans and financial aid processes.

Sample of Publications and Aid Applications

- Check with your state agency for publications that are available in Spanish.

- "Student Guide to Financial Aid, 2006–2007 Academic Year," Department of Education. This publication is updated annually and is available at www.studentaid.ed.gov.

- Spanish version of "Free Application for Federal Student Aid (FAFSA)." This form is available at www.fafsa.ed.gov.

- CSS/Financial Aid Profile—Over 350 colleges, universities, and private scholarship foundations use this supplemental financial aid application. Available at www.collegeboard.com.

- New York State offers seamless application for federal and state financial aid for students all in Spanish: www.hesc.com—the link to the Spanish text is at the bottom of the website.

If you are interested in an extensive Internet search for financial aid information in Spanish, type in: "student financial aid in Spanish" for a Google or Yahoo! search for numerous websites. Happy hunting!

There is a thriving industry in financial aid consulting. But not all financial aid consultants are created equal. At their best, financial aid consultants provide valuable services to families whose circumstances warrant hiring a consultant. Financial aid consultants can also provide overpriced services to families who have no need for a consultant. This chapter explained the financial aid consultant business and described some free outside services to assist families. It also provided sources of guidance to families where Spanish is the primary language in the family.

True or False

1. The FTC discovered that some financial aid consultants were providing incorrect information and filling out forms late, incorrectly, or not at all.
2. Financial aid offices will assist families in completing aid applications.
3. There are numerous websites to assist families in calculating their expected family contribution.
4. If you want to appeal an aid package, you need to hire a consultant.
5. Financial aid offices won't scrutinize an aid application completed by a consultant.
6. Some employers will offer scholarship opportunities to employees' children.
7. Students should begin researching scholarship opportunities in their freshman/sophomore year.
8. Legitimate scholarship search companies will charge a fee for their services.
9. Some scholarship search companies provide a legitimate and worthwhile service.
10. If you use a consultant, you are not responsible for the information submitted on the FAFSA form.

Fill in the Blanks

1. Students and parents can handle the _____ of a student aid award letter with the aid office.
2. Many private scholarships range from _____ to _____ of thousands of dollars.

3. _____ _____, _____, and _____ are websites that provide private scholarship opportunities.

4. _____ _____ _____ investigates scholarship scams.

5. www.collegeboard.com and www.ed.gov are two websites that provide information in both _____ and _____ languages.

6. If you plan to use a financial aid consulting firm, you should ask what _____ them to serve as a financial aid consultant.

7. The Spanish version of the FAFSA is available at _____ website.

8. Never provide your _____ _____ _____, _____ _____ _____ to a scholarship search company.

9. You can identify a scholarship scam company if they _____ that you will win an award.

10. You should begin the scholarship search at the beginning of your _____ year in high school.

Tips: College search and Financial Aid Process

Do I Need to Read This Chapter?

You need to read this chapter if you need a review about

➡ College planning steps

➡ Understanding college costs

➡ Financial aid application process

➡ Merit, athletic, and private scholarships

➡ Award letter process

➡ Controlling college costs

➡ Parental Involvement

High School First Steps

The following are some suggestions for things you can do early in high school to start thinking about college:

- Consider working part-time in high school and saving a portion of your earnings to help pay for college expenses.

- Look into completing a four-year college degree in less time if you have advanced credit, e.g., AP Courses, college credit courses, and CLEP credit.

- Begin to build a resume for college admissions applications and private scholarships while a freshman in high school:
  - Take challenging academic courses.
  - Participate in high school activities: sports, service clubs, and tutoring.
  - Volunteer in your community.
  - Get to know the school counselors and teachers, so they can write meaningful letters of recommendation.

- Be organized during your college search, including preparing a folder for each college on your college short list.

- Talk to students in your proposed major about any hidden costs, and prepare a realistic budget for books and supplies.

- Visit colleges:
  - Call in advance for an appointment.
  - Talk to students on campus.
  - Talk to faculty.
  - Ask about departmental scholarships.
  - Take a campus tour.
  - Visit when students are on campus.

Understanding Tuition Costs

The following are some ideas for gaining a better understanding of tuition costs:

- Determine the real cost of a particular college by checking college websites and literature and/or calling the financial aid office at the college.

- Determine the current tuition, room and board, and books and supplies for colleges on your short list. Sometimes, tuition, fees, room and board costs listed in guidebooks and on the web may not be up to date.

- Consider using work-study earnings for personal expenses, books and supplies, and entertainment. If you plan to use it to pay for tuition, you may be budgeting too tightly.

Applying for Student Financial Aid

As discussed throughout the book, here is a summary of the student aid application process:

- Submit the FAFSA annually after January 1.

- Apply online at www.fafsa.ed.gov. It is easier and faster.

- Complete the FAFSA thoroughly and accurately. You and your parents should ideally complete the appropriate Form 1040 before completing the FAFSA, or use the previous year's 1040 as a guide.

- Submit the FAFSA according to the college's timetable, usually between January 1 and February 15.

- Both you and one parent or guardian must apply for a PIN in November/December of the your senior year.

- If selected for verification, submit the requested information to the college as soon as possible.

- Consider college even if money is a major concern. Talk to a school counselor, college financial aid administrator, or community agency advisor.

- Apply for aid even if you think you are ineligible. Don't take yourself out of the process.

- Know what the required application forms for each college are and the deadline dates for submission.

- Keep copies of correspondence from all colleges during the admission and financial aid application process.

- If you are a veteran, apply for VA benefits. You have earned them.

- Married students must apply separately for student aid. They will each receive a separate financial aid package.

- Siblings, including twins, must apply separately for student aid; they will each receive an individual financial aid package.

- Graduate students are automatically considered independent for federal graduate loans; however, some professional schools ask for parental income before awarding institutional grants.

- Inform student financial aid offices about special financial circumstances in the family (Chapter 4).

Merit, Athletic, and Private Scholarship Opportunities

As we have seen in earlier chapters, there are various sources of financial aid, including scholarships. The following are some suggestions regarding scholarship opportunities:

- Investigate academic merit scholarship opportunities at colleges on your short list.

- Apply for private scholarships—check various websites for free scholarship search companies.

- Ask the financial aid office how an outside scholarship will affect your financial aid package.

- If you are interested in an athletic scholarship, contact the college coach to discuss athletic money. College coaches award athletic scholarship money, not the financial aid office. Be sure to register with the NCAA clearinghouse.

- Check out the Americorp program at www.americorp.org or call 1-800-942-2677 or TTY 800-833-3722. This program provides a wonderful opportunity for public service and securing an educational award of $4,725 to pay for undergraduate, graduate school, or to pay back qualified student loans.

- If you have a disability, check out the website www.finaid.org, or simply type in "students with disabilities, financial aid" for numerous websites. Also contact your local, state, and federal agencies.

College Selection/Award Letter Process

Upon notification of your financial aid standing, the following are some things to consider:

- You should ask for more aid if you need it; don't be embarrassed that you need more money to attend a particular college.

- When you have picked a college, notify the other colleges that you will not attend that college.

- Mail your tuition deposit early because residence hall assignments may be assigned according to when the college receives the deposit.

- Analyze the different colleges' aid packages carefully, paying attention to such things as percentages of loan, grant, and work in each college aid package.
- Don't be shy about showing a college aid administrator a better financial aid award letter from another college.

Renewing Financial Aid/Individual College Policy

As we discussed, you must reapply for financial aid each year:

- Ask the college's financial aid office what the criteria are for renewing scholarship and grant aid.
- Ask if there are scholarship opportunities for upperclassmen and what the criteria are to apply for them.
- Ask about the college's aid philosophy for returning students. For example, find out if the freshman grant aid amount is guaranteed for the next three years.
- Review the college's policy on Satisfactory Academic Progress. Be careful to stay on track when setting your class schedule each semester.
- If you wish to have a study abroad experience during college, check each college's policy on the treatment of financial aid for that semester.

Student Loans

Think carefully about borrowing money. Student loans are a serious responsibility. The following are some things to consider:

- Study student loan provisions carefully. Loans must be repaid.
- You should calculate the total cost of the loan, i.e., principal and interest.
- Remember—taking out a loan is an investment in your future. College graduates earn significantly more money than high school graduates.
- Student loans are serious obligations: If you experience difficulty in making loan payments, contact the school or your student loan lender.
- Most student aid for graduate students is in the form of long-term loans.
- Remember to consolidate your loans at graduation or when you leave college; this strategy will save you interest over the life of the loans.

Cutting College Costs

College is expensive and regardless of your source of funds, it is worth cutting costs when you can. The following are some ways to control expenses:

- Shop around for books. You may be able to find less expensive books online or at used bookstores. Be careful to get the current editions.

- Ask the college bookstore about its return policy.

- If you live within commuting distance of your selected college, consider commuting. You can reduce your direct educational costs significantly.

- When purchasing a cell phone, shop around for competitive prices and a realistic plan.

- Leave the car at home.

- Select a realistic meal plan which fits your lifestyle.

- Check into car pooling, bus and rail service to reduce traveling cost when traveling home.

- Investigate the possibility of completing your degree in three years.

- Don't go overboard on purchasing clothes for college.

Parents

The parents' role in financing college includes a great deal of paperwork, that we have hopefully made less intimidating in this book. The following is a summary of parental tasks in the financial aid process:

- Parents should calculate an Expected Family Contribution (EFC) when children are freshmen or sophomores in high school to get a feel for the family's financial strength. Subtract the EFC from the college's cost of attendance to obtain your financial need at a particular school. Use an EFC calculator to assist you in this exercise (Chapter 4).

- Parents usually pay the EFC from savings, current income, and future loan payments.

- Unmet need is often greater than the EFC because colleges have limited funds.

- Remember that the parental contribution is divided by the number of children enrolled in college at least half-time.

- Remember the simplified Need Analysis Formula. If the total family income is less than $49,999, family assets are not considered in the Federal Need Analysis Formula, so long as the family files a Form1040A or EZ, or does not file any tax return. However, if you filed a 1040 only to claim a Hope Scholarship or a Lifetime Learning Tax Credit and you would have otherwise been eligible for a 1040A or 1040EZ, you would still be eligible. (Refer to Dean's Tip in Chapter 4.)

- Start a savings plan at an early age for your children.

- Investigate 529 plans and other savings vehicles (Chapter 1).

- Use Hope Scholarships and Lifetime Learning Tax Credits to reduce federal taxability when your children are enrolled in college (Chapter 1).

- Investigate the differences between home equity loans and Federal PLUS loans (Chapter 8).

Some of the objectives of this book are to teach you and your parents to adopt a systematic approach to the student aid process, understand college costs, and explore loan options and the benefits of starting an early college savings program. Some families perceive the student aid process as an intimidating undertaking. However, if you read and follow the tips listed here, the financial aid and college search should be easier to navigate and understand. Realize that there are numerous college and borrowing options.

Test Yourself

True or False

1. Tuition and fees costs are always current in guidebooks or on the web.
2. Using work-study earnings to pay for tuition is a wise way to budget for this expense.
3. Submitting the FAFSA online is easier and faster than a paper application.
4. Twins must apply separately for student aid.
5. Graduate students are not considered independent for federal student aid.
6. College coaches award athletic scholarship money, not the financial aid office.
7. Don't negotiate for more aid; it is a waste of time and effort.
8. Living at home during college can reduce your direct educational cost significantly.
9. The family contribution is never divided by the number of children enrolled in college at least half-time.
10. The simplified needs analysis formula will always include assets.
11. Hope Scholarship and Lifetime Learning Tax Credits will reduce federal tax liability when your child is enrolled in college.

Test Yourself

Fill in the Blanks

1. Name three ways that a student can earn advance college credits: _____, _____, and _____.

2. Students should submit the FAFSA annually after _____.

3. Both _____ and one _____ or _____ must apply for a PIN number.

4. If the student is selected for _____ you will have to submit information requested by the college.

5. Married students must apply _____ for student aid.

6. When comparing different colleges' aid packages, check the percentages of _____, _____, and _____ in each college aid package.

7. You should always ask the _____ to renew a scholarship.

8. College graduates _____ significantly _____ money than high school graduates.

9. Student loans are serious _____.

10. Parents usually pay the expected family contribution from _____, _____ _____, and _____ _____ _____.

Appendix

Answers to Review Questions

CHAPTER ONE

True or False
1. F   2. F   3. T   4. T   5. T   6. F   7. F   8. F   9. T   10. T

Fill in the Blanks
1. savings, disposable income, and borrowing (future income)
2. parental asset, 5.6%
3. 970
4. 5.6% and 35%
5. personal residence, life insurance, retirement plan, and personal property
6. consumer debt
7. application
8. children, half-time
9. CSS/Profile Form
10. Hope Scholarship, Lifetime Learning

CHAPTER TWO

True or False
1. F   2. T   3. T   4. F   5. F   6. F   7. F   8. F   9. T   10. F

Fill in the Blank
1. tuition, fees, room and board
2. college cost
3. articulation, public and private colleges
4. 4168
5. 73%
6. tuition discounting

CHAPTER THREE

True or False
1. T   2. T   3. T   4. F   5. F   6. T   7. T   8. F   9. F   10. F   11. T

Fill in the Blanks
1. gift
2. January 1, February 15
3. electronic, parent and applicant
4. CSS/Profile Form
5. $4,050, $400
6. financial need
7. annually
8. Student Aid Report
9. 30, 90–100%

CHAPTER FOUR

True or False
1. T   2. F   3. F   4. F   5. F   6. F   7. T   8. T   9. T   10. T

Fill in the Blanks
1. not
2. independent

3. financial need

4. 5.6%, 35%

5. divided, children

6. expected family contribution

7. non-custodial, not

8. assets

9. unmet need

10. $20,000

CHAPTER FIVE

True or False
1. F   2. T   3. T   4. F   5. F   6. T   7. T   8. F   9. T   10. T

Fill in the Blanks
1. unsubsidized

2. larger

3. significantly

4. colleges

5. phone, writing

6. gift aid, loans, work

7. financial aid

8. influence

9. family's responsibility

10. merit

11. impact, change, alter

CHAPTER SIX

True or False
1. T   2. T   3. F   4. T   5. T   6. F   7. F   8. F   9. T   10. T

Fill in the Blanks
1. $51,000, $28,000

2. 5.2%

3. automatic monthly payments

4. income sensitive plan

5. more

6. loan consolidation

7. supplement

8. $15,982, $18,206

9. standard, income sensitive, consolidated, extended repayment, graduated repayment

10. cost, financial aid

Chapter Seven

True or False
1. T   2. T   3. F   4. F   5. T   6. T   7. F   8. T   9. F   10. F

Fill in the Blanks
1. car pooling

2. used

3. budget, semesters

4. basic

5. Federal Trade Commission

Chapter Eight

True or False
1. T   2. F   3. T   4. T   5. F   6. T   7. F   8. T   9. F   10. F

Fill in the Blanks
1. loan, line of credit

2. educational

3. collateral

4. 8.5%

5. primary residence

6. retirement plan, IRA

7. ten monthly payment, installment loan, long-term loan

8. 85%

9. Federal Trade Commission

10. second mortgage

Chapter Nine

True or False

1. T   2. T   3. T   4. F   5. F   6. T   7. T   8. F   9. T   10. F

Fill in the Blank

1. appeal

2. $50, couple

3. www.collegeboard.com, www.ed.gov, www.fastweb.com, www.finaid.org, and www.wiredscholar.com

4. Federal Trade Commission

5. English and Spanish

6. qualifies

7. www.fafsa.ed.gov

8. credit card number, or checking account number

9. guarantee

10. sophomore

Chapter Ten

True or False

1. F   2. F   3. T   4. T   5. F   6. T   7. F   8. T   9. F   10. F   11. T

Fill in the Blank

1. AP Courses, College Credit Courses, CLEP Credit

2. January 1

3. student, parent, or guardian

4. verification

5. separately

6. loan, grant, work

7. criteria

8. earn, more

9. obligations

10. savings, current income, future loan payments

A

Office of Student Financial Aid

Phone 716-888-2300 | toll free 800-541-6348 | fax 716-888-2377

May 13, 2005

ID XXXXX

Telephone (XXX) XXX-XXXX

John Smith
205 Smith St.
Buffalo, NY

On behalf of the Student Financial Aid Committee, it is a pleasure to inform you that you have been awarded the financial assistance indicated below for the **Academic Year 2005 - 2006**. **In order to fully understand your rights and responsibilities regarding this student aid award and to determine your approximate cost, please read the accompanying literature carefully.**

STUDENT FINANCIAL AID AWARD

Your award was based on full time attendance at Canisius College as a **Returning Undergrad Off Campus**.

TYPE OF AWARD	Summer 2005	Fall 2005	Spring 2006	TOTAL
Academic Scholarship	0	3,100	3,100	6,200
Canisius College Grant	0	1,250	1,250	2,500
Frances G. Churchill Schol.	0	1,250	1,250	2,500
Federal Work Study Program	1,550	1,100	1,100	3,750
T.A.P.	0	910	910	1,820
Fed. Subsidized Stafford Loan	0	2,750	2,750	5,500
TOTAL	1,550	10,360	10,360	22,270

ALL CANISIUS COLLEGE SCHOLARSHIPS/GRANTS ARE APPLIED TO TUITION & FEES FIRST.

Please complete the acceptance form on the reverse side of one copy and return it to this office within two weeks.

Sincerely yours,

Curtis C. Gaume
Director of Student Financial Aid

ACCEPTANCE OF FINANCIAL AID

PLEASE MARK YOUR RESPONSE:

1.   I accept this award.

2. ☐   I accept this award in part. I do not accept: _____

_____

(Please read conditions for re-evaluation in accompanying materials.)

I wish to reduce my Federal Stafford Loan and/or Federal Unsubsidized Loan. The total amount I want to borrow is:

$_____ Stafford
$_____ Unsubsidized

3. ☐   I decline this Financial Aid Award.

Reason:

_____

4. ☐   Please allow me more time to consider this Financial Aid Award. I will respond by:

_____

The Student Financial Aid Office reserves the right to adjust this award based on your change of division, credit hours, residence status, income verification or receipt of other outside funds. Financial Aid awards also may be adjusted contingent on final appropriation bills passed by the federal and New York State governments.

_____	_____
Student Signature	Date

SAMPLE FINANCIAL AID AWARD LETTER

This example is from a selective, high cost, private institution that meets full need of its students.

Dear

This Financial Aid Award Letter reflects the financial assistance you have been awarded for the 2005/2006 academic year based on a thorough review of your application for financial aid. Please refer to the Financial Aid Conditions and Information enclosure for details related to this award.

Financial Aid Award	Fall	Spring	Total	Accept	Decline
University Scholarship	$10,000.00	$10,000.00	$20,000.00		
Federal Pell Grant	$1,950.00	$1,950.00	$3,900.00		
Federal SEO Grant	$2,000.00	$2,000.00	$4,000.00		
Federal Work-Study	$1,150.00	$1,150.00	$2,300.00		
Fed Subsidized Stafford Loan	$1,312.00	$1,312.00	$2,625.00		
TOTAL AID	$16,412.50	$16,412.50	$32,825.00		

Please submit each item (by the date listed below) in order to finalize your award and/or note other related information:

- Scholarship Information Release Form
- Refer to the Federal Stafford Loan Online Master Promissory Note Instructions if you wish to borrow funds from this loan program.

If you have any questions or need additional information, please contact our office.

Office of Financial Aid

CERTIFICATION STATEMENT

I certify that I have read, understand and agree to the conditions of this award as outlined on the Financial Aid Conditions and Information. I accept or decline each award as indicated above.

PLEASE SIGN AND RETURN ONE COPY BY May 1, 2005.
(Retain one copy for your records)

_____   _____

Student's Signature   Date

Canisius
C O L L E G E
Where leaders are made

Office of Student Financial Aid
Old Main 100 | phone 716-888-2300 | toll free 1-800-541-6348

Canisius College PLUS Loan Pre-Approval

Dear Parent,

You may find it necessary to obtain additional funding toward your child's education. We believe one of the best sources to support your investment in your student's future is the Federal Parent Loan for Undergraduate Students (PLUS). Use this pre-approval form to initiate the application process.

Please complete and fax the form on the reverse side to ONE lender of your choice. Of special note to **previous PLUS borrowers**, if your lender is not listed, please write its name next to the PLUS amount you are requesting.

The lender will determine your eligibility for the PLUS Loan by performing a credit check to determine pre-approval status. Both you and the Office of Student Financial Aid will be notified of the results.

For pre-approved borrowers, Canisius will electronically transmit the loan certification to New York State Higher Education Services Corporation (NYSHESC). The PLUS Master Promissory Note (MPN) will then be generated and mailed to you. For subsequent borrowing on behalf of this student, only the Canisius College PLUS Loan Pre-Approval form will be required.

The PLUS Loan allows you to borrow up to the cost of attendance minus any financial aid received. The loan will disburse in two equal payments, minus the 3% origination fee.

If the parent is denied the PLUS Loan, the student may be eligible for Federal Unsubsidized Stafford Loan funds. The amount of the loan is limited, and will be determined by the Office of Student Financial Aid.

As always, our office staff would be pleased to answer all your questions and guide you through the financial aid process. Please feel free to call us at (716)888-2300, or 1-800-541-6348 for assistance.

Sincerely,

Curtis C. Gaume

Curtis C. Gaume
Director
Student Financial Aid

Federal PLUS Loan Pre-Qualification Form

I authorize the lender and its affiliates checked below to obtain a credit bureau report for the purpose of making a preliminary credit determination of whether I qualify for a Federal PLUS Loan. I also authorize you to release the results of the preliminary credit determination to the school listed below and to provide the results to me.

Please choose only one lender:

❑ M&T Bank
Code: 808036
FAX: (877) 290-4585

❑ Chase Bank
Code: 807807
FAX: (800) 377-4269

❑ Bank of America
Code: 824421
FAX: (213) 345-2104

❑ HSBC Bank
Code: 808047
FAX: (888) 595-4722

❑ AMS Educ. Loan Trust
Code: 833067-02
FAX: (508) 235-2869

❑ Wachovia Educ. Finance
Code: 830005
FAX: (888) 451-0733

Parent Borrower Information

$ _____
PLUS Amount Requested by Parent

_____
Last Name   First Name   MI

_____
Social Security Number

_____
Date of Birth (Month/Date/Year)

_____
Permanent Street Address

_____
City   State   Zip

(___)_____   (___)_____
Home Phone   Work Phone

_____
Driver's License Number   State

US Citizen/Eligible Non-Citizen __Yes __No

Check the proper academic period:
___Fall/Spring
___Fall Only   ___Spring Only
___Summer/Fall/Spring   ___Summer Only

Academic Year: ____2004-05   ____2005-06
****
Student Information

_____
Last Name   First Name   MI

_____
Social Security Number

_____
College ID Number   Date of Birth

CANISIUS COLLEGE
002681
FAX (716) 888-2377

By signing below, I understand that any conditional approval I receive based upon the review of my credit report will be subject to such financial information verification as the lender requires (including in some cases, an updated credit bureau report), verification that I am eligible to borrow under the Federal PLUS Loan Program, and receipt by the lender of a signed, completed Federal PLUS Loan Application and Master Promissory Note within forty-five (45) days of the date of any conditional approval.

_____   _____
Parent Signature   Date

If the PLUS Loan is not approved, does the student wish Canisius College to evaluate for, and initiate the process for Federal Unsubsidized Stafford Loan funds?   _____Yes   _____No

_____   _____
Student Signature   Date

Decision Notice (For Lender/Servicer Use Only)	
_____Conditionally Approved	Date_____
_____Denied	By_____

Scholarships and Financial Aid

The mission of The University of Scranton is to provide a high-quality education in the Jesuit tradition. As you and your family prepare for your first year in college, financing your education is an important consideration. While you are primarily responsible for your educational expenses, there are resources and options available to help you meet these costs. The University provides a comprehensive financial aid and scholarship program that includes grants, merit scholarships, loans and work study. Monthly installment and family tuition reduction plans are also available.

For the 2005-2006 academic year, University of Scranton freshmen will receive over $17,000,000 in financial aid and scholarships, $8,000,000 of which will be provided by the University. Of the freshman aid applicants who are enrolled for the fall semester, 89.9% were offered funding from University scholarships and need-based grants. Of those who received University funding, 34% received academic scholarships-only averaging $8,052, 39% were awarded combined academic and need-based awards averaging $12,900 and 34% received an average of $9,037 in awards based solely on need. The average freshman aid package, exclusive of parent loans, is $14,500.

UNIVERSITY OF SCRANTON PROGRAMS
Figures are based on the 2005-06 freshman class.

Presidential Scholarships

These merit-based, full-tuition scholarships are awarded for exemplary academic achievement. Presidential scholars are typically valedictorians and salutatorians of their high school class, have a minimum SAT score of 1400, and have demonstrated leadership and community service. National Merit Finalists will be given preference for these prestigious awards. Eight Presidential scholars are enrolled as freshmen for the 2005 fall semester.

Dean's Scholarships

These merit-based partial-tuition scholarships are awarded to students who demonstrate the highest level of academic achievement. Recipients are typically in the top 20% of their class and have a minimum SAT score of 1200. Ninety-one freshmen were awarded Dean's scholarships for the 2005 fall semester. The average Dean's Scholarship award is $10,000.

Loyola Scholarships

These merit-based, partial-tuition scholarships are awarded to students who demonstrate a strong level of academic achievement, are in the top 30% of their high school class and have a minimum SAT score of 1100. Three hundred forty freshmen were awarded Loyola scholarships for the 2005 fall semester. The average award is $6,300.

Xavier Grants

Four hundred eighty-four members of the freshman class were awarded these need-based grants for the 2005 fall semester. The average Xavier grant is $6,159.

Claver Awards and Arrupe Scholarships

Under-represented groups of students are considered for the Arrupe merit-based scholarship and the Claver need-based grant. The average Arrupe scholarship is $8,720. Fifty awards were made to members of the 2005 freshman class. Under-represented groups of students who are in the top 30% of their high school class and have a minimum SAT score of 1000 are considered for this award. The average Claver grant is $7,232. Fifty-three Claver awards were made to members of the 2005 freshman class.

Family Tuition Reduction Plan

Families with two or more dependent children in attendance at the University during the same semester as full-time undergraduate students are eligible for a tuition discount. Each student receives a 10% discount on tuition. The discount also applies when at least one parent is enrolled as a full-time undergraduate student. Students are required to make a formal application to the bursar each academic year.

2005-2006 Budgets
Undergraduate & Graduate
(Based on Full-Time Enrollment)

	DEPENDENT ON CAMPUS	DEPENDENT OFF CAMPUS	INDEPENDENT ON CAMPUS	INDEPENDENT OFF CAMPUS	GRADUATE
**TUITION	$23,380	$23,380	$23,380	$23,380	$11,610
**ROOM & BOARD	7,526	0	7,526	0	0
SUBTOTAL	30,906	23,380	30,906	23,380	11,610
BOOKS & SUPPLIES	1,000	1,000	1,000	1,000	1,000
PERSONAL EXPENSES	750	750	0	0	0
AT HOME LIVING EXPENSES	0	3000	0	0	0
TRANSPORTATION	800	1400	0	0	0
SUBTOTAL	33,456	29,530	31,906	24,380	12,610
**ACTIVITY FEE	250	250	250	250	0
LOAN FEE	166	166	166	166	166
INDEPENDENT STUDENT ALLOWANCE	0	0	4084	11320	11320
TOTAL COST	**$33,872**	**$29,946**	**$36,406**	**$36,116**	**$24,096**

** Items billed by JCU

Students registered for less than 12 hours will be assessed at a credit hour rate of $708. Please note that the amount of financial aid awarded to a student is in part determined by the total cost of education. Resident status <u>may</u> help qualify a student for additional financial assistance.

GRADUATE

ARTS & SCIENCES

$645 per credit hour

MBA PROGRAM

$793 per credit hour

John Carroll University reserves the right to change its charges if economic conditions make it necessary. The new rates will apply to all students. Notice of any change will normally be published in advance.

Glossary[1]

The following are some financial aid terms and abbreviations used throughout the book and found in financial aid information.

A.A.: Associate of arts degree, which can be earned at some two-year colleges.

A.A.S.: Associate of applied science degree, which can be earned at some two-year colleges.

Ability to Benefit: Basis on which a student without a high school diploma or equivalent, may qualify for federal student financial assistance. The Department of Education maintains a list of approved tests for measuring a student's ability to benefit from the educational program applied for.

Academic Year: A period of time schools use to measure a quantity of study. For example, a school's academic year may consist of a fall and spring semester, during which a student must complete 24 semester hours. Academic years vary from school to school, and even from program to program at the same school.

Acceptance Form: The written acknowledgement by the student of receipt of an award letter. The form usually provides for acceptance of offered aid, possible declination of all or part of the package, and some means of requesting an appeal, if that is desired, to modify the award. Frequently, acceptance letters and award letters are combined in a single document.

Accrued Interest: Interest that accumulates on the unpaid principal balance of a loan.

---

[1]A significant portion of this glossary was reproduced with permission from the College Board and Sallie Mae. Also, material was used from the U.S. Department of Education publications and websites.
2005 College Costs and Financial Aid Handbook. Copyright © 2005 by the College Board reproduced with permission. All rights reserved. www.collegeboard.com.
Sallie Mae Glossary. www.salliemae.com Copyright © 2005 SallieMae, reproduced with permission. All rights reserved.

ACT: Test published by American College Testing, which is located in Iowa City, Iowa. The ACT measures a student's aptitude in English, mathematics, reading, and science reasoning. Many colleges in the South and Midwest require students to take this test and submit their test scores when they apply for admission. Some colleges accept this test *or* the SAT. (See SAT.) Most students take the ACT or the SAT during their junior or senior year of high school.

Actual Interest Rate: The annual interest rate a lender charges on a loan, which may be equal to or less than the applicable or statutory interest rate on that loan.

Adjusted Available Income: The portion of family income remaining after deducting federal, state, and local taxes; a living allowance; and other factors used in the Federal Need Analysis Methodology.

Adjusted Gross Income (AGI): All taxable income as reported on a U.S. income tax return.

Administrative Wage Garnishment: Process by which a guarantor, under federal law, may intercept a portion of the wages of borrowers with a defaulted FFELP loan.

Advanced Placement (AP): Credit and/or advanced standing in certain course sequences that postsecondary institutions may offer to high school students who have taken high-level courses and passed certain examinations.

AFROTC: Air Force Reserve Officer Training.

AGI: See Adjusted Gross Income.

America Counts and America Reads: Federally-funded programs that allow students attending postsecondary educational institutions to work with children who need assistance in mastering the fundamentals of math and reading. College students must file a FAFSA and be granted a Federal Work-Study award in order to qualify for a paid position as a reading or math tutor in one of the local elementary schools.

Americorps Program: A program established through the National and Community Service Trust Act of 1993 designed to reward individuals who provide community service with educational benefits. A college student can work before, during, or after postsecondary education, and can use the funds to pay current educational expenses or to repay federal student loans.

Annual Percentage Rate (APR.): The interest maintained on a loan for a one-year period.

Army College Fund: A program that provides Army enlistees in certain job specialties and who score at least 50 on the Armed Forces Vocational Aptitude Battery test educational benefits to attend college.

Army Reserve Student Loan Repayment Program: Student loan repayment program available to Army Reservists; amount of repayment is based on years of service and job specialty.

Assets: Cash on hand in checking and savings accounts; trusts, stocks, bonds, other securities; real estate (excluding home), income-producing property, business equipment, and business inventory. Considered in determining Expected Family Contribution (EFC).

Associate's Degree: A degree given for successful completion of some courses of study at a two-year college.

Automatic Debit: The automatic deduction of funds from the borrower's checking or savings accounts to cover monthly education loan payments. Borrowers may receive a 0.25% interest rate reduction on eligible loans during active periods of repayment as long as payments are made on time.

Award Letter: A means of notifying admitted financial aid applicants of the financial assistance being offered. The award letter usually provides information on the types and amounts of aid offered, as well as specific program information, student responsibilities, and the conditions that govern the award. Generally provides students with the opportunity to accept, decline, or clarify the aid offered. (See Financial Aid Notification.)

B.A. or B.S.: Bachelor of Arts and Bachelor of Science. Both degrees can be earned at four-year colleges.

Bachelor's Degree: The degree given for successful completion of the undergraduate curriculum at a four-year college or a university. Also called a baccalaureate degree.

Base Year: For need analysis purposes, the base year is the calendar year preceding the award year. For instance, 2005 is the base year used for the 2006–2007 award year.

BIA Grant: See Bureau of Indian Affairs Grant.

Borrower-Specific Deferment: Refers to the federal requirement that eligibility for deferment be applied to all of a borrower's loans, rather than to each separate loan. For example, a borrower who has used the maximum 24 months of internship deferment is not entitled to an additional internship deferment.

Budget: See Cost of Attendance.

Bureau of Indian Affairs (BIA) Grant: A federal grant program administered by the Bureau of Indian Affairs for needy students who are members of an Indian, Eskimo, or Aleut tribe enrolled in accredited postsecondary institutions in pursuit of an undergraduate or graduate degree.

Bursar's Office: The university office that is responsible for the billing and collection of university charges.

Business Assets: Property that is used in the operation of a trade or business, including real estate, inventories, buildings, machinery, and other equipment, patents, franchise rights, and copyrights. Considered in determining an Expected Family Contribution (EFC) under the Federal Methodology formula.

Byrd Scholarship: A federally sponsored, merit-based scholarship for outstanding high school students.

Campus-Based Programs: The term commonly applied to those U.S. Department of Education federal student aid programs administered directly by postsecondary institutions, including Federal Perkins Loan, Federal Supplemental Educational Opportunity Grant (FSEOG), and Federal Work-Study (FWS) programs.

Cancellation (Discharge) of a Federal Loan: The result of a borrower meeting specific requirements established by law that releases the borrower from all obligation to repay a federal education loan. Cancellation results in the principal and interest being paid by the federal government. Cancellation is not automatic, and the appropriate loan agency must be contacted for more information.

Cancellation Options: The conditions for federal loan cancellation or discharge are based on the loan program (e.g., FFELP, FDLP, and Perkins). The total and permanent disability or death of a borrower are the only conditions that justify 100% cancellation of a loan in any of the programs. Conditions such as being a full-time teacher (in designated studies or demographic areas), nurse or medical technician, Vista or Peace Corp volunteer, or a member of the US Armed Forces *may* qualify the borrower for 50–100% discharge on Perkins Loans only. Bankruptcy may be a valid condition for discharge. However, this may occur only if repaying the loans would cause the borrower or his/her family "undue hardship."

Candidates Reply Date Agreement (CRDA): A college subscribing to this College Board-sponsored agreement will not require any applicants offered admission as freshmen to notify the college of their decision to attend (or to accept an offer of financial aid) before May 1 of the year the applicant applies. The purpose of the agreement is to give applicants time to hear from all the colleges to which they have applied before having to make a commitment to any of them.

Capitalization of Loan Interest: The process of deferring interest payments as they come due and adding the accrued interest to the principal amount of the loan. Although capitalizing is a way to postpone interest payments, it adds to the amount of the principal and, consequently, increases both the interest (based on the higher principal) and the overall amount that must eventually be repaid.

Central Processing System (CPS): The computer system to which the student's need analysis data is electronically transmitted by the FAFSA processor. The Central Processing System performs database matches, calculates the student's official Expected Family Contribution (EFC), and prints out the Student Aid Report (SAR). The CPS mails a SAR to the student or sends one electronically.

Certificate: The formal acknowledgement of successful completion of a particular program or course of study, particularly in a vocational school, trade school, or junior college.

Citizen/Eligible Non-Citizen: A student must be one of the following to receive federal student aid:

- U.S. citizen,
- U.S. national (includes natives of American Samoa or Swain's Island), or
- U.S. permanent resident who has an I-151, I-551 or I-551C (Alien Registration Receipt Card).

If a student is not in one of these categories, he or she must have an Arrival-Departure Record (I-94) from the U.S. Immigration and Naturalization Service (INS) showing one of the following designations:

- Refugee,
- Asylum Granted,
- Cuban-Haitian Entrant (Status Pending), or
- Conditional Entrant (valid only if issued before April 1, 1980).

If a student has only a Notice of Approval to Apply for Permanent Residence (I-171 or I-464), he or she is not eligible for federal student aid.

If a student is in the U.S. on an F-1 or F-2 student visa, or on a J-1 or J-2 exchange-visitor visa only, he or she can't get federal student aid. Also, persons with G series visas (pertaining to international organizations) are not eligible for federal student aid.

Citizens of the Federated States of Micronesia, the Republic of the Marshall Islands, and the Republic of Palau are eligible only for Federal Pell Grants, Federal Supplemental Educational Opportunity Grants, Federal Work-Study, and Byrd Scholarships. These applicants should check with their schools' financial aid administrators for more information.

CLEP: See College-Level Examination Program.

Clock Hour: A measure of educational or academic work in real time at a proprietary school. A clock hour consists of:

- A 50-minute to 60-minute class, lecture, or recitation in a 60-minute period; or
- A 50-minute to 60-minute laboratory, shop training or internship in a 60-minute period; or
- 60 minutes of preparation in a correspondence course of study.

COA: See Cost of Attendance.

Collection Agency: A business organization that accepts, from schools and lenders, loan accounts that have become delinquent or are in default, and attempts to collect on those accounts. A fee is charged for the service.

CollegeCredit Education Loans: An array of government and private loans sponsored by the College Scholarship Service of the College Board. Federal Stafford Loans, Federal PLUS Loans, and privately sponsored Student Signature Education and Private Parent loans are available to students and parents in 31 states and the District of Columbia.

College-Level Examination Program (CLEP): A series of College Board examinations demonstrating a student's proficiency in a subject area, for which some postsecondary institutions offer credit based on their own policies.

College Scholarship Service (CSS): A division of the College Board that collects additional information used by colleges, universities, and scholarship programs in awarding private financial aid funds.

Commercial Lender: Generally, lenders are commercial banks, savings and loan associations, credit unions, stock savings banks, trust companies, mutual savings banks, or state agencies created specifically for this purpose. Commercial lenders provide services offered through the Federal Family Education Loan Programs as well as a variety of other loan programs for both students and parents.

Commuter Student: A student who does not live on campus; typically, commuter refers to a student living at home with his or her parents, but can also mean any student who lives off-campus.

Comprehensive Fee: If the college combines tuition, fees, room, and board expenses, that single figure is called a comprehensive fee.

Consolidation Loan: A loan made to enable a borrower with different types of loans to obtain a single loan with one interest rate and one repayment schedule. Federal Perkins, Federal Stafford (subsidized and unsubsidized), Direct Subsidized and Direct Unsubsidized, Health Education Assistance Loans (HEAL), Health Professions Student Loans, and Loans for Disadvantaged Students may be combined for purposes of consolidation, subject to certain eligibility requirements. A consolidation loan pays off the existing loans; the borrower then repays the consolidated loans.

Consumer Price Index (CPI): A measure of inflation or deflation at the consumer level, updated monthly by the U.S. Bureau of Labor Statistics.

Cooperative Education: A program through which a college student alternates periods of classroom instruction with periods of off-campus related employment.

Cosigner: A person who signs the promissory note in addition to the borrower and is responsible for the obligation if the borrower does not pay.

Cost of Attendance (COA): Generally, this includes the tuition and fees normally charged to a student, together with the institution's estimated cost of room and board, transportation and commuting costs, books and supplies, and miscellaneous personal expenses. In addition, student loan fees, dependent care, reasonable costs for a study abroad or cooperative education program, and/or costs related to a disability may be included, when appropriate. Also referred to as cost of education or budget.

Coverdell Education Savings Account (ESA): Formerly referred to as the Education IRAs, this federal income tax provision enables taxpayers to establish a college savings plan. A maximum of $2,000 may be contributed annually, according to income.

CPS: See Central Processing System.

Credit (or Credit Hour): The unit of measurement some institutions give for fulfilling course requirements.

Credit Bureau: An agency that gathers and stores credit information on individuals. When a credit report is needed for a loan application, a credit bureau produces a report to the lender based on the gathered data. The lender also reports back to credit bureaus how frequently an individual makes payments when due. This information is then available to potential employers and creditors in the future.

Credit Report: A report that contains details about individual borrowing habits and money-management skills. Lenders use credit reports to determine if they should approve a loan and to set the terms (interest rate, fees, and length) of the loan.

Credit-Scoring: A method, based on statistical analysis of applicant characteristics, through which lenders determine the applicant's qualification for credit.

Credit-Worthy: An individual with no negative credit history per the criteria established by the lender.

Custodial Parent: The parent with whom the dependent student lives, and whose financial information is used in the need analysis formula when parents are divorced or separated.

Default: Failure to repay a student loan according to the agreed-upon terms of a promissory note. Default occurs at 180 days when the delinquency date is prior to 10/7/98, and 270 days when the delinquency date is on or after 10/7/98. The school, lender, and state and federal governments may take legal action against the borrower to recover defaulted loan funds.

Default Rate: The default rate is the percentage of students who took out federal student loans to help pay their expenses but did not repay them properly.

Deferment (of Loan): A condition during which payments of principal are not required, and, for Federal Perkins Loan and subsidized Federal Stafford and Direct Subsidized Loans, interest does not accrue. The repayment period is extended by the length of the deferment period.

Department of Education, U.S. (ED): The federal government agency that administers assistance to students enrolled in postsecondary educational programs under the following programs: Federal Pell Grant, Federal Perkins Loan,

Federal Supplemental Educational Opportunity Grant (FSEOG), Federal Work-Study (FWS), Federal Family Education Loan (FFEL) Programs, and William D. Ford Federal Direct Loan (Direct Loan) Program.

Departmental Scholarship: An award of gift assistance that is specifically designated for a recipient in a particular academic department within the institution.

Dependent Student: A student who does not qualify as an independent student and whose parental income and asset information is used in calculating an Expected Family Contribution. (See Independent Student.)

Direct Costs: Costs that the college or university directly bills to the student. For example, tuition and fees are direct costs.

Direct Loan: A student loan issued under the William D. Ford Federal Direct Student Loan (Direct Loan) Program. The program includes Federal Direct Stafford/ Ford (Direct Subsidized) Loans, Federal Direct Unsubsidized Stafford/Ford (Direct Unsubsidized) Loans, Federal Direct PLUS (Direct PLUS) Loans, and Federal Direct Consolidation (Direct Consolidation) Loans.

Direct PLUS Loan: Long-term loans made available to parents of dependent students, and graduate/professional students. The interest rate is fixed at 8.5%. May be used to replace the EFC; amount borrowed is limited to the cost of attendance minus estimated financial assistance.

Direct Subsidized and Direct Unsubsidized Loans: Long-term, low-interest loans administered by the Department of Education and institutions. Fixed interest rates are set at 6.8%. Direct Unsubsidized Loans can be used to replace EFC.

Disability: A medically determined condition that renders a person unable to work and earn money, or to attend school. A borrower (or his spouse or dependent) is considered to be temporarily totally disabled if the condition is expected to be of a short and finite duration; a borrower is considered totally and permanently disabled if this condition is expected to continue for a long or indefinite period of time, or to result in death.

Disbursement: The process by which financial aid funds are made available to students for use in meeting educational and related living expenses. Funds may be disbursed directly to the student, or applied to the student's account.

Disclosure Statement: Statement explaining specific terms and conditions of student loans, such as interest rate, loan fees charged, and gross amount borrowed. Disclosure statements must accompany each loan disbursement.

Early Action: A college admissions program that consists of earlier deadlines and notification dates than the regular admissions process, but that does not require a binding commitment from the student if admission is offered. The student applying under this program may apply to many schools. The student will not know what financial aid will be awarded prior to committing.

Early Decision: A program with earlier deadlines and notification dates than the regular admissions process. Students who apply to an early decision program commit to attending the school if admitted (thus, early decision can be applied to only one school). The student will not know what financial aid will be awarded prior to committing.

Economic Hardship: A period during which the borrower is working full time but is earning an amount that does not exceed the greater of the minimum wage or the poverty line for a family of two. Economic hardship also exists if a borrower's monthly payments on federal education loans are equal to or greater than 20% of the borrower's total monthly gross income, as defined in FFELP regulations.

Educational Benefits: Funds, primarily federal, awarded to certain categories of students (veterans, children of deceased veterans or other deceased wage earners, and students with physical disabilities) to help finance their postsecondary education regardless of their ability to demonstrate need in the traditional sense.

Education IRA: An education IRA is a tax-deferred savings and investment account for educational expenses. Parents are allowed to put away $500 a year for each child or grandchild under the age of 18. Like the Roth IRA, contributions aren't tax deductible, but withdrawals are tax free. The money must be used for college or graduate school tuition, room, board, or books by the time the student turns 30. At that point, the funds will be distributed to the beneficiary and will be subject to a 10% penalty and income taxes. Before then, however, the funds can be transferred to a new Education IRA for another family member.

ED: See Education Department, U.S.

EFC: See Expected Family Contribution.

Electronic Funds Transfer (EFT): Transfer of funds initiated through electronic means, such as data transmission by computer rather than a paper-based transaction, such as a check.

Eligible Institution: A higher education institution, vocational school, or postsecondary vocational institution, or a proprietary institution of higher education that meets all criteria for participation in the federal student aid programs.

Eligible Non-Citizen: Someone who is not a US citizen but is nevertheless eligible for federal student aid. Eligible non-citizens include US permanent residents who are holders of valid green cards, US nationals, holders of Form I-94 who have been granted refugee or asylum status, and certain other non-citizens. Non-citizens who hold a student visa or an exchange visitor visa are not eligible for federal student aid.

Eligible Program: A course of study that requires a certain minimum number of hours of instruction and period of time and that leads to a degree or certificate at a school participating in one or more of the federal student aid programs. Generally, to get student aid, a student must be enrolled in an eligible program.

Employment: With reference to financial aid, the opportunity for students to earn money to help pay for their education. Federal Work-Study is one program by which needy students can work to defray their educational expenses.

Employment Allowance: An allowance to meet expenses related to employment when both parents (or a married independent student and spouse) are employed or when one parent (or independent student) qualifies as a surviving spouse or as head of a household. Used in need analysis formula for parents and student, if eligible.

Endowment: Funds owned by an institution and invested to produce income to support the operation of the institution. Many educational institutions use a portion of their endowment income for financial aid.

Enrolled: The status of a student who has completed the registration requirements (except for the payment of tuition and fees) at the school the student is attending or will attend, and has attended at least one day of classes at the school at which the student is enrolled, or has been admitted into a correspondence study program and has submitted one lesson, completed by the student after acceptance for enrollment and without help of a representative of the school.

Enrollment Status: An indication of whether a student is full time or part time. Generally, a student must be enrolled at least half time (and in some cases full time) to qualify for financial aid.

Entitlement Program: Entitlement programs award funds to all qualified applicants. The Pell Grant is an example of such a program.

Entrance Counseling: Students with federal educational loans are required to receive counseling before they receive their first loan disbursement, during which the borrower's rights and responsibilities and loan terms and conditions are reviewed with the student. This session may be conducted online, by video, in person with the FAA or FAO, or in a group meeting.

Estimated Financial Assistance (EFA): The school's estimate of the amount of financial assistance that a student has been or will be awarded for the enrollment period for which a loan is sought. The EFA includes assistance from federal, state, institutional, scholarship, grant, financial need-based employment, or other sources.

Exceptional Need: An eligibility criterion in the FSEOG and Federal Perkins Loan programs. Exceptional need for FSEOG is defined in statute as the lowest expected family contributions at an institution. The law does not define the term for the Federal Perkins Loan Program.

Expected Family Contribution (EFC): An amount, determined by a need analysis formula that is specified by federal law, and that indicates how much a student and parent(s) can reasonably be expected to pay for postsecondary expenses. Factors such as taxable and non-taxable income, assets (such as savings and checking accounts), and benefits (for example, unemployment or Social Security) are all considered in this calculation. The EFC is used in determining eligibility for federal and institutional need-based aid.

Extended Repayment Plan: A repayment plan under which the length of the borrower's repayment period is increased and monthly payments are reduced. The repayment period cannot exceed 25 years.

FAFSA: See Free Application for Federal Student Aid.

FAFSA Express: New electronic method for students to apply for federal student financial assistance directly to the Department of Education.

Federal Academic Competitiveness Grants: These are federal, Pell-eligible grants for postsecondary students. Grants for first- and second-year undergraduates will be known as an Academic Competitiveness Grant in the amount of $750 for the first year award and $1,300 for second year awards. Grants for third- and fourth-year undergraduates will be known as a National Science and Mathematic Access to Retain Talent Grant (SMART) and will be in the amount of $4,000. Students' coursework must meet the rigorous standards established by the state, local educational agency, or school.

Federal Family Education Loan (FFEL) Programs: The collective name for the Federal Stafford (subsidized and unsubsidized), Federal PLUS Loan, and Federal Consolidated Loan programs. Funds for these programs are provided by private lenders and the loans are guaranteed by the federal government.

Federal Loan: Loans guaranteed by the U.S. government.

Federal Methodology (FM): See Federal Need Analysis Methodology.

Federal Need Analysis Methodology: A standardized method for determining a student's (and family's) ability to pay for postsecondary education expenses; also referred to as Federal Methodology (FM). The single formula for determining an Expected Family Contribution (EFC) for Pell Grants, campus-based programs, FFEL programs, and Direct Loan program; the formula is defined by law.

Federal Pell Grants: These are federal need-based grants for postsecondary students who have not yet received a baccalaureate or first professional degree. This grant is administered by the U.S. Department of Education. In academic year 2005–2006, the maximum Pell Grant was $4,050.

Federal Perkins Loans: This is a federal financial aid program for undergraduates and graduate students with financial need. Loans are awarded by the school. This is a long-term, low-interest program. The interest rate as of July 1, 2006, was 5%.

Federal PLUS Loan (FPLUS): Long-term loans made available to parents of dependent students and graduate/professional students. The fixed interest rate is 8.5%. May be used to replace EFC; annual amount borrowed limited to the cost of attendance minus estimated financial assistance.

Federal Processor: The organization that processes the information submitted on the Free Application for Federal Student Aid (FAFSA) and uses it to compute eligibility for federal student aid. There are two different federal processors serving specific geographic regions.

Federal SEOG (Supplemental Educational Opportunity Grant): This is a federal award that helps undergraduates with exceptional financial need, and the actual dollar amount is awarded by the school. The SEOG does not have to be paid back. Priority for this award must be given to Pell Grant recipients with the lowest expected family contribution.

Federal Stafford Loan (Subsidized and Unsubsidized): Student loans offered by the federal government. There are two types of Stafford Loans: one need-based and the other non-need-based. Under the Stafford Loan programs, students can borrow money to attend school and the federal government will guarantee the loan in case of default. Under the Stafford Loan programs, the combined loan limits are $2,625 for the first year, $3,500 for the second year, and $5,500 for the third or more years. However, effective July 1, 2007, the first-year loan limit will increase from $2,625 to $3,500 and second year from $3,500 to $4,500. An undergraduate cannot borrow more than a total of $23,000 and the fixed interest rate is set at 6.8%. An unsubsidized Federal Stafford Loan may be used to replace the E.F.C.

Federal Student Aid Programs: Programs administered by the U.S. Department of Education:

- Federal Pell Grants,
- Federal Academic Competitiveness Grants
- Federal Supplemental Educational Opportunity Grants (FSEOG),
- Federal Work-Study (FWS),
- Federal Perkins Loan,
- Federal Direct Stafford/Ford Loans (both subsidized and unsubsidized),
- Federal Direct PLUS Loans (for parents and graduate/professional students),
- Federal Direct Consolidation Loans,
- Federal Stafford Loans (both subsidized and unsubsidized),
- Federal PLUS Loans (for parents and graduate/professional students),
- Federal Family Education Loan (FFEL) Consolidation Loans,
- Leveraging Educational Assistance Partnership (LEAP) Program grants (SSIG), and
- Robert C. Byrd Honors Scholarship Program (Byrd Program).

Federal Work-Study Program: This programs is offered by many colleges. It allows both undergraduate and graduate students to work part time during the school year as part of their financial aid package. To obtain a work-study position, students must demonstrate financial need. The jobs are usually on campus and the money earned is used to pay for educational and living expenses.

Fees: These are charges that cover costs not associated with the student's tuition and room and board, such as costs of technology use, some athletic activities, clubs, and special events.

Fellowship: A form of aid given to graduate students to help support their education. Some fellowships include tuition waivers or payments to universities in lieu of tuition. Most fellowships include a stipend to cover reasonable living expenses (e.g., just above the poverty line). Fellowships are a form of gift aid and do not have to be repaid.

FFELP: See Federal Family Education Loan Program.

Financial Aid: Financial aid in this book refers to money available from various sources to help students pay for college. This money may be need-based or merit. It includes scholarships, grants, loans, and employment.

Financial Aid Administrator: An individual who is responsible for preparing and communicating information pertaining to student loans, grants, and scholarships, and employment programs, and for advising, awarding, reporting, counseling, and supervising office functions related to student financial aid. These individuals are accountable to the various publics that are involved and are managers or administrators who interpret and implements federal, stat, and institutional policies and regulations. They are capable of analyzing student and employee needs and making changes where necessary.

Financial Aid Award Letter: An offer of financial assistance to help a student meet postsecondary educational expenses.

Financial Aid Consultant: A person who, for a fee, provides a variety of services to students and parents, including preparing the FAFSA and other financial aid forms, estimating the Expected Family Contribution (EFC), and estimating financial need.

Financial Aid Notification: The letter from the postsecondary institution that lets the student know whether aid has been awarded. If the student will be receiving assistance, the notification also describes the financial aid package. State agencies and private organizations may send students financial aid notifications separately from the postsecondary institution. (See Award Letter.)

Financial Aid Package: The total amount of financial aid a student receives. Federal and non-federal aid such as grants, loans, or work study are combined in a "package" to help meet the student's need. Using available resources to give each student the best possible package of aid is one of the major responsibilities of a school's financial aid administrator.

Financial Aid Transcript (FAT): A record of all federal aid received by students at each school attended.

Financial Need: In the context of student financial aid, financial need is equal to the cost of education (estimated costs for college attendance and basic living expenses) minus the expected family contribution (the amount a student's family is expected to pay, which varies according to the family's financial resources).

Financial Need Equation: Cost of attendance minus Expected Family Contribution equals financial need (COA – EFC = Need).

Five Twenty-Nine Plans (529 Plans): An education savings plan operated by a state or educational institution designed to help families set aside funds for future college costs. 529 Plans are usually categorized as either prepaid or savings.

Fixed interest: On a fixed interest loan, the interest rate remains the same for the life of the loan.

FM: See Federal Need Analysis Methodology.

Forbearance: Permitting the temporary cessation of repayments of loans, allowing an extension of time for making loan payments, or accepting smaller loan payments than were originally scheduled.

FPLUS: See Federal PLUS Loan.

Free Application for Federal Student Aid (FAFSA): An application completed and filed by a student who wishes to receive federal student aid. The application collects household and financial information used by the federal government to calculate the Expected Family Contribution (EFC) to postsecondary education costs.

Front-Loading: The practice of awarding a very attractive financial aid package to first-year students to entice them to enroll and then aiding them at a lower rate for their remaining years. Before accepting a financial aid offer, ask whether you can expect comparable aid for all four years, assuming your financial status remains the same.

FSEOG: See Federal Supplemental Educational Opportunity Grant.

FTC: Federal Trade Commission.

Full-Time Student: A student enrolled in an institution of higher education (other than a student enrolled in a program of study by correspondence) who is carrying a full academic workload as determined by the school under standards applicable to all students enrolled in that student's particular program. The student's workload may include any combination of courses, work, research, or special studies, whether or not for credit, that the school considers sufficient to classify the student as a full-time student.

Full-Need: Colleges that meet all of a student's demonstrated financial need through loans, scholarships, grants, and work study.

FWS: See Federal Work-Study.

General Educational Development (GED) Diploma: The certificate students receive if they have passed a high school equivalency test. Students who do not have a high school diploma but who have a GED will still qualify for federal student aid.

GI Bill Benefits: Special assistance provided by the federal government to eligible veterans for the purpose of financing education or training programs.

Gift Aid: Student financial aid that does not require repayment or that work be performed. This generally includes grants and scholarships.

Gift Aid Grant: A grant is money given to a student for the purposes of paying at least part of the cost of college. A grant does not have to be repaid. It is free money.

GPA: Grade Point Average.

Grace Period: The period of time that begins when a loan recipient ceases to be enrolled at least half time and ends when the repayment period starts. Loan principal need not be paid, and generally, interest does not accrue during this period.

Grade Level: A student's academic class level, as provided by a school official on the student's application and promissory note. Undergraduate students are 01 (freshman/first year) through 05 (fifth year/other undergraduate); graduate and professional students are A (first year) through D (fourth year and beyond).

Grade Point Average (GPA): An average of a student's grades where the grades have been converted to a numerical scale, with 4.0 being an A, 3.0 being a B, and 2.0 being a C.

Graduate or Professional Student: A student who is enrolled in a program or course above the baccalaureate level at an institution of higher education, or enrolled in a program leading to a first professional degree; has completed the equivalent of at least three years of full-time study at an institution of higher education, either before entrance into the program or as part of the program itself; and is not receiving Title IV aid as an undergraduate student for the same period of enrollment.

Graduated Repayment: A repayment schedule where the monthly payments are smaller at the start of the repayment period and become larger later on.

Grant: A type of financial aid that does not have to be repaid; usually awarded on the basis of need, possibly combined with some skills or characteristics the student possesses. (See Gift Aid.)

Gross Income: Income before taxes, deductions, and allowances are subtracted.

Guarantee Fee: A fee charged by a guarantor for each loan it guarantees.

Guarantor or Guarantee Agency: State or private non-profit agencies that insure student loans for lenders and administer the student loan insurance program for the federal government.

Half-Time Student: A student who is enrolled in a participating school; is carrying an academic workload that amounts to at least half of the workload of a full-time student, as determined by the school; and is not a full-time student.

HEAL (Health Education Assistance Loan): The HEAL program provides federal insurance for educational loans made by participating lenders to eligible graduate students in schools of medicine, osteopathy, dentistry, veterinary medicine, optometry, podiatry, public health, pharmacy, chiropractic, or in health administration and clinical psychology programs. Please note that no new HEAL loans are being issued.

Health and Human Services, U.S. Department of (HHS): The section of the federal government that provides assistance to future health care practitioners. The Nursing Student Loan, Health Profession Student Loan, and Health Education Assistance Loan are some of the aid programs administered by HHS.

Health Professions Programs: Federal student assistance programs administered by the U.S. Department of Health and Human Services for students preparing for careers in the health sciences.

HHS: See Health and Human Services, U.S. Department of.

Home Equity: The portion of a home's value that the homeowner owns outright; it is the difference between the fair market value of the home and the sum of the principal balances remaining on mortgage loans held by the homeowner for that home.

Home Equity Line of Credit (HELOC): A variation of the home equity loan that allows a homeowner to draw money (i.e., write checks) against the home's equity on an ongoing basis. Generally, a home equity line of credit features a variable interest rate, a specific time period during which money may be withdrawn, and a repayment period following any withdrawal. The credit also revolves on a home equity line of credit as soon as principal is repaid, it may be borrowed again.

Home Equity Loan: A loan based on a homeowner's equity in the home. The home equity loan features a fixed rate, payment, and term.

Home-Schooled Student: A student who is taught at home by a parent or a tutor instead of attending a traditional public or private institution.

Hope Scholarship Tax Credit: An income tax credit available to taxpayers financing a student's postsecondary education. The credit is based on a student's college tuition and fee charges, minus grants and scholarships, and other tax-free educational assistance. It can be claimed during the first two years of schooling, up to a maximum of $1,500.

HPL: Health Professional Student Loan.

HPSL Loans (Health Professions Student Loans): Low-interest loans for graduate health profession students with exceptional financial need.

Income: Amount of money received from any or all of the following: wages, interest, dividends, sales or rental of property or services, business or farm profits, certain welfare programs, and subsistence allowances such as taxable and non-taxable Social Security benefits and child support.

Income-Contingent Repayment: A repayment schedule for some HEAL loans under which the monthly payment amount is adjusted annually, based on the total amount of the direct loans, the family size, and the adjusted gross income (AGI) reported on the most recently filed federal income tax return. In the case of a married borrower who files a joint income tax return, the AGI includes the spouse's income.

Income Protection Allowance: An allowance against income for the basic costs of maintaining family members in the home. The allowance is based upon consumption and other cost estimates of the Bureau of Labor Statistics for a family at the low standard of living.

Income-Sensitive Repayment Schedule: A repayment schedule for some FFELP loans under which the borrower's monthly payment amount is adjusted annually, based solely on the borrower's expected total monthly gross income received from employment and other sources during the course of the repayment period.

Independent Student: A student who meets the following criteria:

- will be 24 years of age by December 31 of the academic year for which aid is being pursued, or who:
- is an orphan or a ward of the court;
- is a veteran;
- is married or is a graduate or professional student;
- has legal dependents other than a spouse; or
- active duty members of the armed forces for purpose other than training;
- presents documentation of other unusual circumstances demonstrating independence to the student financial aid administrator.

Indirect Costs: Costs associated with a student's enrollment that are not billed by or incurred through the college. Transportation and miscellaneous costs are examples of indirect costs.

Individual Retirement Account (IRA): An individual tax-deferred savings and investment account meant to accumulate funds for retirement.

Ineligible Borrower: A borrower or potential borrower who does not meet federal eligibility criteria for a Federal Stafford Loan or, in the case of a parent-borrower, a Federal PLUS Loan.

In-School and Grace Interest Subsidy: Interest the federal government pays on certain loans while borrowers are in school, an authorized deferment, or grace periods.

Institutional Loan: Loans specific to a college, university, or other postsecondary educational institution. Eligibility and loan characteristics will vary among institutions.

Institutional Methodology: The formula a college or university uses to determine financial need for allocation of the school's own financial aid funds.

Institutional Student Information Record (ISIR): An electronic record for schools that contains a student's Expected Family Contribution (EFC) as calculated by

ED's Central Processing System (CPS) and all the financial and other data submitted by the student on the Free Application for Federal Student Aid (FAFSA). (See Student Aid Report.)

Interest on a Loan: The fee a lender charges a borrower for using money. In regard to federal student loans, the interest that is accruing while the borrower is enrolled at least half time, during the grace period and during any other approved deferment period is

- paid by the federal government on the borrower's behalf for the Federal Stafford Subsidized Loan, or
- billed to the student for the Federal Stafford Unsubsidized Loan.

For all loan programs, once repayment of loan principal begins, interest is charged.

Interest Rate—Fixed: An interest rate that remains the same for the life of the loan.

Interest Rate—Variable: An interest rate that is recalculated on a periodic basis, usually based on the prime rate or the T-bill rate.

International Baccalaureate (IB): A comprehensive and rigorous two-year curriculum (usually taken in the final two years of high school) that is similar to the final year of secondary school in Europe. Some colleges award credit or advanced placement to students who have completed an IB program.

International Student: A student who is not a citizen or resident of the U.S. and who intends to attend or is attending a college, university, or other postsecondary educational institution.

Internship: A part-time job during the academic year or the summer months in which a student receives supervised practical training in their field.

Investment Plans: Educational savings programs, usually sponsored by commercial banking institutions.

IPA: See Income Protection Allowance.

IRS: Internal Revenue Service.

ISIR: Institutional Student Information Record.

Late Fee: A fee that may be assessed if a scheduled payment is not made by the due date.

Leave of Absence: A break in enrollment, not including semester or spring break(s), that is requested by the student and sanctioned by the school. The leave of absence may be no longer than 60 days, and the student may be granted no more than one leave of absence during a 12-month period.

Legal Dependent (of Applicant): A biological or adopted child, or person for whom the applicant has been appointed legal guardian, and for whom the applicant provides more than half the support. In addition, a person who lives with and receives at least half the support from the applicant, and will continue to receive that support during the award year. For purposes of determining dependency status, a spouse is not considered a legal dependent.

Lender: The organization that furnishes loan funds, whether a bank, a college, the government, or another establishment.

Lifetime Learning Credit: An income tax credit available to taxpayers financing a student's postsecondary education. The credit is based on a student's college tuition and fee charges, minus grants and scholarships, and other tax-free educational assistance. It is available for any level of postsecondary study, up to a current maximum of $1,000.

Loan: A loan is a type of financial aid that is available to students and to the parents of students. An education loan must be repaid. In many cases, however, payments do not begin until the student finishes school. A promissory note is signed when a student receives a loan.

Loan Balance: The total unpaid amount of a specific loan. This sum includes outstanding principal, capitalized interest, accrued interest, late charges, and any miscellaneous fees such as returned check fees.

Loan Interviews: Required counseling sessions with a financial aid administrator (FAA) that the federal student loan borrower must attend before receiving their first loan disbursement and again before leaving school. During these counseling sessions, called entrance and exit interviews, the FAA reviews the repayment terms of the loan and the repayment schedule with the student.

Loan Repayment Program: A special program available to qualified students who have attended college on federally-funded student loans and who subsequently enlist in the Army for at least three years in any job specialty.

Loan Servicer: The agent designated to track and collect a loan on behalf of a lending institution.

Merit-Based Financial Aid: This kind of aid is given to students who meet requirements not related to financial need. Most merit-based aid is awarded on the basis of academic performance; service to the community; talent in a particular area, such as music or athletics; and the aid is given in the form of scholarships or grants. This type of student aid does not require repayment. It is free money.

Methodology: Refers to the system used to calculate the Expected Family Contribution (i.e., the Federal Need Analysis Methodology).

Military Scholarships: Reserve Officer Training Corps (ROTC) scholarships available for the Army, Navy, and Air Force at many colleges and universities throughout the United States. These scholarships cover tuition and fees, books and supplies, and include a subsistence allowance.

Multiple Disbursements: The disbursement of Federal Stafford, Federal PLUS, or Federal SLS Loan funds at pre-designated times, usually in two or more installments of approximately equal increments.

National Health Service Corps Scholarship (NHSC): Scholarship program for students who pursue full-time courses of study in certain health professions disciplines, and are willing to serve as primary care practitioners in underserved areas after completing their education.

National and Community Service (AmeriCorps): A program established through the National and Community Service Trust Act of 1993 designed to reward individuals who provide community service with educational benefits and/or loan forgiveness or cancellation.

National of the United States: A citizen of the United States or, as defined in the Immigration and Nationality Act, a non-citizen who owes permanent allegiance to the United States.

National Service Trust: A national community service program whereby students who participate in this program before attending school may be able to use funds to pay educational expenses. If students participate after graduating, the funds may be used to repay their federal student loans. Eligible types of community service include education, human services, the environment, and public safety.

Need: See Financial Need.

Need Analysis: A system by which a student applicant's ability to pay for educational expenses is evaluated and calculated. Need analysis consists of two primary components: (a) determination of an estimate of the applicant's and/or family's ability to contribute to educational expenses; and (b) determination of an accurate estimate of the educational expenses themselves.

Need Analysis Formula: Defines the data elements used to calculate the Expected Family Contribution (EFC). There are two distinct formulas: regular and simplified. The formula determines the EFC under the Federal Need Analysis Methodology.

Need-Based Financial Aid: This kind of financial aid is given to students who are determined to be in financial need of assistance based on their income and assets and their families' income and assets, as well as some other factors.

Need-Gapping: The practice of awarding students only part of the financial aid they need. Also called unmet need.

Non Need-Based Aid: Aid based on criteria other than need, such as academic, musical, or athletic ability. Also, refers to federal student aid programs where the Expected Family Contribution (EFC) is not part of the need equation.

Non-Subsidized Loan: A loan that is not eligible for federal interest benefits. The borrower is responsible for paying the interest on the outstanding principal balance of a non-subsidized loan throughout the life of the loan. During the in-school, grace, and deferment periods, these interest payments are normally made on a monthly or quarterly basis, or are capitalized. Non-subsidized loans were guaranteed by some guarantors before the introduction of unsubsidized Federal Stafford Loans.

NROTC: Naval Reserve Officers Training Corps.

Open Admissions: This term means that a college admits most or all students who apply to the school. At some colleges it means that anyone who has a high school diploma or a GED can enroll. Open admissions, therefore, can mean slightly different things at different schools.

Origination Fee: A fee charged to offset the cost of interest, special allowance, and reinsurance payments by the federal government on FFELP and Direct Loans. This fee, like the guarantee fee, is subtracted from the borrower's proceeds.

Over-Award: The disbursement of funds to a student in excess of his/her demonstrated need as determined by the need analysis system utilized by the institutions. Two-hundred dollars ($200) over need is considered an over-award by the Department of Education.

Overpayment: Any amount paid to a student in excess of the amount (s)he was entitled to or eligible to receive.

Packaging: The process of combining various types of student aid (grants, loans, scholarships, and employment) to attempt to meet full amount of student's need.

Parent: A student's natural or adoptive mother or father.

Paul Douglas Teacher Scholarship: A scholarship program administered by the states to enable and encourage outstanding high school graduates who demonstrate an interest in teaching to pursue teaching careers at the elementary or secondary levels.

PC: See Parent Contribution.

Parent Contribution: A quantitative estimate of the parents' ability to contribute to postsecondary educational expenses based on Federal Methodology and in some cases Institutional Methodology.

Permanent Resident of the United States: A person who meets certain requirements of the Immigration and Naturalization Service (INS). Valid documentation of permanent residency includes the following: I-551, I-151, I-181, I-94, or a passport stamped processed for I-551: Temporary evidence of lawful admission for permanent residence.

Personal Identification Number (PIN): The code that serves as a financial aid applicant's unique identifier, allowing the student access to personal information in various U.S. Department of Education systems. It is similar to the PIN provided by a bank that enables a customer to access account information. The PIN can be used to file the FAFSA or the Renewal FAFSA online. A request for the PIN may be made on the website of the U.S. Department of Education.

Postsecondary: This term means after high school and refers to all programs for high school graduates, including programs at two-and four-year colleges and vocational and technical schools.

Preferential Packaging: When colleges offer better students or students who meet other criteria more grants (free money), as opposed to loans or work study.

Presidential Access Scholarships: Scholarship available to undergraduate students who are eligible for Federal Pell Grants and who demonstrate academic achievement.

Principal Balance: The outstanding amount of the loan on which the lender charges interest. As the loan is repaid, a portion of each payment is used to satisfy interest that has accrued and the remainder of the payment is applied to the outstanding principal balance.

Principal (of a Loan): The amount of money borrowed through a loan; it does not include interest or other charges, unless they are capitalized.

Principal (Savings): This refers to the face value or the amount of money you place in a savings instrument on which interest is earned.

Professional Judgment (PJ): Aid administrator discretion, based on special circumstances of the student, to change data elements used in determining eligibility for federal student aid.

PROFILE: A CSS/Financial Aid PROFILE™ is a customized financial aid application form required at certain colleges to collect additional financial information to determine eligibility for institutional aid.

PROFILE Online: An electronic application option available for students required to complete the CSS/Financial Aid PROFILE. By connecting to www.collegeboard.com, students can choose to register for a paper PROFILE application or complete the entire application online.

Promissory Note: A binding legal document that a borrower signs to get a loan. By signing this note, a borrower promises to repay the loan, with interest, in specified installments. This promissory note also includes any information about

- grace periods,
- deferment or cancellation provisions, and
- a borrower's rights and responsibilities with respect to that loan.

Proprietary Schools: These schools are private and are legally permitted to make a profit. Most proprietary schools offer technical and vocational courses.

Proration: A reduction of the standard annual loan limit for an undergraduate student. Proration of the loan amount is required if the student's program or the remainder of the student's program is less than a full academic year in length.

PSAT/NMSQT (Preliminary Scholastic Assessment Test/National Merit Scholarship Qualifying Test): A practice test that helps students prepare for the Scholastic Assessment Test (SAT I). The PSAT is usually administered to tenth or eleventh grade students. Although colleges do not see a student's PSAT/NMSQT score, a student who does very well on this test and who meets many other academic performance criteria may qualify for the National Merit Scholarship Program.

Reference: An individual to whom inquiries may be made regarding another person's character, ability, or whereabouts. A lender generally will ask a borrower to provide the names, phone numbers, and addresses of at least three individuals to be used as references for the borrower. In the event that the lender loses track of the borrower's whereabouts, the lender will contact these individuals to try to find the borrower.

Refund: The credit balance, usually made up of financial aid, exceeding the charges a student owes to a college for a particular semester. Financial aid must first be used to pay for tuition and fees, and on-campus room and board expenses, if any. If excess remains, a refund will be released to the student either in the form of a paper check, or as a direct deposit to a private lending institution account.

Rehabilitation Training Program: A program of the Department of Veterans Affairs that provides rehabilitation training to disabled individuals or a program of a state agency responsible for vocational rehabilitation, drug or alcohol abuse treatment, or mental health services.

Renewal FAFSA: One type of FAFSA that resembles a SAR and has the same questions as the FAFSA. The Renewal FAFSA is preprinted with the student's prior year responses to certain data items that are likely to remain constant from year to year.

Repayment: The time during which a borrower actively pays back an education loan.

Repayment Period: The period during which interest accrues on the borrower's loan and principal payments are required. For FFELP loans, the repayment period excludes any period of authorized deferment or forbearance; however, interest will continue to accrue during these periods for unsubsidized Federal Stafford, Federal SLS, and Federal PLUS Loans.

Repayment Start Date: The date the repayment period begins. For Federal Stafford Loans, repayment begins on the day following the last day of the grace period. For Federal PLUS Loans repayment begins on the date the loan is fully disbursed.

Repayment Schedule: A plan that is provided to the borrower at the time he or she ceases at least half-time study. The plan should set forth the principal and interest due on each installment and the number of payments required to pay the loan in full. Additionally, it should include the interest rate, the due date of the first payment, and the frequency of payments.

Reserve Officer Training Program: See ROTC Scholarship Program.

Resources: Student financial aid that must be taken into account to prevent over-awarding of aid in the campus-based programs. Resources are called estimated financial assistance in determining a student's eligibility for federal student loans.

ROTC (Reserve Officers Training Corps): A scholarship program wherein the military covers the cost of tuition, fees, and textbooks and also provides a monthly allowance. Scholarship recipients participate in summer training while in college and upon graduation a full-time active duty commitment of at least four years.

SAR: See Student Aid Report.

SAR Acknowledgement: A federal output document, similar to the SAR, that ED's central processor sends to a student who does not provide a valid email address when he or she files the FAFSA through *FAFSA on the Web*, files through a postsecondary school, or makes changes through *Corrections on the Web*. (See Student Aid Report (SAR).)

SAT (Scholastic Assessment Test): Published by the College Board, a non-profit organization with headquarters in New York City. The SAT is a test that measures a student's mathematical, verbal reasoning, and writing abilities. Many colleges in the East and West require students to take the SAT and submit their test scores when they apply for admission. Some colleges accept this test *or* the ACT. (See ACT). Most students take the SAT or the ACT during their junior or senior year of high school.

SAT Reasoning Test: The College Board's test of developed verbal and mathematical reasoning abilities, given on specified dates throughout the year at test centers in the United States and other countries. The SAT is required by many colleges and sponsors of financial aid programs. In March 2005, the SAT included a writing test.

SAT Subject Test: SAT subject tests (also known as SAT II tests) are offered in many areas of study including English, mathematics, many sciences, history, and foreign languages. Some colleges require students to take one or more SAT subject tests when they apply for admission.

Satisfactory Academic Progress (SAP): To be eligible to receive federal student aid, a student must maintain satisfactory academic progress toward a degree or certificate. The student must meet the school's written standards of satisfactory progress. Check with the school to find out about its standards.

Savings Plan: A methodical approach to periodically putting money into an account with a financial institution with the goal of reaching a target amount that is to be used for a stated purpose. The account preferably is an interest-bearing account.

SC: See Student Contribution.

Scholarship: A form of financial assistance that does not require repayment or employment and is usually made to students who demonstrate or show potential for distinction, usually in academic performance.

Scholarship Search Services: Organizations that claim to help students find little-known and unused financial aid funds. Families who are interested in using such a service should carefully investigate the company first.

School Code: For financial aid purposes, the federal ID number assigned to postsecondary educational institutions by the U.S. Department of Education.

School Lender: A school, other than a correspondence school, that has been approved as a lender under the FFELP and has entered into a contract of guarantee with the Department or a similar agreement with a guarantor.

Section 529 Plans: State tuition savings plans, named for the section of the IRS code authorizing their existence.

Selective Service Certification: Documentation that must be collected to verify that all male students (who were born on or after 1/1/60) are registered with Selective Service. If required by law, a student attending a postsecondary educational institution must register with the Selective Service before receiving federal financial aid.

Self-Help Aid: Financial aid loan programs or employment opportunity programs awarded to a student by a postsecondary institution as a form of educational financial assistance.

Self-Help Expectation: The assumption that a student has an obligation to help pay for a portion of his/her education. This obligation is usually in the form of summer savings, student loans, or employment during the school year.

Service Academy: The five postsecondary institutions administered by branches of the military: U.S. Military Academy, U.S. Air Force Academy, U.S. Naval Academy, U.S. Coast Guard Academy, and U.S. Merchant Marine Academy.

Servicer: Organization that administers and collects loan payments. May be either the loan holder or an agent acting on behalf of the holder.

Simplified Needs Test: An alternate method of calculating the expected family contribution for families with adjusted gross incomes of less than $50,000, who have filed, or are eligible to file, an IRS Form 1040A or 1040EZ, or are not required to file an income tax return. Excludes all assets from consideration.

SSN: See Social Security Number.

Social Security Number (SSN): The nine-digit number assigned to an individual by the Social Security Administration. The SSN is used as an identifier for tracking the borrower's loan account(s), skip tracing, and reporting to the Department. A borrower must have an SSN in order to apply for federal aid, including a FFELP loan.

Special Condition: Several specific circumstances that require expected 2006 income—instead of 2005—to be used to calculate a student's Pell Grant eligibility. These conditions accommodate certain situations where a family's financial circumstances would be worse in 2006 than in 2005. In these cases, using 2006 income would more accurately reflect the family's financial status.

Standard Repayment Schedule: A repayment schedule under which the borrower pays the same amount for each installment payment throughout the entire repayment period or pays an amount that is adjusted to reflect annual changes in the loan's variable interest rate. The Standard Repayment Schedule cannot exceed 10 years, excluding in-school, grace, deferment, or forbearance periods.

State Lender: In any state, a single state agency or private not-for-profit agency designated by the state that has been approved as a lender and that has entered into a contract of guarantee with the Department or a similar agreement with a guarantor.

Statement of Educational Purpose: A statement a student must sign in order to receive federal student aid at a postsecondary educational institution. By signing, a student agrees to use federal Title IV financial assistance solely for educational expenses. This statement appears on the FAFSA and renewal applications.

Student Aid Report (SAR): A student's official notification of the results of processing his/her Free Application of Federal Student Aid (FAFSA).

Student Contribution: For dependent students, the amount the student is expected to contribute from summer earnings, previous savings, and other resources such as Social Security, Veterans, and War Orphans benefits. For self-supporting students, a quantitative estimate of the student's ability to contribute toward their living and educational costs during the year.

Student Expense Budget: A calculation of the annual cost of attending a college that is used to determine financial need. Student expense budgets usually include tuition and fees, books and supplies, room and board, personal expenses, and transportation. Sometimes additional expenses are included for students with special education needs, students who have a disability, or students who are married or have children.

Student Resources: The funds available to the student to meet educational costs from sources such as student employment, savings, trust accounts, child support, alimony, V.A. benefits, Social Security benefits, personal loans, welfare, Aid to Dependent Children; or for married students, spouse's earnings.

Subsidized Loan: A loan eligible for interest benefits paid by the federal government. The federal government pays the interest that accrues on subsidized loans during an in-school, grace, authorized deferment, and (if applicable) post-deferment grace periods if the loan meets certain eligibility requirements.

Subsidized Stafford Loans: Need-based loans.

Subsidy: The money the federal government uses to help underwrite student aid programs; primarily refers to government payments to lenders of the in-school interest on Federal Stafford Loans.

Taxable Income: Income earned from wages, salaries, and tips, as well as interest income, dividend income, business or farm profits, and rental or property income.

TERI Loan: An alternative loan for students, parents, or other creditworthy individuals issued by The Education Resource Institute.

Title IV Programs: Those federal student aid programs authorized under Title IV of the Higher Education Act of 1965, as amended, including the Federal Pell Grant, Federal Supplemental Educational Opportunity Grant, Federal Work-Study, Federal Perkins Loan, Federal Stafford Loan, and (both subsidized and unsubsidized) Federal PLUS Loan, and Direct Loan.

Total Amount Outstanding: Unpaid balance of the loan including late fees, outstanding principal balance, and interest.

Transcript: A list of all the courses a student has taken with the grades earned in each course. A college will require a student to submit his or her high school transcript when the student applies for admission to the college.

Tuition: This is the amount of money that colleges charge for classroom and other instruction and use of some facilities such as libraries. Tuition can range from a few hundred dollars per year to more than $33,000. A few colleges do not charge any tuition.

Tuition and Fee Waivers: Some colleges waive the tuition or tuition and fees for some categories of students such as adults, senior citizens, or children of alumni. Check individual college websites or literature to determine if they offer tuition and fee waivers.

Tuition Payment Plans: A strategy by which payment for present costs of postsecondary education is extended into a future period of time.

Unconsummated Loan: Loan proceeds that the school returned to the lender prior to the borrower having cashed the check (if an individual check) or the school having applied the proceeds to the student's account (if included in a master check or EFT—electronic funds transfer transmission). This includes checks that may have been released by the school but remain uncashed by the 120th day following disbursement, and EFT and master check transactions that have not been completed by the 120th day following disbursement.

Undergraduate Student: A degree-seeking student at a college or university who has not earned a first bachelor's degree.

Unemployment Benefits: Temporary and partial wage replacement to workers who have become unemployed through no fault of their own.

Unmet Need: The difference between a student's total cost of attendance at a specific institution and the student's total available resources. This will include family contribution and all financial aid awarded to the student.

Uniform Transfer to Minors Act (UTMA): This law offers the same advantages as the Uniform Gifts to Minors Act, but allows the adult to control the custodial account for a longer period of time. The monies in an UTMA account can be invested in mutual funds, bank accounts, or stocks and extends the definition of gifts to include real estate, paintings, royalties, and patents.

Unsubsidized Loan: A non need-based loan such as an unsubsidized Federal Stafford Loan or a Federal PLUS Loan. The borrower is responsible for paying the interest on an unsubsidized loan during in-school, grace, and deferment periods, and to repayment periods.

Unsubsidized Stafford Loans: Non need-based loans.

U.S. Department of Education (ED, DOE, USED, DE): Government agency that administers federal student financial aid programs, including the Federal Pell Grant, the Federal Work-Study Program, the Federal Perkins Loan, the FFELP, and the FDLP.

U.S. Department of Health and Human Services (DHHS, HHS): Government agency that administers several federal health education loan programs, including the HEAL, HPSL, and NSL loan programs.

Untaxed Income: All income received that is not reported to the Internal Revenue Service or is reported but excluded from taxation. Such income would include but not be limited to any untaxed portion of Social Security benefits, Earned Income Credits, welfare payments, untaxed capital gains, interest on tax-free bonds, dividend exclusion, and military and other subsistence and quarter's allowances.

VA: Veteran's Administration.

Variable Interest on a Loan: Interest rates that change periodically (e.g., quarterly or annually). The interest rate for Federal Stafford Loans, subsidized and unsubsidized, and Parent PLUS Loans are set by the government each year and change annually or on the first of July for loans borrowed before June 30, 2006.

Verification: A procedure whereby the school checks the information the student reported on the financial aid application, usually by requesting a copy of the tax returns filed by the student and, if applicable, the student's spouse and parent(s). Many schools conduct their own form of verification. In addition, schools must verify students selected through the Federal Central Processing System, following the procedures established by regulation. The processor will print an asterisk next to the Expected Family Contribution (on the Student Aid Report) to identify students who have been selected for verification.

Verification Worksheet: A form sent by the college to students who are selected for verification by the Department of Education's Central Processing System (CPS).

Veteran: For federal financial aid purposes, such as determining dependency status, a veteran is a former member of the US Armed Forces who served on active duty and was discharged other than dishonorably.

Veterans Educational Benefits: Assistance programs for eligible veterans and/or their dependents for education or training.

Vocational Rehabilitation: Programs administered by state departments of vocational rehabilitation services to assist individuals who have a physical or mental disability, defined as a substantial handicap to employment.

W2 Form: The form listing an employee's wages and tax withheld. Employers are required by the IRS to issue a W2 form for each employee before January 31.

Ward of the Court: A ward of the court is someone under the protection of the courts. The ward of the court may have a guardian appointed by the court. The legal guardian is not personally liable for the ward's expenses and is not liable to third parties for the ward's debts.

William D. Ford Federal Direct Loan (Direct Loan) Program: The collective name for the Direct Subsidized, Direct Unsubsidized, Direct PLUS Loan, and Direct Consolidation Loan Programs. Loan funds for these programs are provided by the federal government to students and parents through postsecondary institutions that participate in the program. With the exception of certain repayment options, and origination fees, the terms and conditions of loans made under the Direct Loan Program are identical to those made under the FFEL program.

Index

Academic Common Market, 83–84
Academic success, and secular wor, 54–55
Advanced placement, 175–176
Aid packages
   appeal procedure, 148–149
   how differ, 142–148
   how outside private scholarships affect,
      149–151
Air Force. *See* military financial assistance
   opportunities
Alabama
   college savings plans, 17
   costs of colleges in, 36, 44
   state grant, scholarship, and loan programs, 78
   state residency guidelines, 72
Alaska
   costs of colleges in, 36
   reduced tuitions, 49
   state grant, scholarship, and loan programs, 78
Alternative loan programs
   overview, 161–166
   private student loan lenders, 164–166
   what to look for in, 187–188
Ambassadorial Scholarship, 96–97
Application process, 213
Arizona
   college savings plans, 17
   costs of colleges in, 36
   state grant, scholarship, and loan
      programs, 78
   state residency guidelines, 72

Arkansas
   college savings plans, 18
   costs of colleges in, 36
   state grant, scholarship, and loan
      programs, 78
Army. *See* military financial assistance
   opportunities
Army College Fund, 95
Articulation agreements, 43
Assets, and Expected Family Contribution
   (EFC), 28–29
Athletic funding
   National Association of Intercollegiate
      Athletics (NAIA), 90–91
   National Collegiate Athletic Association
      (NCAA), 87–90
   overview, 87, 214
ATM machines, 173
Automatic qualification for zero Expected
   Family Contribution (EFC), 129
Award letters
   comparing, 140–141
   notification, 137–139
   overview, 214–215
   reviewing, 139–141
   sample of, 226

BA/BS programs, three-year, 175–176
Back end prices, 158
Bank accounts, 173
Bonds, 12

Books, 172
Business and farm net worth adjustment, 123

California
  college savings plans, 18
  costs of colleges in, 36
  state residency guidelines, 72
  tuition discounts, 48
Canisius College (Buffalo, New York), 35
Capital gains earnings, 29
Cash back program, 159
Clothing expenses, 176
Club sports, 176
Coast Guard. *See* military financial assistance
    opportunities
College credit courses, 175–176
College Fund program, 95
College Goal Sunday, 196
College Level Examination Program (CLEP),
    175–176
College planning calendar
  freshman year, 102
  junior year, 103–104
  middle school, 102
  senior year, 104–106
  sophomore year, 102–103
  Summer before college, 106–107
Colleges, types of in U.S., 35
College Scholarship Service (CSS) Profile
    form, 30–32, 70
College-sponsored aid programs, 86–87
College-sponsored payment and loan
    programs, 182–183
Colorado
  college savings plans, 18
  costs of colleges in, 36
  state grant, scholarship, and loan
    programs, 78
  state residency guidelines, 72
"Compare Your Financial Aid Awards" online
    service, 139
Compounding, 4
Connecticut
  college savings plans, 18
  costs of colleges in, 36
  state grant, scholarship, and loan
    programs, 78
Consultants. *See* financial aid consultants
Cost of college education. *See also* debt;
    paying college expenses; savings plans

Cost of college education (*Cont.*):
  average costs, 45
  chart of, 36–42, 47
  controlling
    cars, 172
    cell phones, 170–171
    checking accounts, 173–174
    credit cards, 171
    meal plans, 173
    overview, 169–170
    school supplies, 172–173
    three-year BA/BS programs, 175–176
    traveling to and from college, 173
  cutting, 216
  direct costs vs. indirect costs, 45
  estimating, 2–4, 45–46
  and financial need, 49–50
  and minorities, 52
  myths about student financial aid, 50–57
  net cost, 46–48
  online calculators for, 45
  overview, 33–35, 212–213
  public colleges and universities for nonstate
    residents, 43–45
  published tuition discounts, 48
  range of college options, 35
  two-year colleges, 43
  whether unaffordable, 51
Coverdell Education Savings Account
    (Formerly Education IRA), 11–12, 31
Credit score, 181
Cultural Ambassadorial Scholarships
    program, 96–97
Custodial accounts, 12, 31

Debt
  from credit cards, 171
  effect on Federal and Institutional
    Methodology, 190
  overview, 155
  reasonable amount of, 157–158. *See also* loans
Deficit Reduction Act of 2005
  changes to Federal Family Education Loan
    Program (FFELP), 77
  explanation of eligibility for automatic zero
    income cap, 129
  explanation of eligibility for Simplified
    Needs Test, 129
  National Science and Mathematic Access to
    Retain Talents Grant (SMART), 73–74

Deficit Reduction Act of 2005 (*Cont.*):
  overview, 46
  reduction or phasing out of origination fees, 161
Delaware
  college savings plans, 18
  costs of colleges in, 36
  state grant, scholarship, and loan
      programs, 78
  state residency guidelines, 72
Dependent students, 128–129, 132–133
Direct costs, 45
Disabilities, aid for students with
  health impairments, 99
  hearing loss/deafness, 99
  learning disabilities, 100
  mobility impairments, 100
  overview, 97–98
  Social Security: Supplemental Security
      Income (SSI), 101
  visual impairments, 100–101
District of Columbia. *See* Washington DC
Divorced parents, 130, 131
Domicile, 71
Dormitory, living at, 55
Dorm room items, 172

Education IRA. *See* Coverdell Education
    Savings Account
Education Savings and Asset Protection
    Allowance, 122–123
Education savings and asset protection
    allowance, 123–126
Education tax credits
  Hope Scholarship Tax Credit, 13–14
  Lifetime Learning Tax Credit, 14, 17
  overview, 13
Employment Expense Allowance, 127–128
Expected Family Contribution (EFC)
  adjustments made by Financial Aid
      Administrators to calculations, 133
  automatic qualification for zero EFC,
      129–130
  calculating under Federal Methodology (FM)
    and financial need calculation, 128
    overview, 112–113
    principles of need analysis, 113
    process, 113–128
  lowering, 28
  overview, 28–29
  simplified

Expected Family Contribution, simplified (*Cont.*):
  automatic qualification for zero Expected
      Family Contribution (EFC), 129–130
  dependent students, 128–129
  independent students, 129
Expense. *See* cost of college education
Experts, financial-aid, 194–199
Extended loan repayment plan, 160

Federal Family Education Loan (FFEL),
    75, 77, 157
Federal financial aid programs, 63–70
Federal loans, 185–187
Federal Methodology (FM), calculating
    EFC under
  and financial need calculation, 128
  overview, 112
  principles of need analysis, 113
  process, 113–128
Federal Need Analysis Methodology. *See*
    Federal Methodology (FM)
Federal Parent Loan for Undergraduate
    Students (FPLUS), 139
Federal Pell Grant, 73
Federal Perkins Loan, 74
Federal PLUS Loan, 30
Federal Stafford Loans, 75, 76
Federal student aid programs, 73–77
Federal Supplemental Educational
    Opportunity Grant, 74
Federal Trade Commission (FTC),
    174, 194, 199
Federal Work-Study (FWS) Program, 74
Financial aid, defined, 60
Financial aid consultants
  hiring, 198–199
  negative experiences, 198–199
  overview, 194–195
  selling points for, 195–198
Financial Aid for Students with
    Disabilities, 98
Financial Aid Office
  negotiating with, 148–149
  post-enrollment activity with, 151–152
Financial Aid Profile application, 70
Financial aid source books, 199
Financial planning strategies
  education tax credits
    Hope Scholarship Tax Credit, 13–14
    Lifetime Learning Tax Credit, 14, 17

Financial planning strategies (*Cont.*):
  overview, 13
  estimating future college cost, 2–4
  financial aid eligibility, 28–30
  overview, 1–2
  savings plans
  529 state college savings plans, 9–10
  bonds, 12
  comparison chart of, 15, 16
  Coverdell Education Savings Account, 11–12
  custodial accounts, 12
  independent 529 plans, 10–11
  power of compounding, 4
  Roth IRA, 12
  savings plan worksheet, 6–7
  savings tips, 7–9
  state college savings plan, 17–27
  taxable accounts, 13
  tools for estimating college savings, 5–6
  state prepaid tuition, 17–27
529 plans
  independent plans, 10–11, 31
  state plans, 9–10, 31
Florida
  college savings plans, 18
  costs of colleges in, 37, 44
  state grant, scholarship, and loan
    programs, 78
  state residency guidelines, 72
Food expenses, 173
Foster parents, 131
Fraud, scholarship-related, 194, 199–203
Free Application for Federal Student Aid
    (FAFSA). *See also* Expected Family
    Contribution (EFC); Federal
    Methodology (FM)
  ease of filling out, 53
  overview, 60
  processing, 61–62
  who is considered a "parent" on, 130–133
Freshman year, planning calendar for, 102

Georgia
  college savings plans, 19
  costs of colleges in, 37
  state grant, scholarship, and loan programs, 78
  state residency guidelines, 72
Grades, 54
Graduated loan repayment plan, 159
Grandparents, 131

Guam, state grant, scholarship, and loan
    programs, 82
Guardians, 131
Guide for College Board Student Athletes,
    The, 87
Guide for Students Transferring from
    Two-Year, A, 90

Hawaii
  college savings plans, 19
  costs of colleges in, 37
  state grant, scholarship, and loan programs, 78
HEALTH (National Clearing House on
    Post-Secondary Education for Students
    with Disabilities), 97–98
Health impairments, aid for students with, 99
Health-related or nursing ROTC programs, 93
Hearing loss/deafness, aid for students with, 99
High school activities in preparation
    for college, 121
Home
  living at instead of dormitory, 55
  whether need to sell for tuition, 56
home equity lines of credit, 184–185
Home equity loans, 185
Home-schooled students, 89, 131
Hope Scholarship Tax Credit, 13–14, 30

Idaho
  college savings plans, 19
  costs of colleges in, 37
  reduced tuitions, 49
  state grant, scholarship, and loan programs, 78
Identity theft prevention, 174
Illinois
  college savings plans, 19
  costs of colleges in, 37
  reduced tuitions, 49
  state grant, scholarship, and loan programs, 78
  state residency guidelines, 72
Income Protection Allowance (IPA), 122
Income sensitive loan repayment plan, 160
Independent 529 plans, 10–11, 31
Independent students, 129, 132–133
Indiana
  college savings plans, 19
  costs of colleges in, 37
  state grant, scholarship, and loan programs, 79
  state residency guidelines, 72
  tuition discounts, 48

Indirect costs, 45
Individual Retirement Accounts (IRAs), 188–189
Inflation rate, 3–4
Initial Eligibility Clearinghouse, NCAA, 89
Installment loans, 183
Institutional aid application, 70–71
Institutional aid programs, 86
Institutional Methodology (IM), 112
Insurance
    cash value of policies, and FAFSA, 190
    fees on loan replacement plans, 161
    renter's, 176
Interest deduction on student loans, 31
Internal Revenue Service (IRS) Publications, 14
Internet resources, 203–208
Iowa
    college savings plans, 19
    costs of colleges in, 37
    reduced tuitions, 49
    state grant, scholarship, and loan programs, 79

Junior year, planning calendar for, 103–104

Kansas
    college savings plans, 20
    costs of colleges in, 37
    state grant, scholarship, and loan programs, 79
Kentucky
    college savings plans, 20
    costs of colleges in, 38
    state grant, scholarship, and loan programs, 79
    tuition discounts, 48

Learning disabilities, aid for students with, 100
Legal guardians, 131
Life insurance loans, 189
Lifetime Learning Tax Credit, 14, 17, 30
Loans. *See also* debt
    alternative loan programs
        overview, 161–164
        private student loan lenders, 164–166
        what to look for in, 187–188
    college-sponsored, 182–183
    consolidation plans, 159–160
    federal loans, 185–187
    to finance parental contribution and
        unmet need
        credit score, 181
        financing options, 181–182
        overview, 180

Loans (*Cont.*):
    home equity loans, 185
    incentives from lenders, 158–159
    life insurance loans, 189
    long-term, 183
    overview, 215
    private student loan lenders, 164–166
    repayment plans, 159–161
        calculating estimated repayments, 161
        college-sponsored, 182–183
        extended, 160
        graduated loan repayment plan, 159
        income sensitive, 160
        overview, 95
    tips for borrowing, 158
    unsubsidized, 75
    viewing as investment, 155–157
    whether will impact student aid formula,
        189–190
Louisiana
    college savings plans, 20
    costs of colleges in, 38
    state grant, scholarship, and loan programs, 79

Maine
    college savings plans, 20
    costs of colleges in, 38
    state grant, scholarship, and loan programs, 79
    tuition discounts, 48
Major, selecting, 176
Marines. *See* military financial assistance
    opportunities
Maryland
    costs of colleges in, 38
    state grant, scholarship, and loan programs, 79
Maryland savings plans, 21
Massachusetts
    college savings plans, 21
    costs of colleges in, 38, 44
    reduced tuitions, 49
    state grant, scholarship, and loan programs, 79
    state residency guidelines, 72
    tuition discounts, 48
Merit scholarships, 52, 214
Michigan
    college savings plans, 21
    costs of colleges in, 38, 44
    state grant, scholarship, and loan programs, 79
    state residency guidelines, 72
Middle school, planning calendar for, 102

Midwest Student Exchange Program (MSEP), 84
Military financial assistance opportunities
  College Fund program, 95
  college loan repayment programs, 95
  Montgomery GI Bill (MGIB), 92–93
  overview, 91–92
  Reserve Officer Training Corps (ROTC), 93
  state educational assistance, 95–96
  United States military academies, 93–94
Minnesota
  college savings plans, 21
  costs of colleges in, 38
  state grant, scholarship, and loan programs, 79
  state residency guidelines, 72
  tuition discounts, 48
Minorities, and student financial aid, 52
Mississippi
  college savings plans, 21–22
  costs of colleges in, 39
  state grant, scholarship, and loan programs, 79
Missouri
  college savings plans, 22
  costs of colleges in, 39
  reduced tuitions, 49
  state grant, scholarship, and loan programs, 79
Mobility impairments, aid for students with, 100
Montana
  college savings plans, 22
  costs of colleges in, 39
  state grant, scholarship, and loan programs, 80
Montgomery GI Bill (MGIB), 92–93, 95
Multi-Year Ambassadorial Scholarships program, 96
Myths about student financial aid, 50–57

National Association of Intercollegiate Athletics (NAIA), 87, 90–91
National Collegiate Athletic Association (NCAA), 87–90
National Science and Mathematic Access to Retain Talents Grant (SMART), 73–74
Navy. *See* military financial assistance opportunities
Nebraska
  college savings plans, 22

Nebraska (*Cont.*):
  costs of colleges in, 39
  state grant, scholarship, and loan programs, 80
Need analysis, 114
Nevada, costs of colleges in, 39
New England Regional Student Program (RSP), 82–83
New Hampshire
  college savings plans, 22
  costs of colleges in, 39
  state grant, scholarship, and loan programs, 80
New Jersey
  college savings plans, 23
  costs of colleges in, 39
New Mexico
  college savings plans, 23
  costs of colleges in, 39
  state grant, scholarship, and loan programs, 80
New York
  college savings plans, 23
  costs of colleges in, 40
  reduced tuitions, 49
  state grant, scholarship, and loan programs, 80
  state residency guidelines, 72
  tuition discounts, 48
New York Student Financial Aid Administrators Association (NYSFAAA), 53
Non-custodial parents, 131
Nonstate residents
  public colleges and universities for, 43–45
  student financial aid programs for
    Academic Common Market, 83–84
    Midwest Student Exchange Program (MSEP), 84
    New England Regional Student Program (RSP), 82–83
    overview, 82
    Western Interstate Commission for Higher Education, 85–86
North Carolina
  college savings plans, 23
  costs of colleges in, 40
  reduced tuitions, 49
  state grant, scholarship, and loan programs, 80
  state residency guidelines, 72

North Dakota
  college savings plans, 24
  costs of colleges in, 40
  state grant, scholarship, and loan
    programs, 80

Ohio
  college savings plans, 24
  costs of colleges in, 40
  reduced tuitions, 49
  state grant, scholarship, and loan
    programs, 80
  state residency guidelines, 72
  tuition discounts, 48
Oklahoma
  college savings plans, 24
  costs of colleges in, 44
  state grant, scholarship, and loan
    programs, 80
On-campus, living, 55
One-Year Academic Ambassadorial
  Scholarships program, 96
On-time payments, 158
Oregon
  college savings plans, 24
  costs of colleges in, 40
  state grant, scholarship, and loan
    programs, 80
  state residency guidelines, 72
  tuition discounts, 48
Origination fees, 161
Outside private scholarships, how affect aid
  packages, 149–151

Parents
  assets of, 189
  role of, 216–217
  who is considered on FAFSA, 130–133
Partial qualifiers, 89–90
Paying college expenses. *See also* cost of
    college education; debt
  alternative loans, 187–188
  college-sponsored payment and loan
    programs, 182–183
  federal loans, 185–187
  home equity lines of credit, 184–185
  home equity loans, 185
  life insurance loans, 189
  loan programs to finance parental
    contribution and unmet need

Paying college expenses, loan programs to
    finance parental contribution and unmet
    need (*Cont.*):
  credit score, 181
  financing options, 181–182
  overview, 180
  overview, 179
  retirement/IRA plans, 188–189
  whether loans will impact student aid
    formula, 189–190
Pennsylvania
  college savings plans, 24
  costs of colleges in, 40
  reduced tuitions, 49
  state grant, scholarship, and loan programs, 81
  state residency guidelines, 72
  tuition discounts, 48
Personal identification number (PIN), 61
Phones, cell, 170
Post-enrollment activity, with Financial Aid
  Office, 151–152
Prenuptial agreements, 130
Prepaid Affordable College Tuition (PACT)
  Program, 17
Princeton University, 35
Principal reduction, 159
Private scholarships, 200–203, 214
Private schools, 55
Private student loan lenders, 164–166
Public colleges and universities for nonstate
  residents, 43–45
Puerto Rico
  costs of colleges in, 41
  state grant, scholarship, and loan programs, 81

Qualified educational expenses, 10

Reapplying for financial aid, 215
Renewing financial aid, 215
Renter's insurance, 176
Repayment plans for loans, 159–161
  college-sponsored, 182–183
  extended, 160
  graduated loan repayment plan, 159
  income sensitive, 160
  overview, 95
Reserve Officer Training Corps
  (ROTC), 93
Residency classification, 73
Retirement/IRA plans, 188–189, 190

Rhode Island
  college savings plans, 24
  costs of colleges in, 41
  state grant, scholarship, and loan programs, 81
Rotary Foundation's Ambassadorial Scholarship, 96–97
Roth IRA, 12
"Rule of 72", 5

Savings plans
  529 state savings plans, 9–10
  bonds, 12
  comparison chart of, 15, 16
  Coverdell Education Savings Account, 11–12
  custodial accounts, 12
  independent 529 plans, 10–11
  power of compounding, 4
  Roth IRA, 12
  savings plan worksheet, 6–7
  savings tips, 7–9
  state college savings plan, 17–27
  and student financial aid, 53
  taxable accounts, 13
  tools for estimating college savings, 5–6
Scams, scholarship-related, 194, 199–203
Scholarships
  Ambassadorial Scholarship, 96–97
  College Scholarship Service (CSS) Profile form, 30–32, 70
  Cultural Ambassadorial Scholarships program, 96–97
  Hope Scholarship Tax Credit, 13–14, 30
  merit scholarships, 52, 214
  Multi-Year Ambassadorial Scholarships program, 96
  One-Year Academic Ambassadorial Scholarships program, 96
  overview, 214
  private, 149–151, 200–203, 214
  Rotary Foundation's Ambassadorial Scholarship, 96–97
  scams, scholarship-related, 194, 199–203
  scholarship search companies, 200–203
  scholarship services, 197
  whether used, 55
Senior year, planning calendar for, 104–106
Simplified need analysis formula
  automatic qualification for zero Expected Family Contribution (EFC), 129–130

Simplified need analysis formula (Cont.):
  dependent students, 128–129
  independent students, 129
Social Security: Supplemental Security Income (SSI), 101
Sophomore year, planning calendar for, 102–103
South Carolina
  college savings plans, 25
  costs of colleges in, 41, 44
  state grant, scholarship, and loan programs, 81
South Dakota
  college savings plans, 25
  costs of colleges in, 41
  state grant, scholarship, and loan programs, 81
Southern Regional Education Board (SREB), 83
Spanish, Internet resources in, 207–208
Sports, 176
Stafford Loan Program, 75
Standard repayment loan plan, 159
State aid programs, 77–82
State college savings plans, 17–27, 31
State educational assistance, 95–96
State residency guidelines, 71–73
Step-parents, 130
"Sticker price" of colleges, 46
Student Aid Report (SAR), 62
Student emancipation, 71
Student Financial Aid Office, 136–137
Subsidized loans, 75
Summer before college, planning calendar for, 106–107

Taxable accounts, 13
Tax credits
  Hope Scholarship Tax Credit, 13–14
  Lifetime Learning Tax Credit, 14, 17
  overview, 13
Tennessee
  college savings plans, 25
  costs of colleges in, 41
  state grant, scholarship, and loan programs, 81
Texas
  college savings plans, 25
  costs of colleges in, 41
  state grant, scholarship, and loan programs, 81

Texas (*Cont.*):
    state residency guidelines, 72
    tuition discounts, 48
Textbooks, 172
TIAA-CREF Tuition Financing Inc., 10
Transfer students, 89
Tuition. *See* cost of college education
Two-year colleges, 43

Undergraduate budgets, 45
Uniform Gifts or Transfers to Minors Act
    Accounts, 12
Unsubsidized loans, 75
U.S. Department of Education Office of
    Post-Secondary Education (OPE), 98
U.S. military academies, 93–94
Utah
    college savings plans, 26
    costs of colleges in, 41, 44
    state grant, scholarship, and loan
        programs, 81

Verification process, for federal financial aid
    programs, 63–70
Vermont
    college savings plans, 26
    costs of colleges in, 41, 44
    reduced tuitions, 49
    state grant, scholarship, and loan
        programs, 81
    tuition discounts, 48
Virginia
    costs of colleges in, 26, 41
    reduced tuitions, 49
    state grant, scholarship, and loan
        programs, 81
Virgin Islands, state grant, scholarship, and
    loan programs, 82
Visual impairments, aid for students with,
    100–101

Voter registration, 71

Washington
    costs of colleges in, 42, 44
    state grant, scholarship, and loan
        programs, 81
    state residency guidelines, 72
    tuition discounts, 48
Washington DC
    college savings plans, 18, 26
    costs of colleges in, 37
    state grant, scholarship, and loan
        programs, 78
Western Interstate Commission for Higher
    Education, 85–86
West Virginia
    college savings plans, 26–27
    costs of colleges in, 42
    reduced tuitions, 49
    state grant, scholarship, and loan
        programs, 81
William D. Ford Direct Loan Program, 75
Williams College (Williamstown,
    Massachusetts), 35
Wisconsin
    college savings plans, 27
    costs of colleges in, 42, 44
    state grant, scholarship, and loan
        programs, 82
Working secularly, and academic success,
    54–55
Wyoming
    college savings plans, 27
    costs of colleges in, 42
    state grant, scholarship, and loan
        programs, 82

Zero Expected Family Contribution (EFC),
    automatic qualification for, 129–130

About the Author

Anthony J. Bellia is Dean Emeritus, Enrollment Management, and former Director of Student Financial Aid at Canisius College, Buffalo, New York.